Broken *yet*

Faithful.

From the Journal of Umm Zakiyyah

Adult Coloring Book

Art by Cynthia Lyles
Quotes by Umm Zakiyyah

Broken yet Faithful. From the Journal of Umm Zakiyyah
Adult Coloring Book
By Umm Zakiyyah

Art by Cynthia Lyles
Accompanying adaptations by Umm Zakiyyah

ISBN: 978-1-942985-07-5

Order information at ummzakiyyah.com/store

Published by Al-Walaa Publications
Camp Springs, Maryland USA

I lived so much of my life as a problem solver. When I was younger, math had been my favorite subject in school, and I'd always looked forward to the challenging problems it presented. Behind all the alphabetic variables, cryptic charts, scrambled values, and geometric shapes was always a single numerical solution.

If you got the wrong answer, it was because you missed something, because you looked away when you should have been paying attention, or because you gave up on yourself when you became too consumed in helplessness to lift your head and see that the answer was literally right in front of you, even if not in the form you found easiest to understand.

And to me, math was the language of life. That is, until I began to live life beyond the confines of a school building and the clarity of a numerical grading system.

Shortly after graduating from college, I found myself at odds with those I loved most because I was pursuing what I valued most—my faith in God. When they expressed anger and disapproval with the evidence of my spiritual growth, I frantically searched my mind for a solution that would give us all what we wanted. And I failed.

It took years of trying and disappointing, hoping and suffering, and giving up even my peace of mind before I realized that they wanted from me something that I could not give. Because my soul did not belong to me. It belonged to God.

But my heart was connected to them, and I valued their happiness more than I valued my own. So began the painful battle between my heart and soul, hence the beginning of my emotional breaking. But by God's mercy, I retained my faith, hence the title *Broken yet Faithful*.

Here I share some of my journal reflections from that difficult time along with abstract art pieces by Cynthia Lyles, which were inspired by my words. You'll also find my personal adaptation of the art beneath each selection of journal excerpts, inspired by the original art piece itself.

Umm Zakiyyah

July 2016

My mother passed away in 2004, and I found myself consumed with so many emotions. My husband comforted me during this time, and he became my muse, the inspiration that gave release to what I was feeling inside.

Without giving much thought to what I was doing or why, I began to doodle on a piece of paper until it was filled with squares and lines. After I finished, I would carefully color inside the lines. Then something unexpected happened. I began to feel relief. It was like the comfort I'd gotten from my husband was being channeled into the lines and shapes on paper. Eventually I began making handmade books of my abstract art, and I would gift them to friends and family. The pages would include quotes from writers who had put into words what I had expressed in lines and shapes.

August 23, 2013 marked thirty-eight years of marriage for me and my husband. But six days after our anniversary, he died. When I'd first found out he had cancer, I didn't know what to do with the energy inside me, so I put it down on canvas. But when he passed away, I stopped my art completely. And I am only now picking it back up again.

~

Pain is a powerful emotion. It can consume you and take you into deep folds of depression. Or you can conquer it, turning your pain into something positive, allowing it to be the fuel for something great. Over twelve years ago, I took that step towards channeling my pain into positivity. Through the mercy of God, I was able to self teach and prescribe "abstract art" as a form of my personal therapy journey.

I discovered that as I created my artwork, I felt the deepest levels of my soul open. I pray that you find your own healing through this book. May you be blessed with many calming and soothing moments while coloring. And please remember to take your time, reflect, and always enjoy!

Cynthia

July 2016

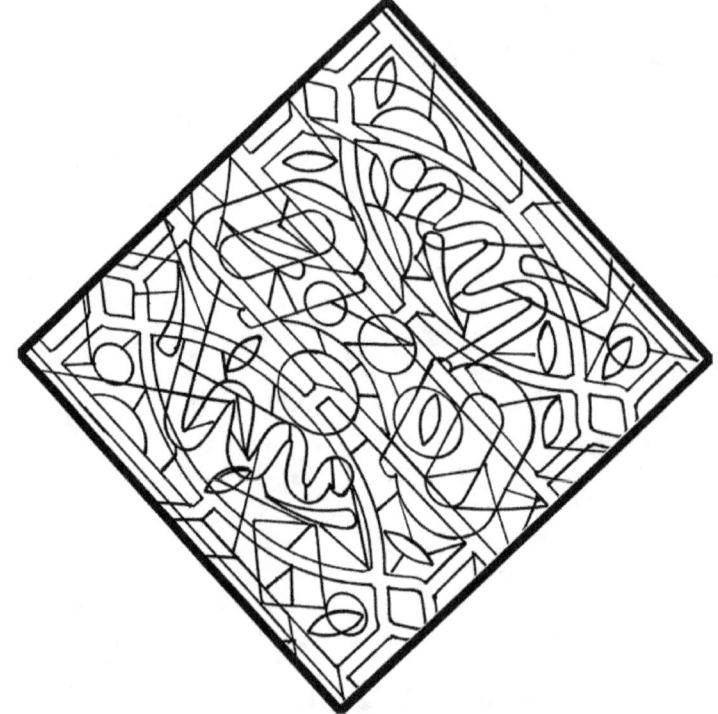

I had to learn the beauty of being broken.
It was a difficult lesson, but a freeing one.
Because as a human in front of God,
I had always been in need of Him keeping me from falling apart.
Yet I, in my zeal and foolishness, had thought I was holding myself together.

—from the journal of Umm Zakiyyah

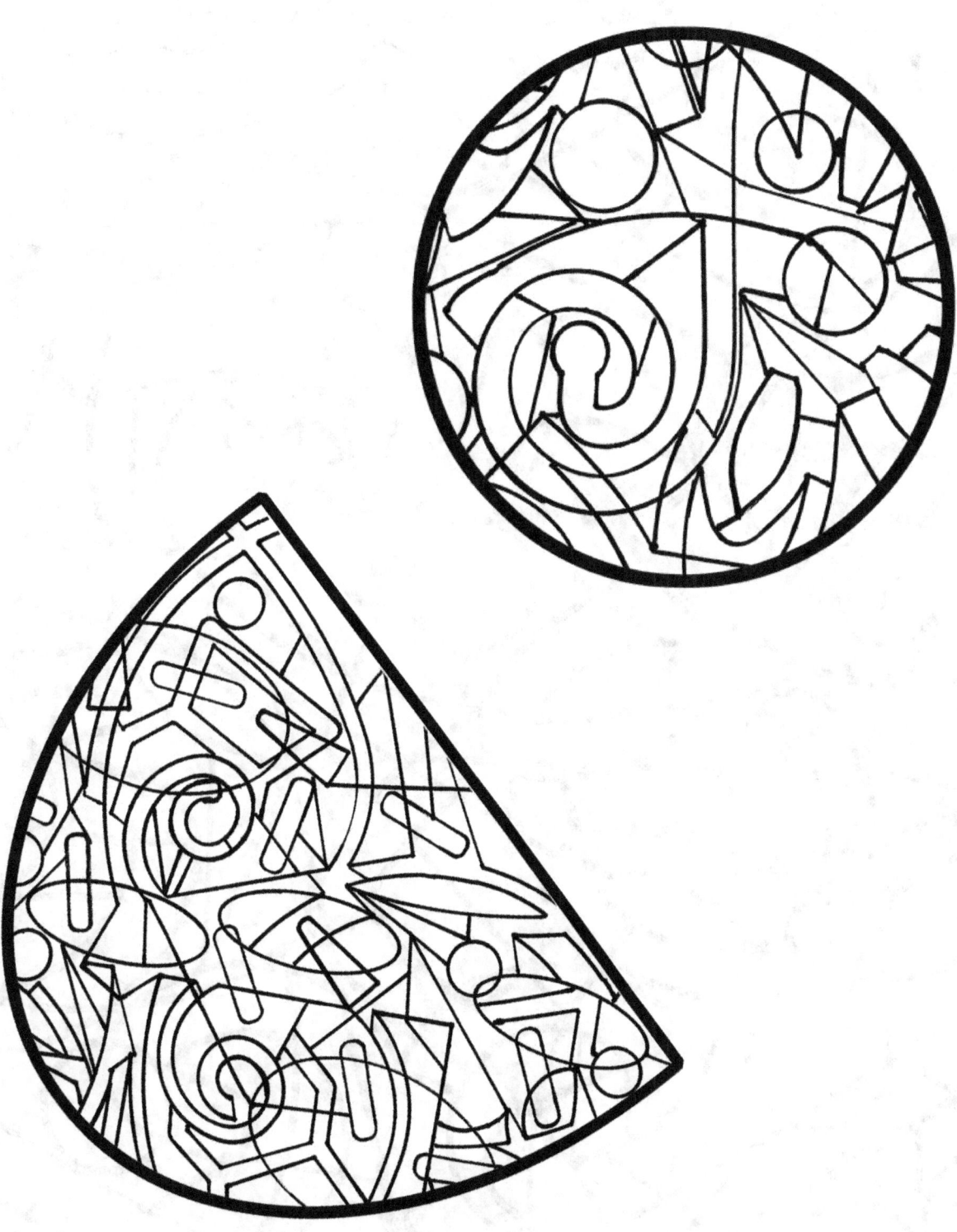

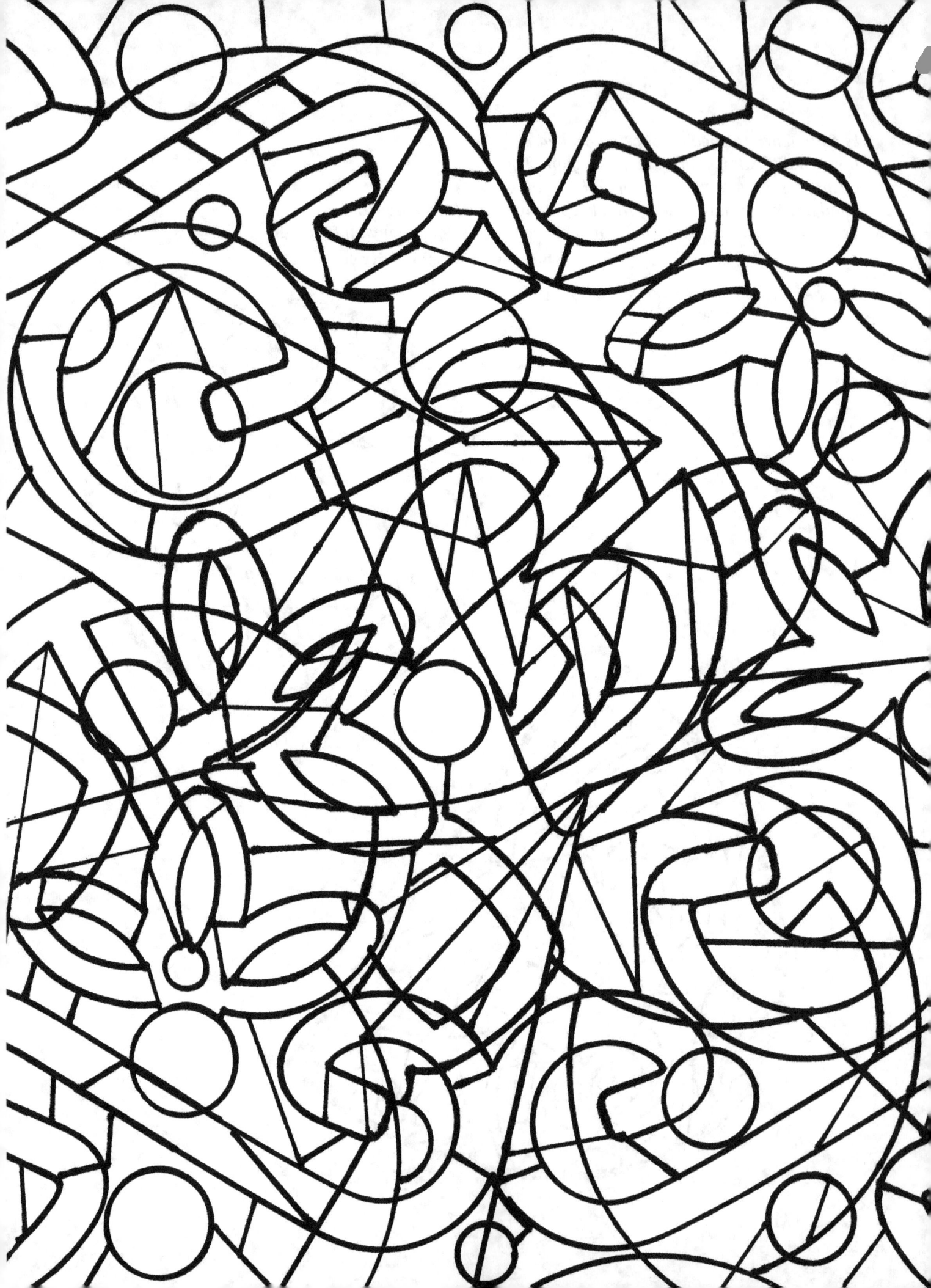

My faults and struggles seem to puzzle and disturb you.
Let me help you better understand my situation: I am a human being.
What are you?

Human.

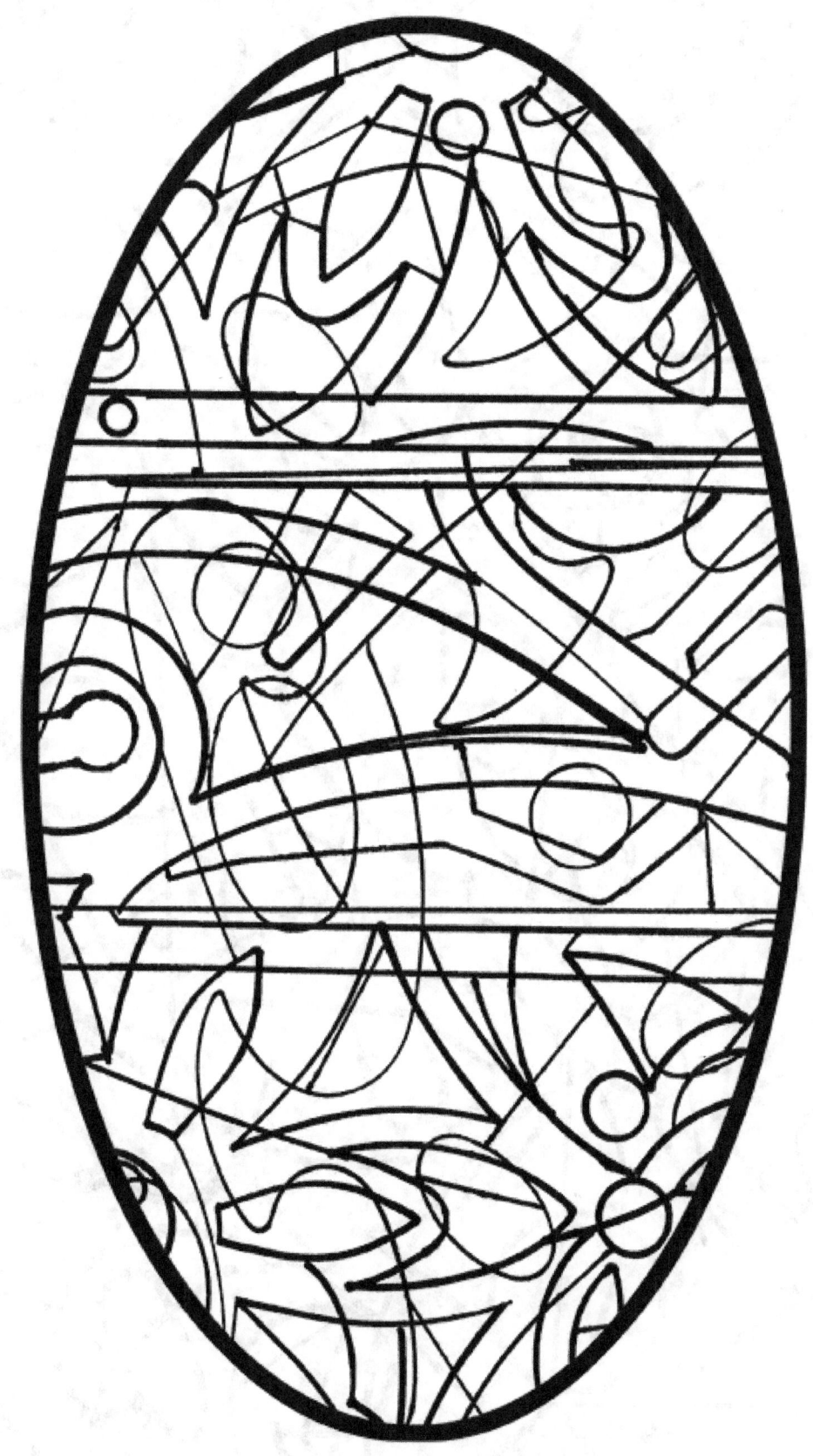

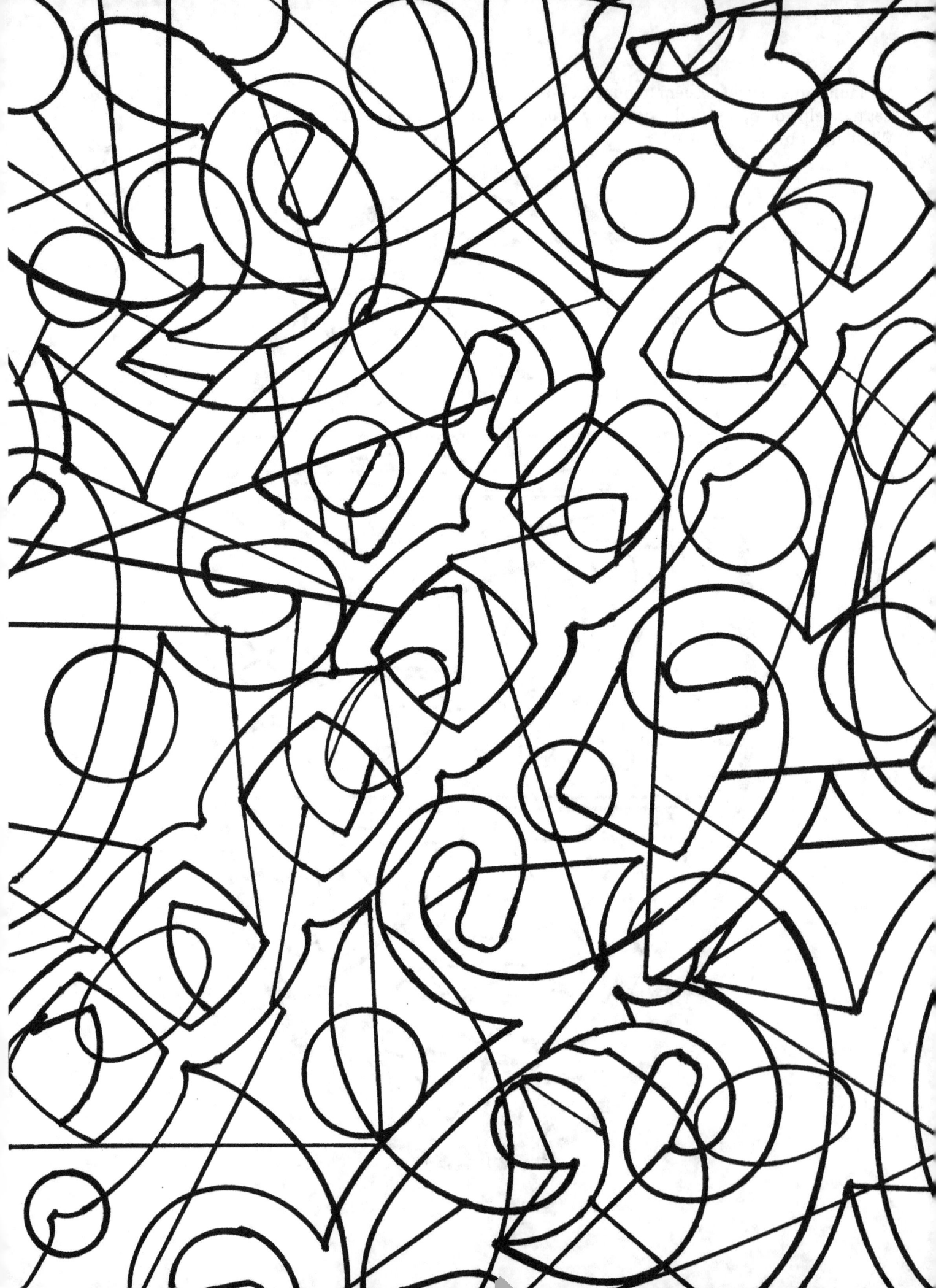

O dear soul who rushes through Prayer,
Is there somewhere you absolutely *must* go...
Other than Paradise?

~

A person has not tasted the sweetness of faith until they find peace and relaxation in Prayer.

~

Do you often feel unmotivated to pray?
Reflect then, dear soul, on the day you'll be lowered into the ground, lifeless,
and mounds of dirt will fall on your face.
Then you'll wish you fell on your face when you could still lower *yourself* to the ground.

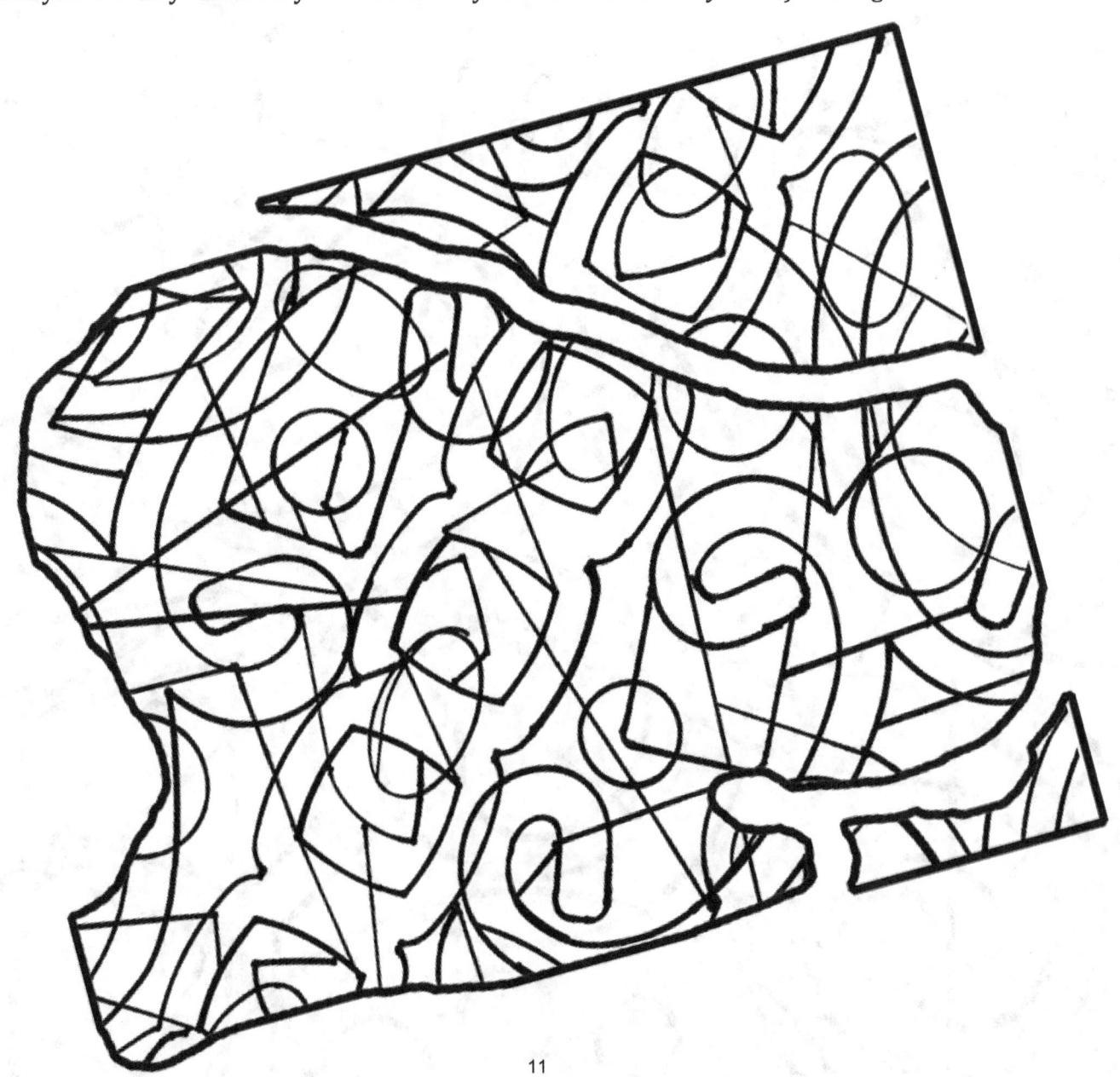

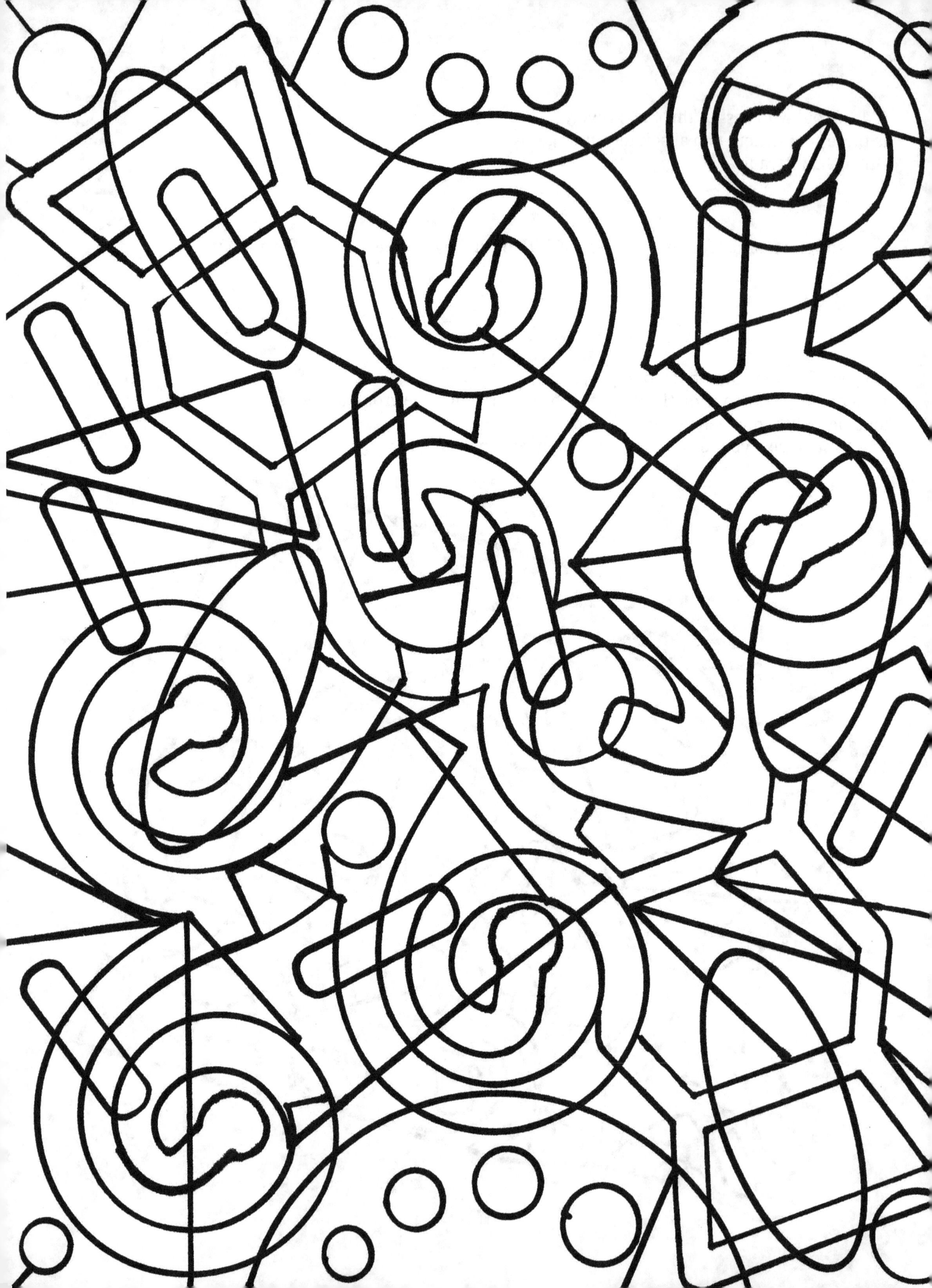

Think good of your Lord, and He will become for you what you think He is.
Expect good from your Lord, and He will grant for you what you expect from Him.
Then think good of yourself, expecting only the best for your life and soul.
How could you not—if you truly think and expect good of your Lord, who you trusted will grant it to you?

Trust.

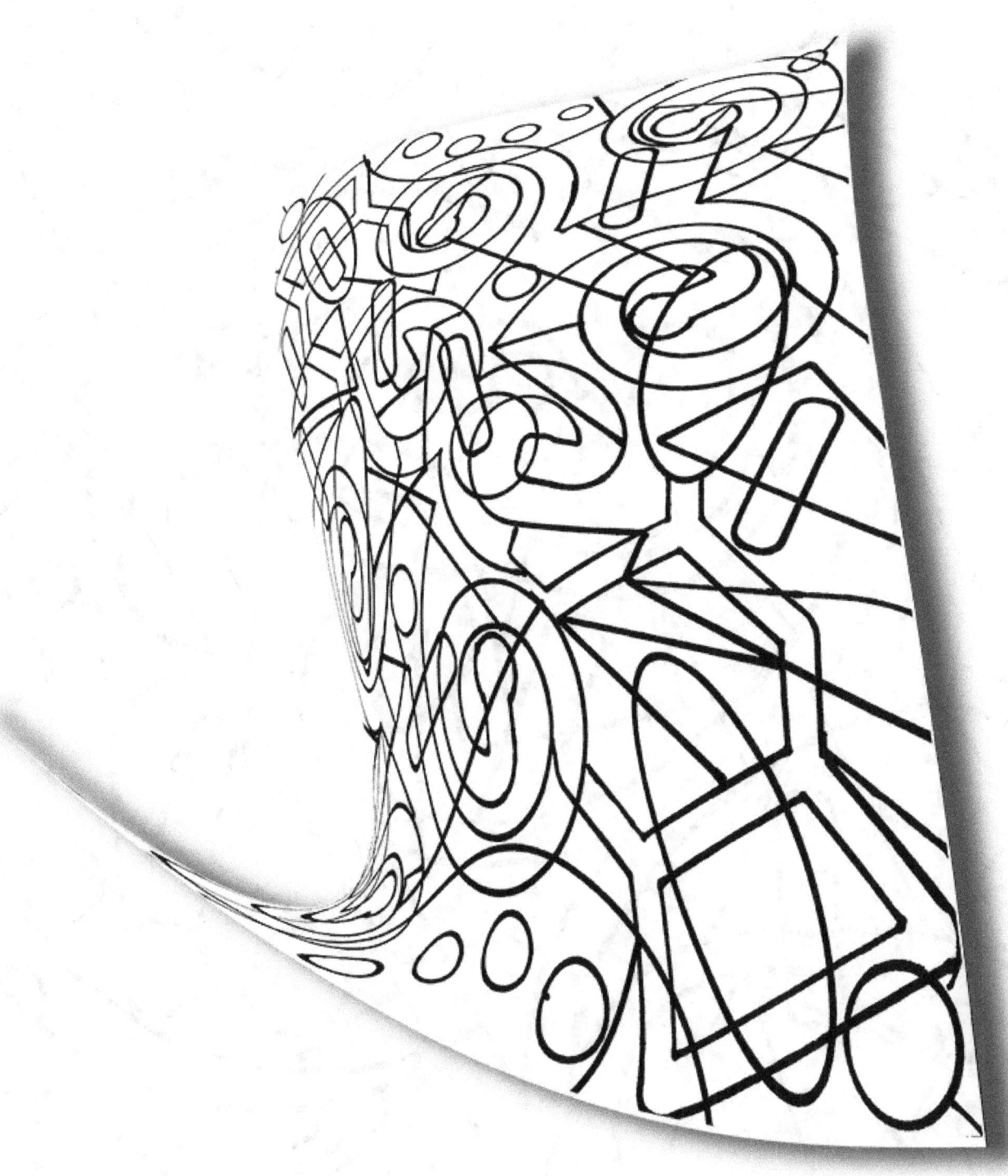

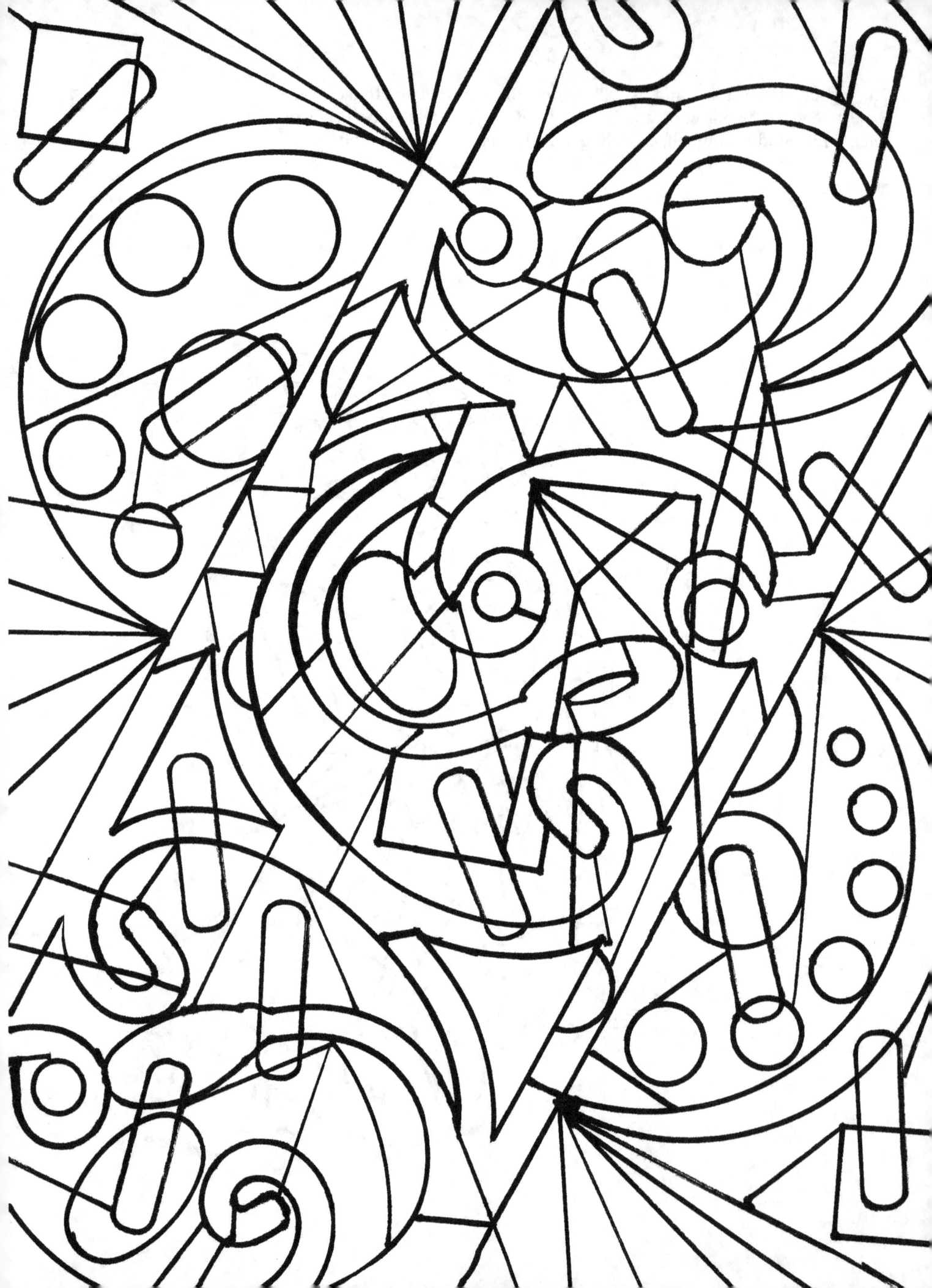

I was afraid I was lost, until I found myself in prayer, begging for direction.
Can one who is lost, I thought, be brought before Him,
except that He had placed them there?
SubhaanAllah.
He had answered my prayer before I'd even thought to make it.

~

Right guidance is not about always knowing what is right.
It is about always remaining on the right path.

~

There are people who do not want to be guided.
Don't be one of them.

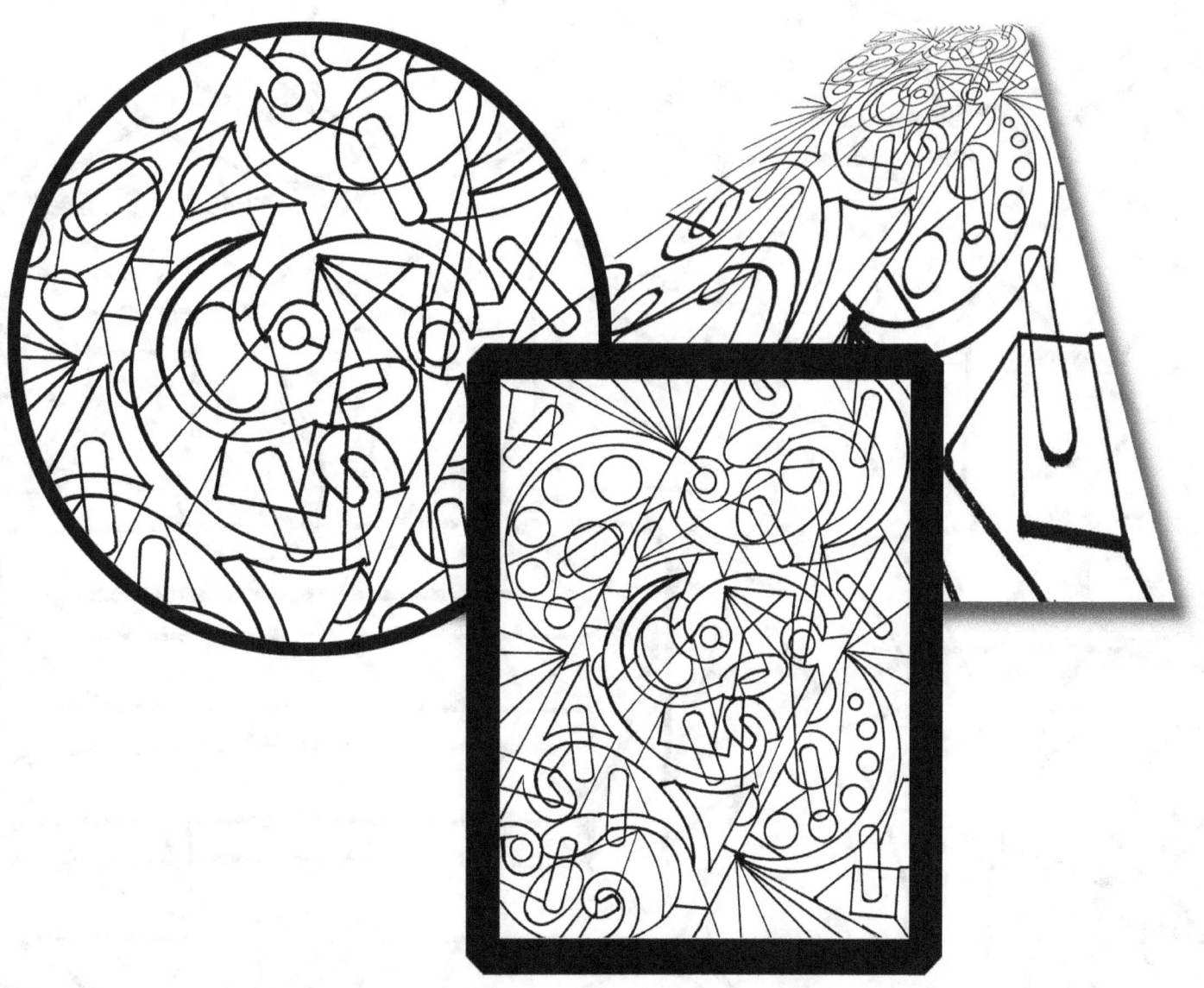

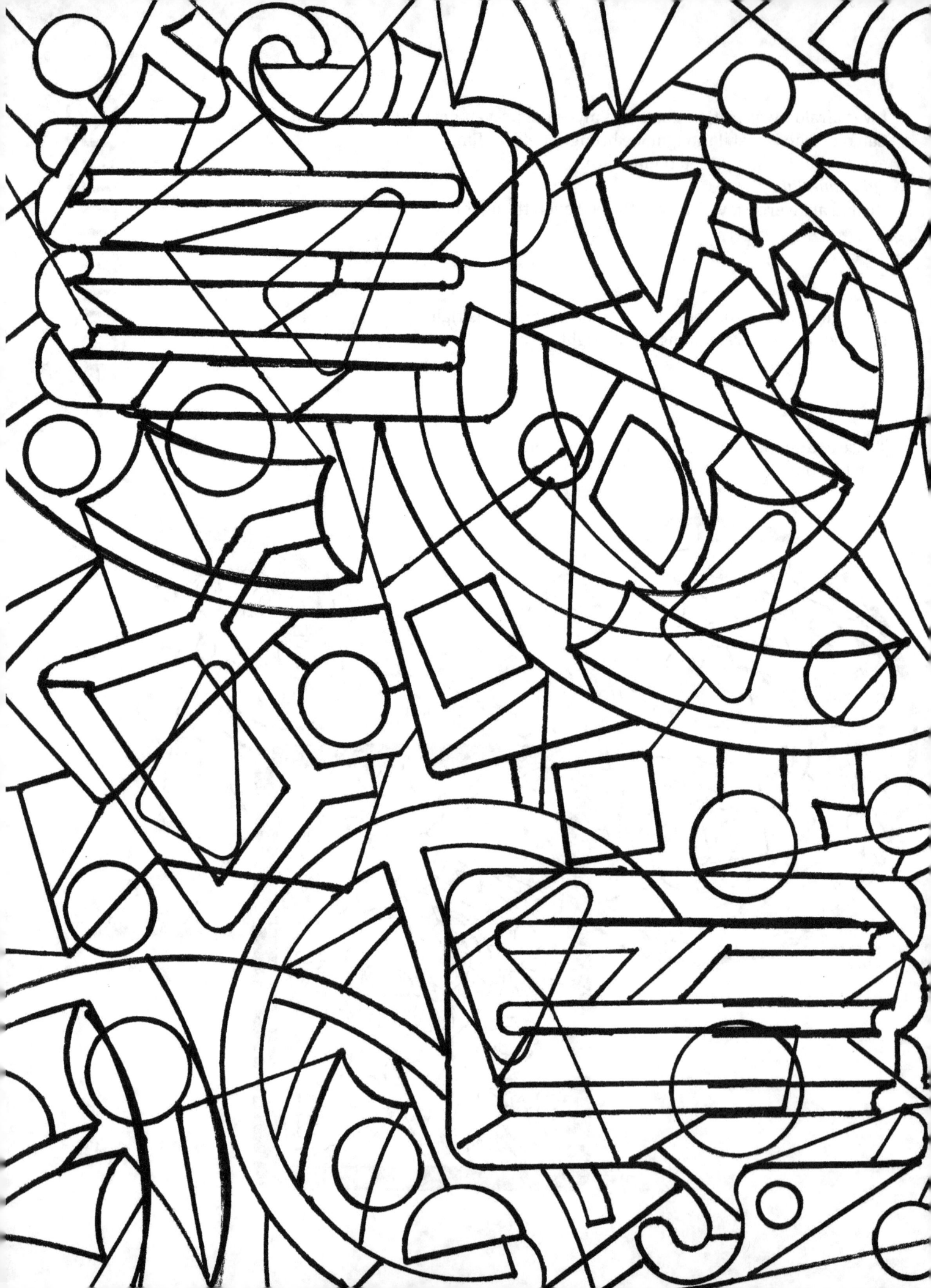

If you find yourself angry or frustrated with God, then there is a deep spiritual sickness in your heart that has led you to believe that God is your servant instead of the other way around. God is not our personal bank teller or wish granter.

Yes, we call on Him and He responds to our prayers. But prayers are not demands. They are sincere, humble requests beseeching The Most Generous, the One who showers blessings upon us while we've done nothing to deserve them.

Thus, to become angry or frustrated when we don't get what we want isn't too different from a child having a tantrum when his or her parents don't bestow every coveted prize or toy.

Dear soul, you need to take an honest look at what you understand your purpose of life to be, then feel anger and frustration—and happiness—to the extent that you fulfill that.

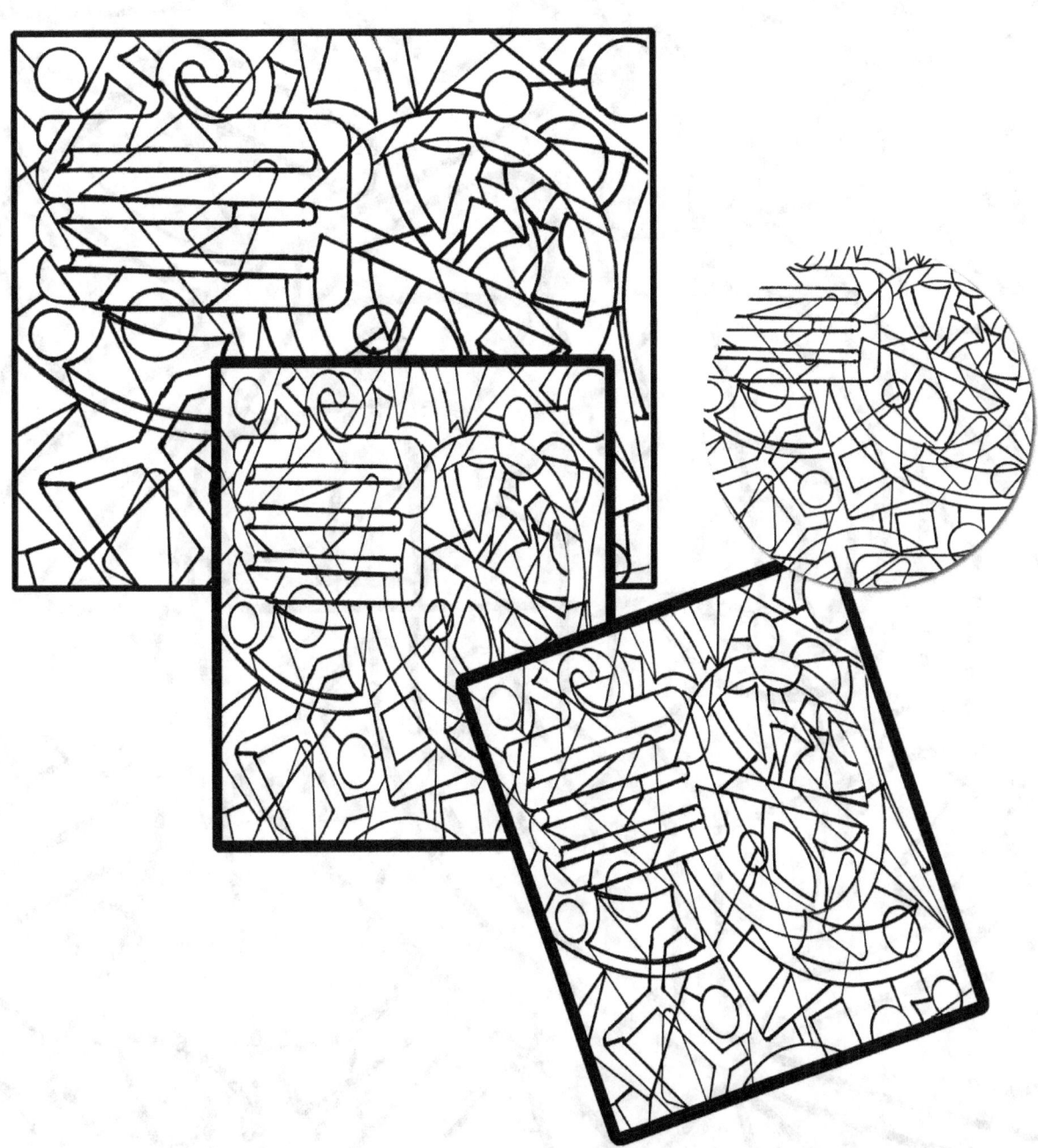

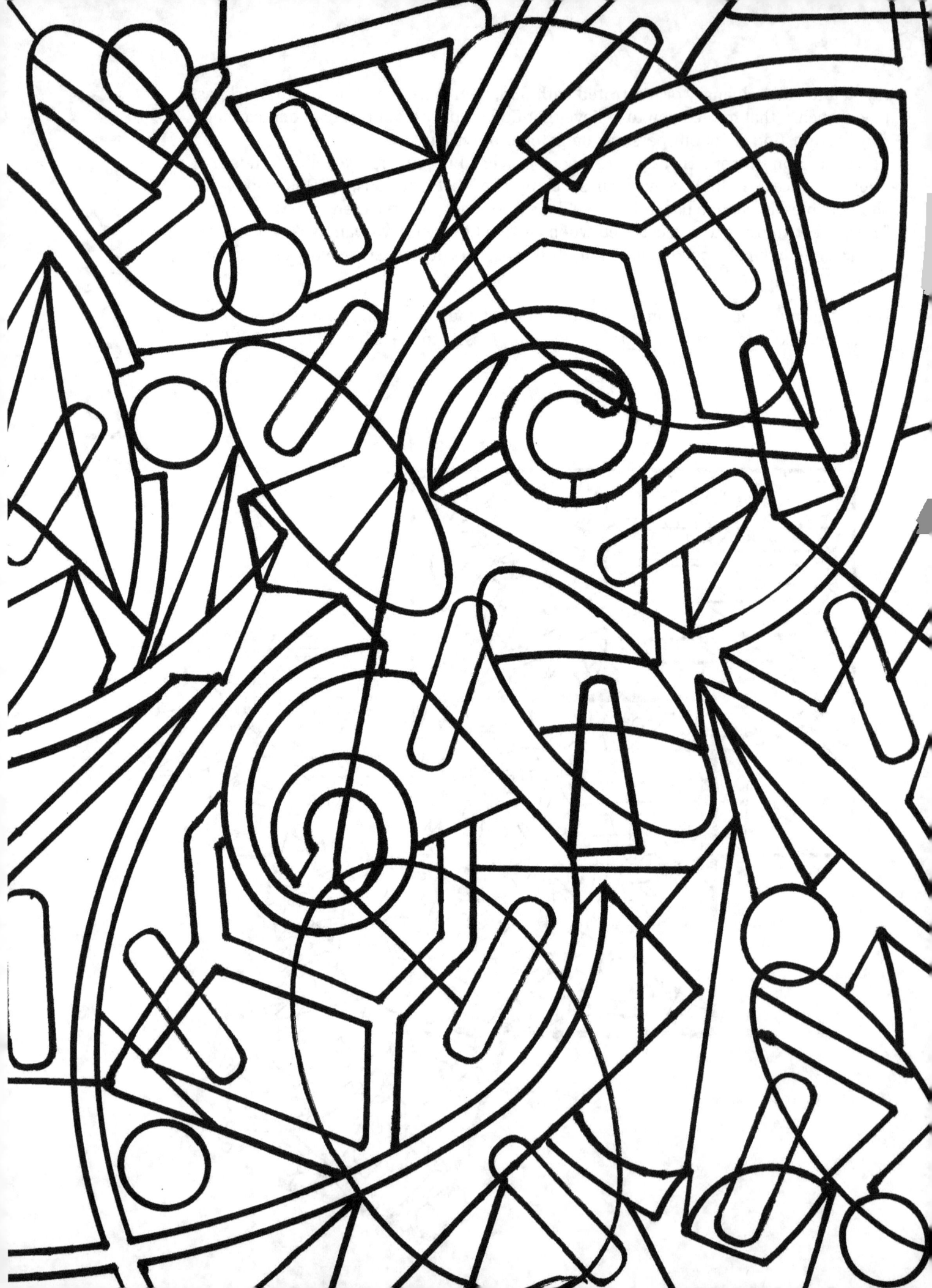

Sins are subtle yet visceral assaults upon the soul.

~

Spiritual diseases, like physical diseases, in the earliest stages manifest in the subtlest, most undetectable ways. Yet it is a rather obvious symptom of spiritual corruption to imagine that only others suffer from the diseases of destructive pride and envy in their lives.

~

The heart tarnished with the deepest envy is blind to its own rust. So it sees its dislike for someone only through the lens of what that person has said or done, but almost never through the lens of its own sight-altering spiritual disease, *hasad*.

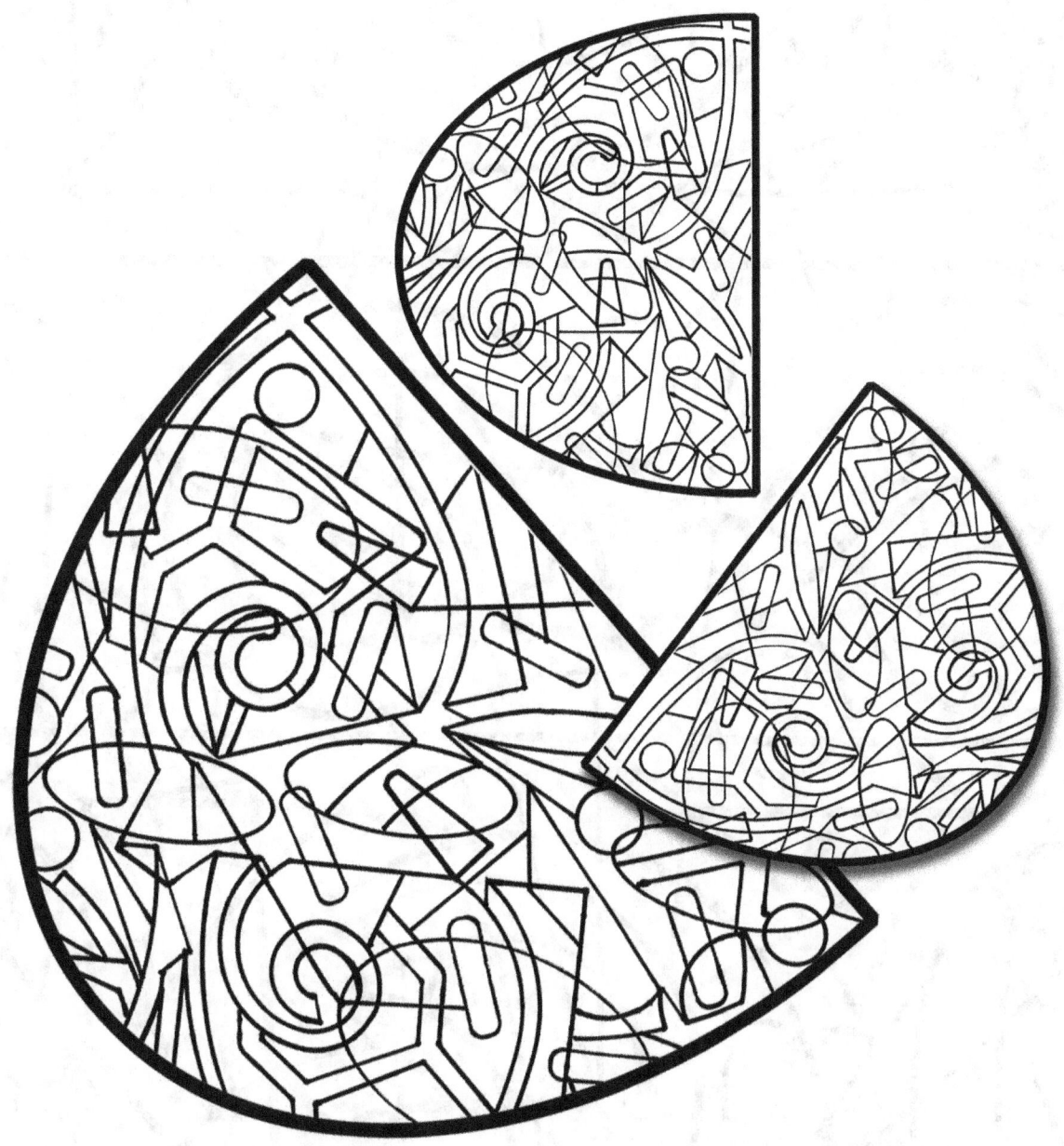

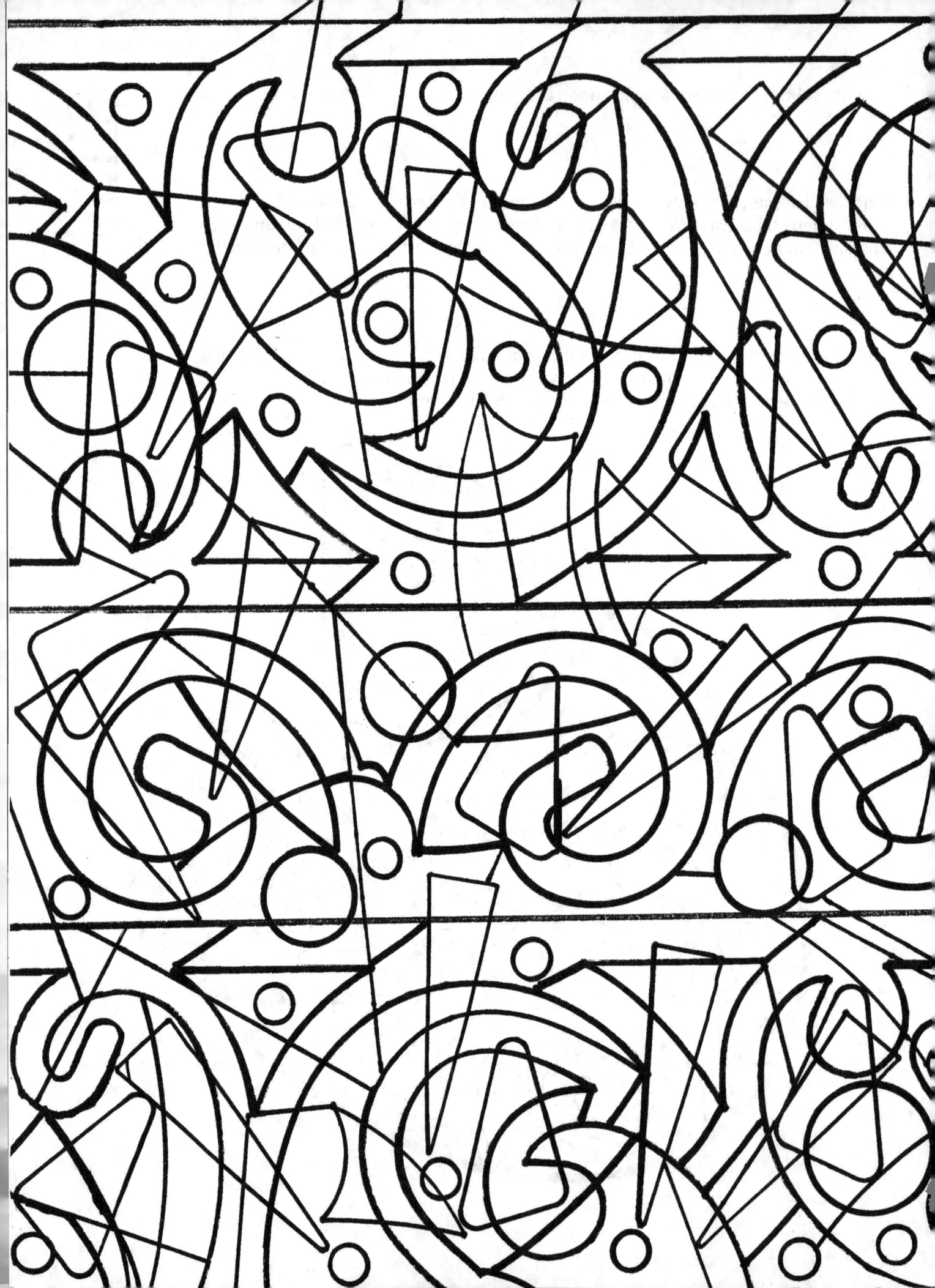

The worst form of prostitution is not of the body, but of the soul.
Only when we tear from ourselves our last shred of spiritual dignity do we lay our hearts bare and willingly open to any coveted corruption that offers the "right price"—thereby selling our souls for the transient pleasures of this world.

But like prostitution of the body, no one sinks to such lows except out of frantic desperation, losing one's way, or severe external pressure—or force.
And no one remains in such lows except out of believing that there is no way out...
Or convincing oneself that this life path was meant to be.

But there is always a way out, even if it is not readily in sight.
And selling neither the body nor the soul is a life path that God meant for any of us on earth. But both physical and spiritual freedom begin with looking deep within ourselves and reclaiming at least a shred of that dignity that God clothed each of us in at birth.

Indignity.

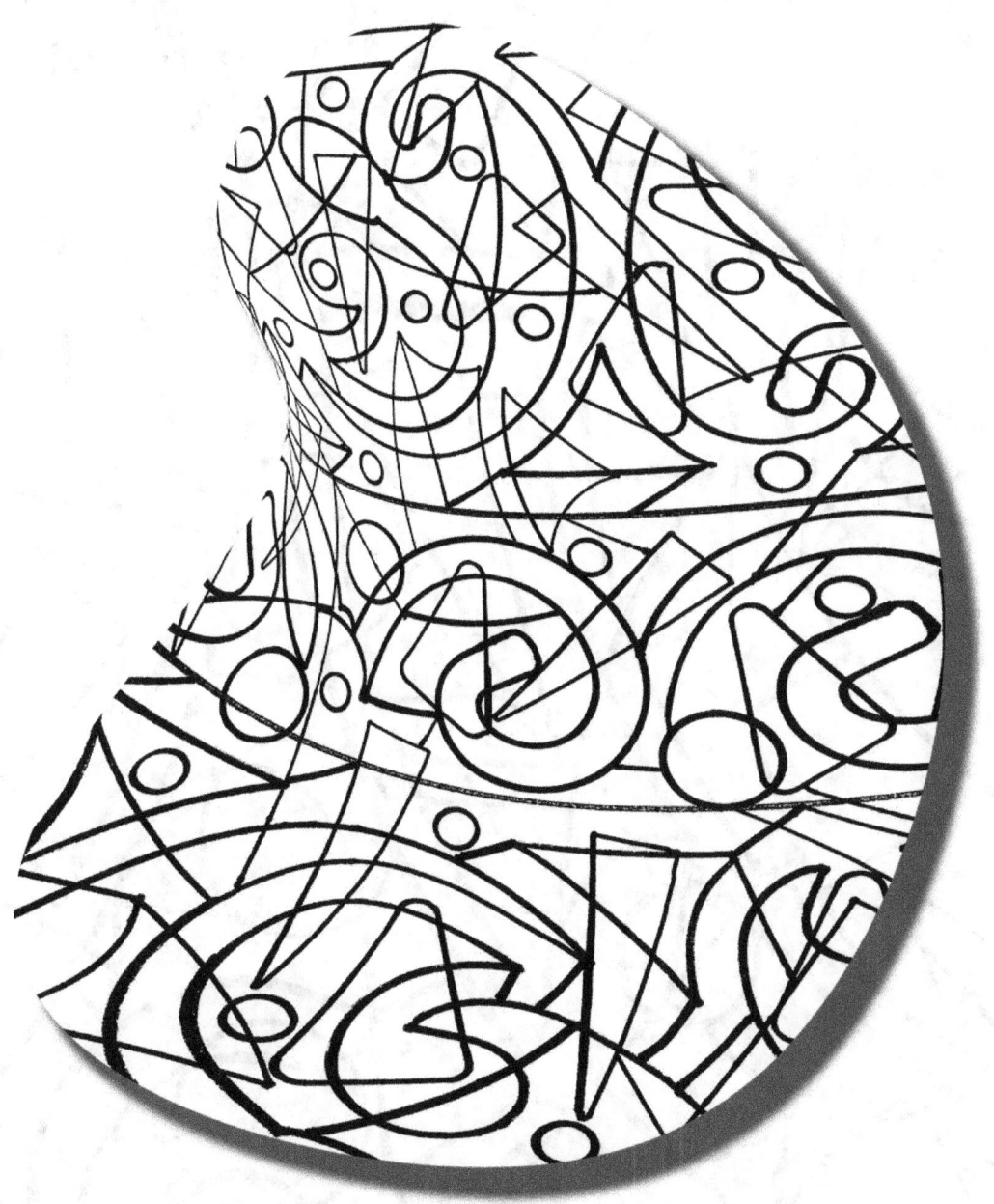

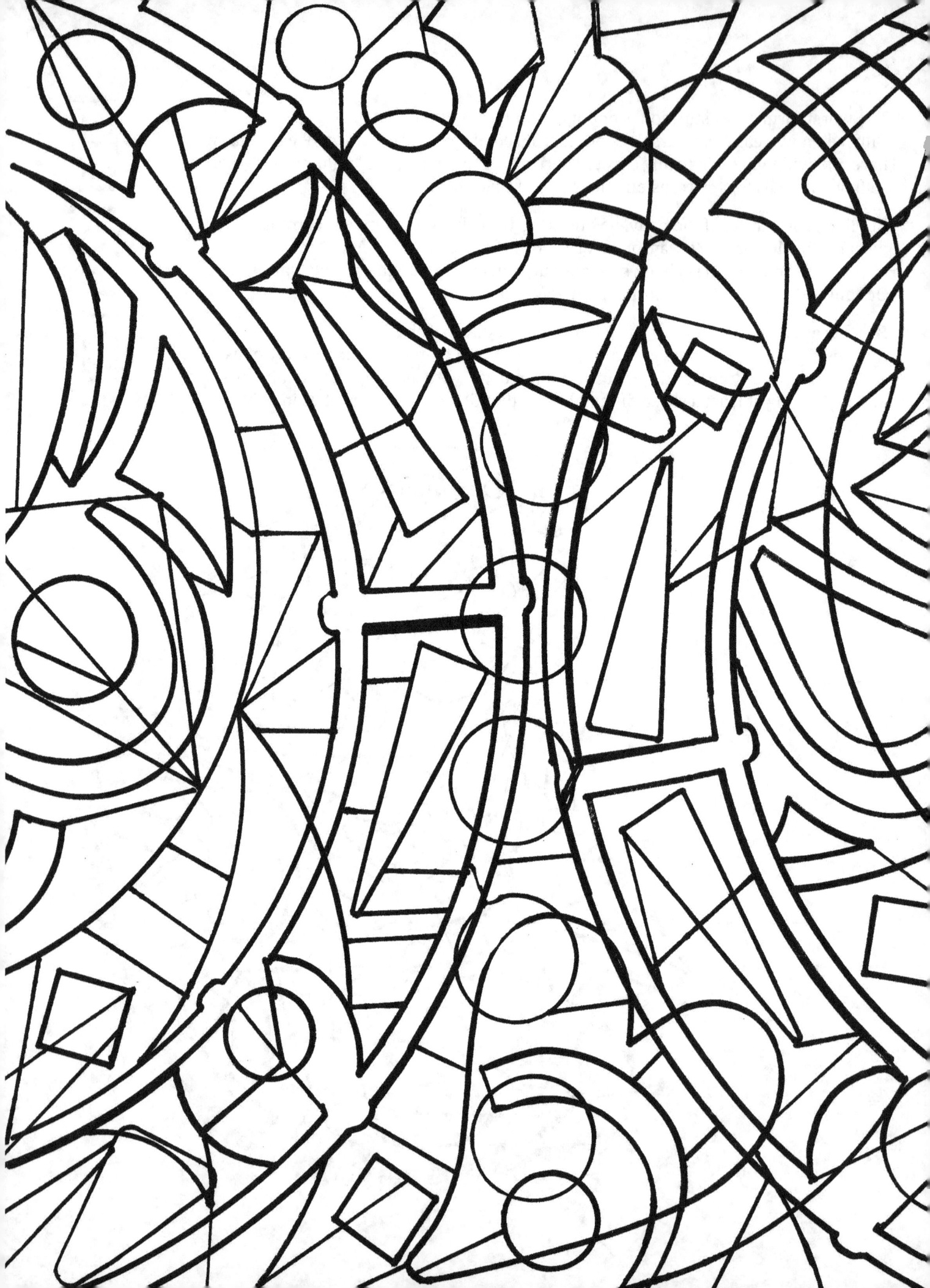

In the end, your failures and successes in life—and ultimately in the Hereafter—boil down to one simple matter: how you spend your time.

~

I'd rather have a difficult, painful road to Paradise than an easy and relaxed, pleasurable path to Hellfire.

~

Do not let your good deeds be your path to Hellfire.
Ask God to remove pride from your heart and scoffing and mocking others from your tongue.

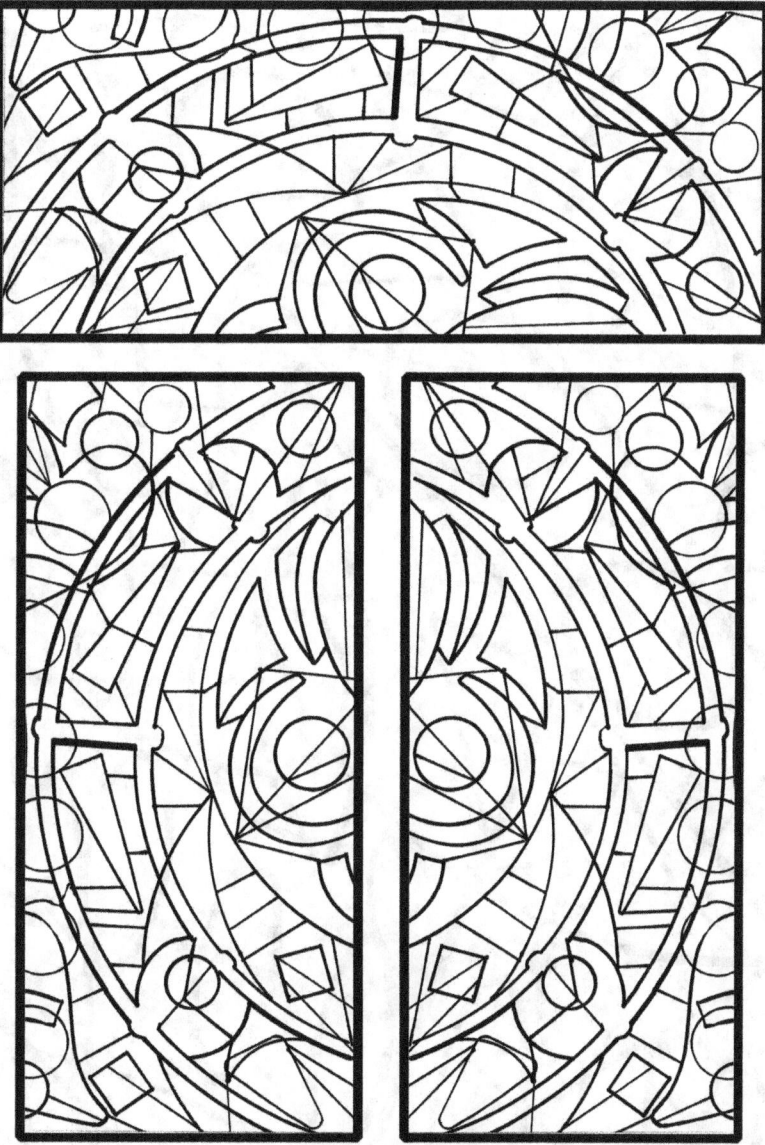

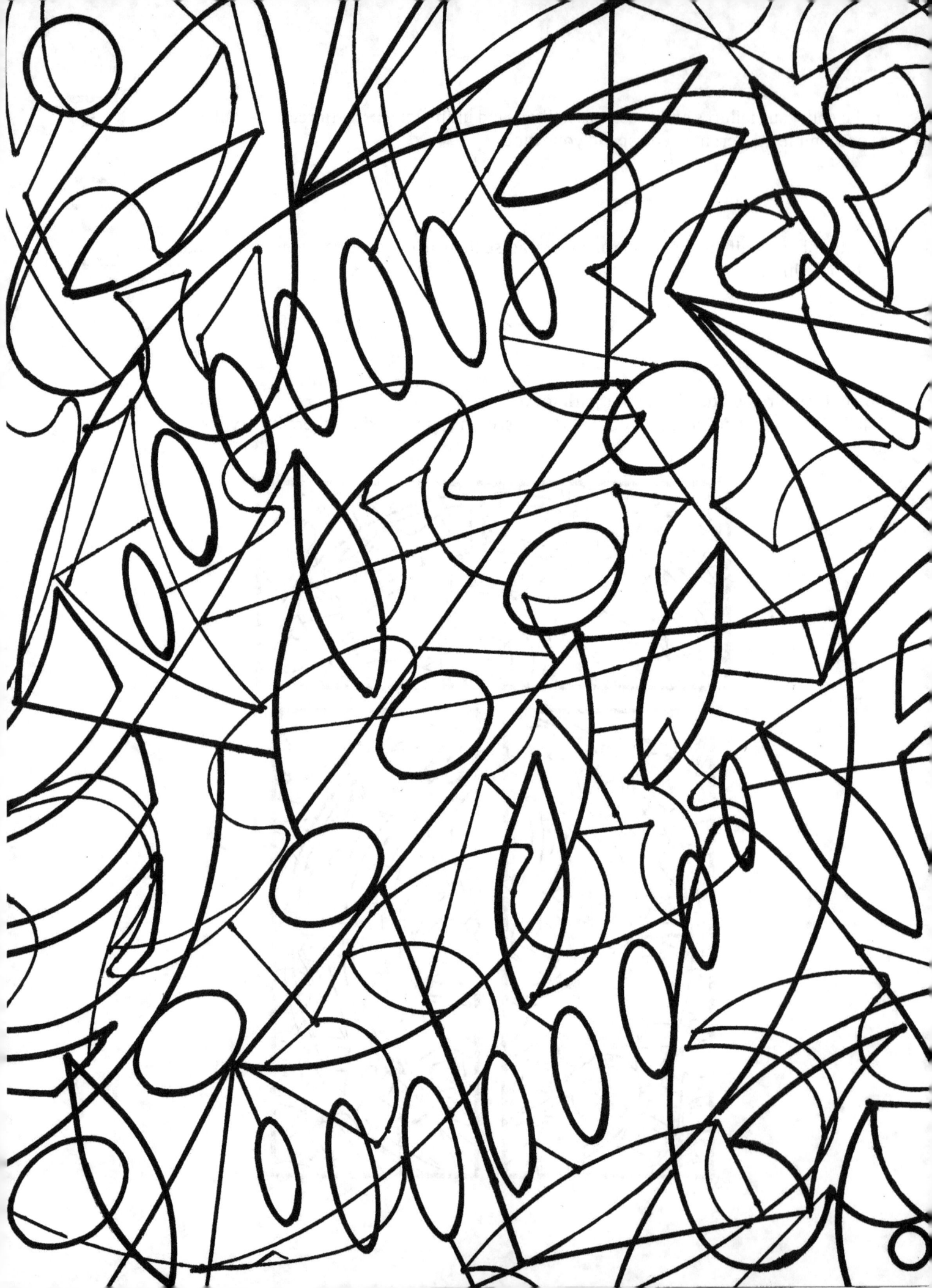

Don't die saying that spiritual truth never reached you, when your soul calls out to you every day. You don't have to take a course in theology or have a religious friend before you realize you should live and die upon sincere belief in God.

Death.

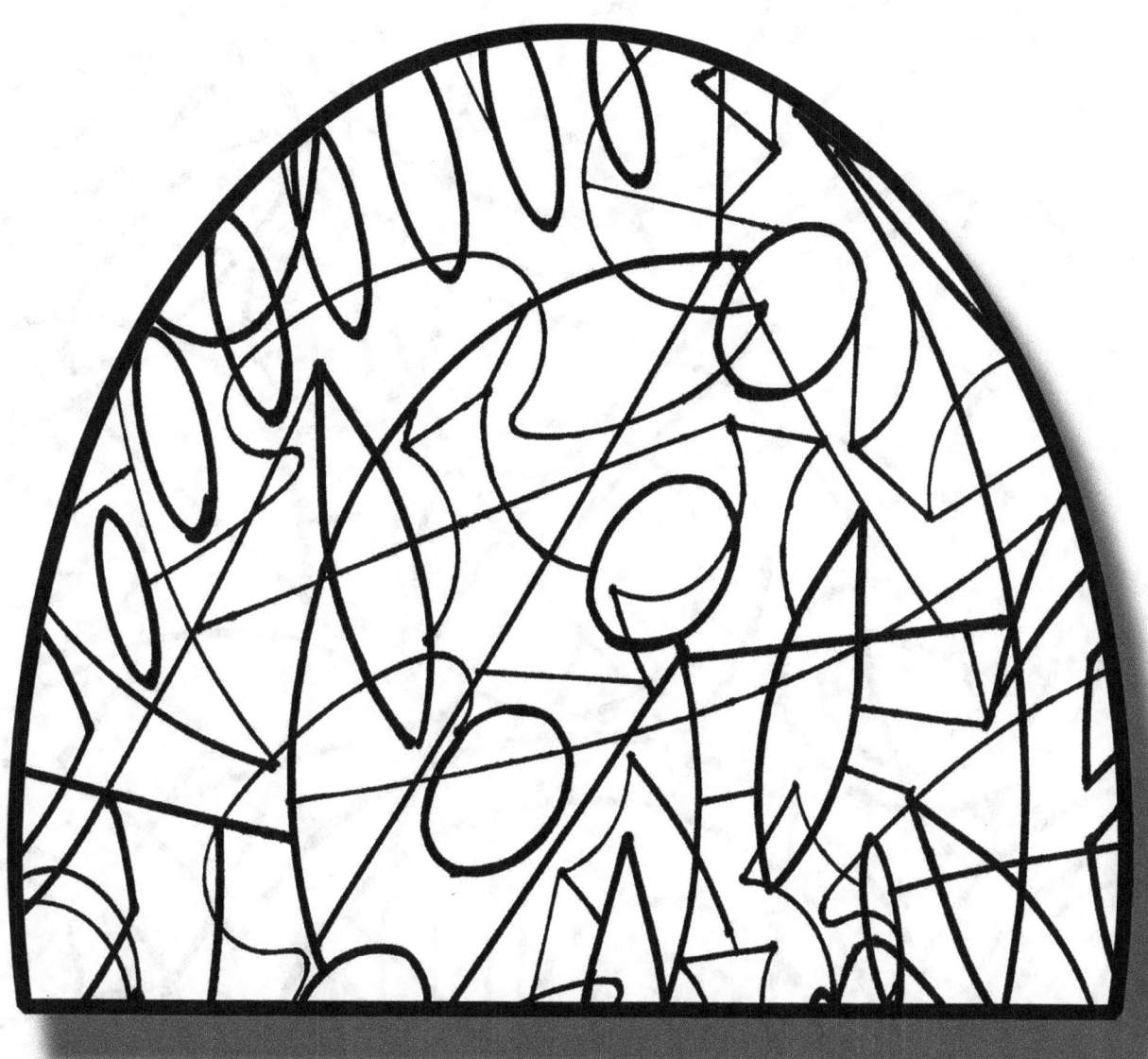

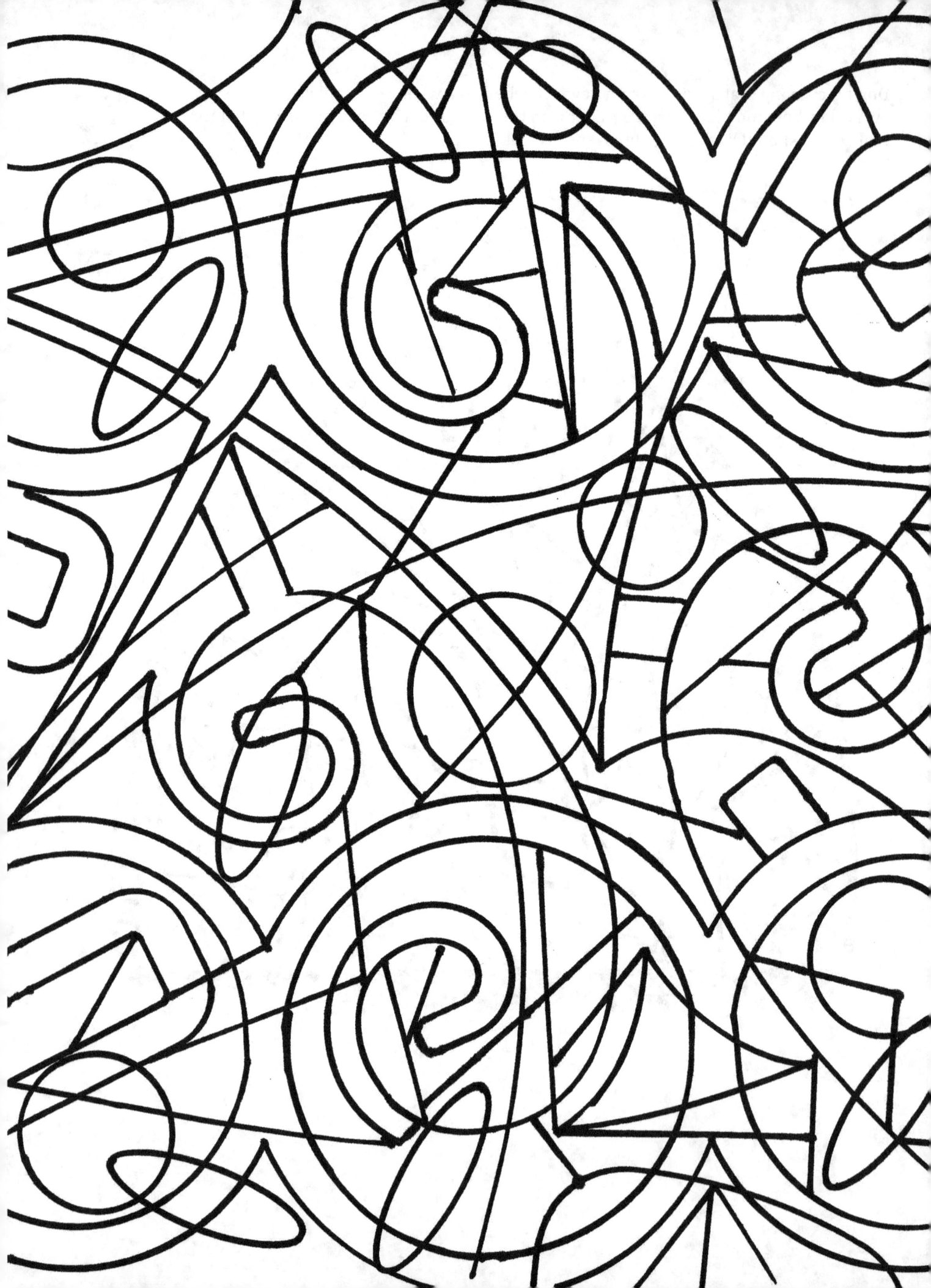

Beware of emotionalism. It is like a cheating spouse.
Faithful to nothing except what excites it at the moment.
Follow it and you'll find yourself constantly off balance, furious, and confused,
even if you've no idea why.
Principles and morality are more dependable.
They remain faithful, no matter what excitement is happening in the world.
So choose principles and morality over emotionalism.
They are the cornerstones of faith.

Emotionalism.

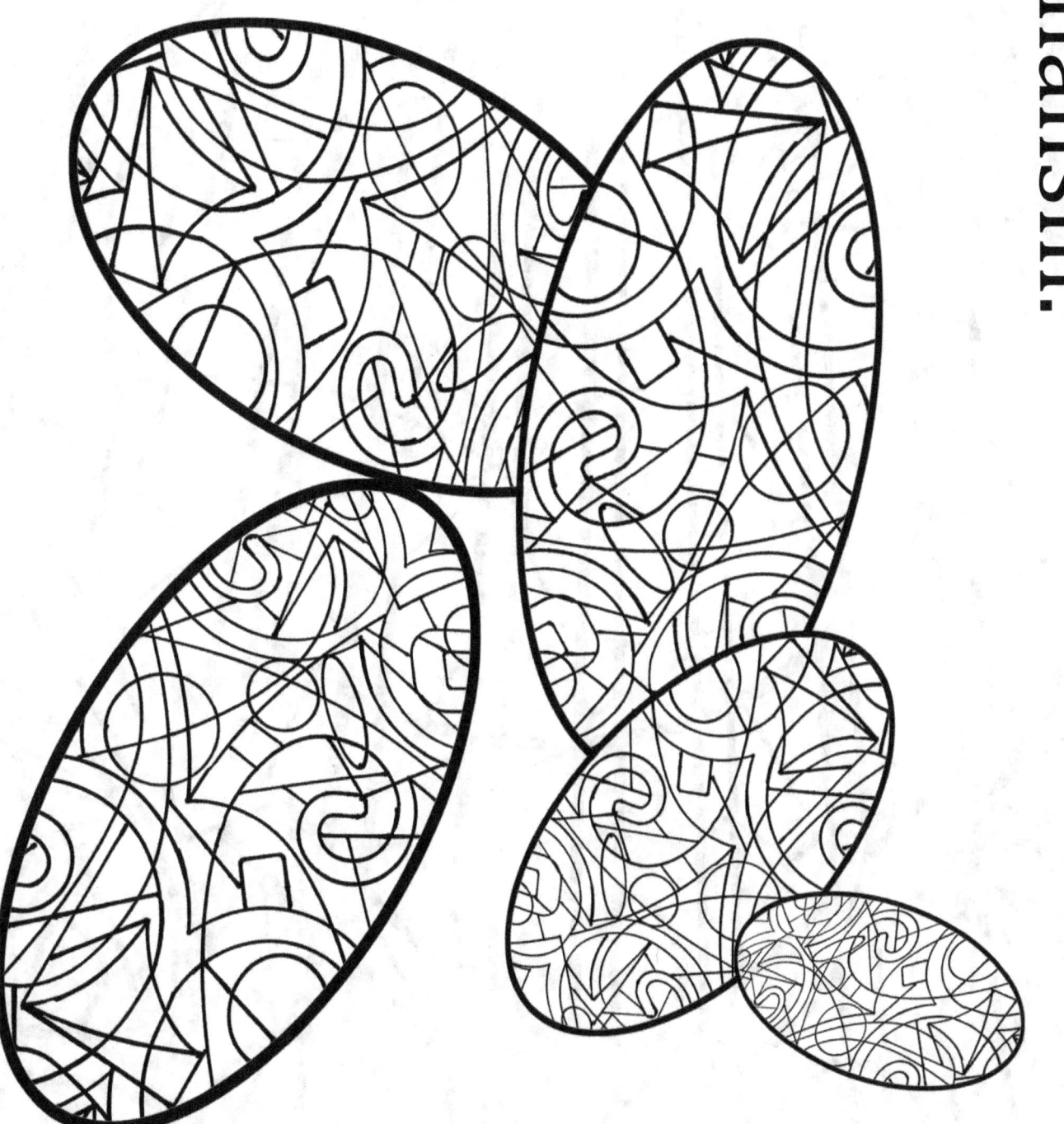

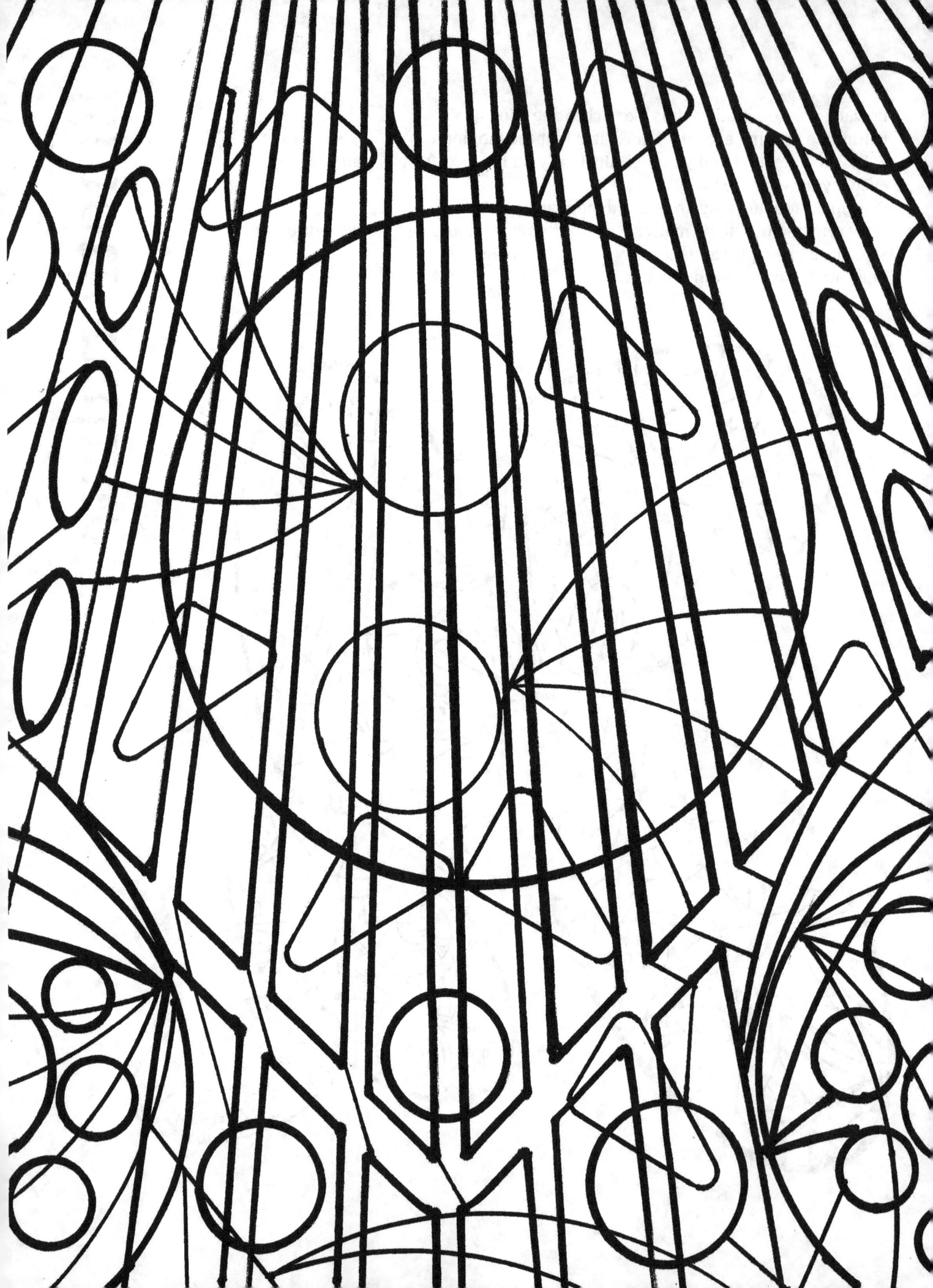

In the eyes of those who seek fault, no good you do is sincere,
and any bad you do reflects who you "really" are.

~

I claim no perfection in conveying the truth. However, I encourage you to sincerely reflect on the fact that your reactions and opinions do not reflect reality. They reflect only your personal feelings, emotions, and opinions. Thus, to use terms like "judgmental attitude" indicate a very faulty path in communication and perception, as they imply that your internal world reflects the reality of the world around you.

~

"I don't care what people think!" many of us boast.
But is that really true?
If it is, why then do we keep saying, "Don't judge"?
The popularity and earnestness of this statement alone means we actually care a great deal about what people think. Otherwise, their judgment (or lack thereof) wouldn't matter to us, and we certainly wouldn't feel the need to keep exclaiming, "Don't judge!"
Be honest with yourself.

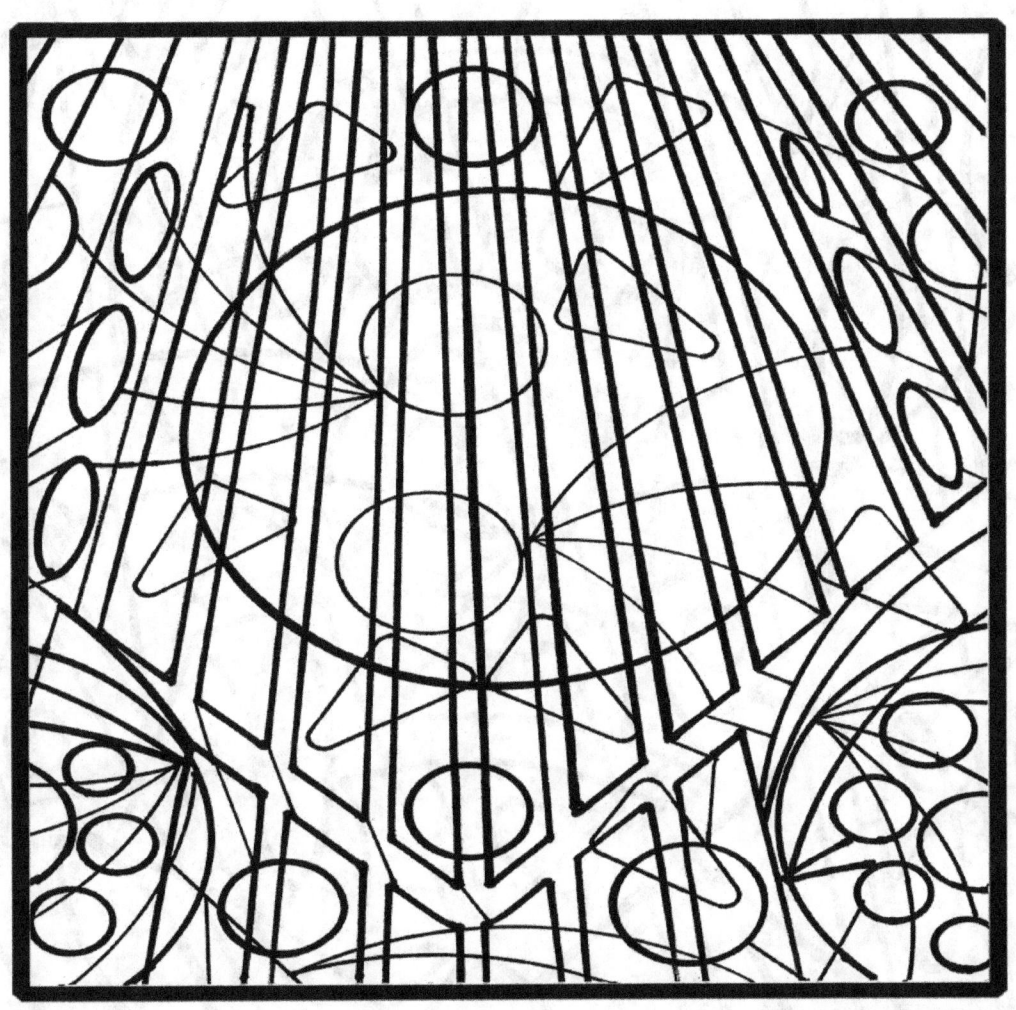

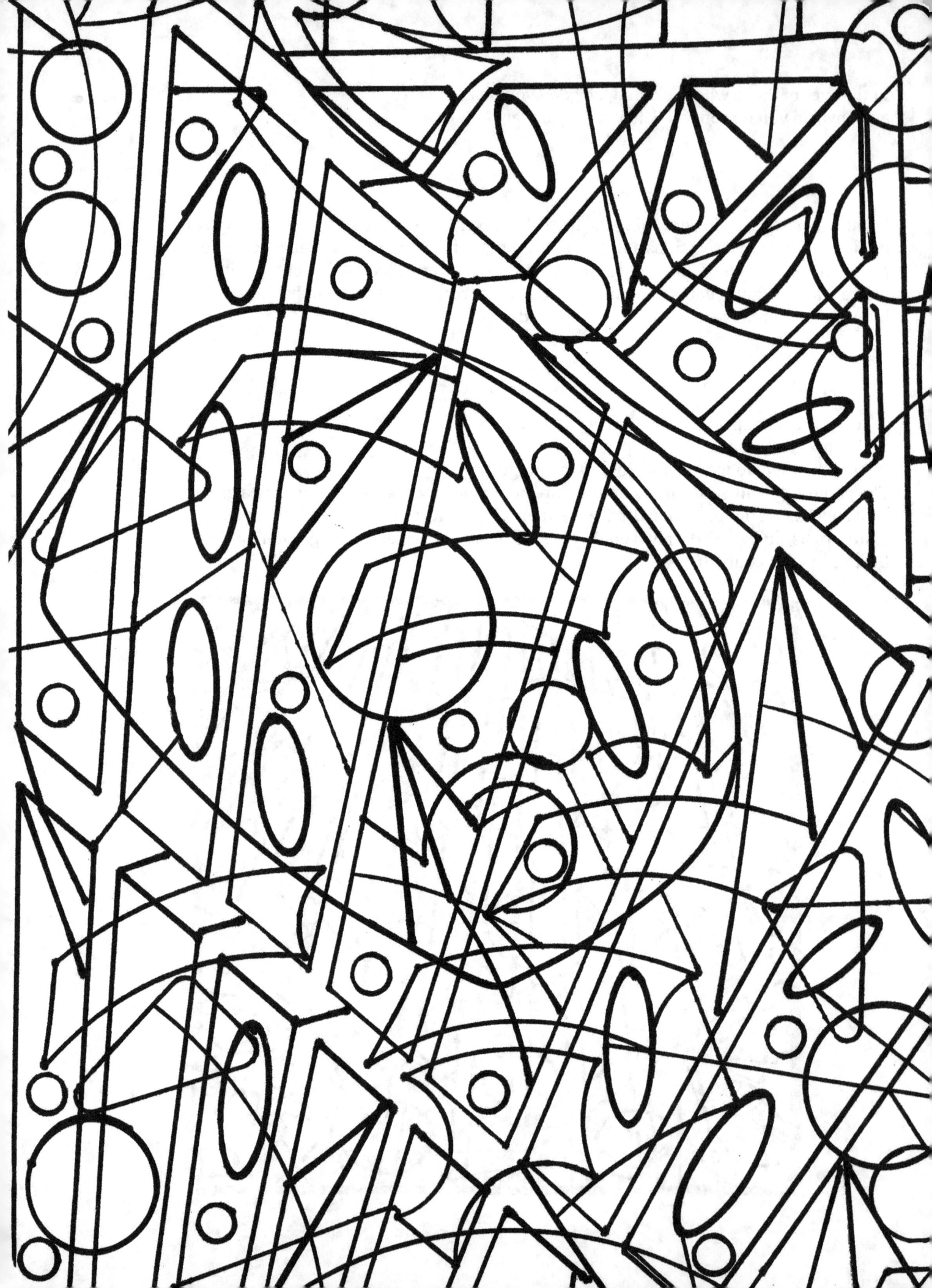

There is a saying, "The eyes are a window to the soul."
I always thought of it as a person seeing into the soul of another by merely looking at him.
But now I think it is a person seeing into their own soul by reflecting on what their eyes
see in others.

Windows.

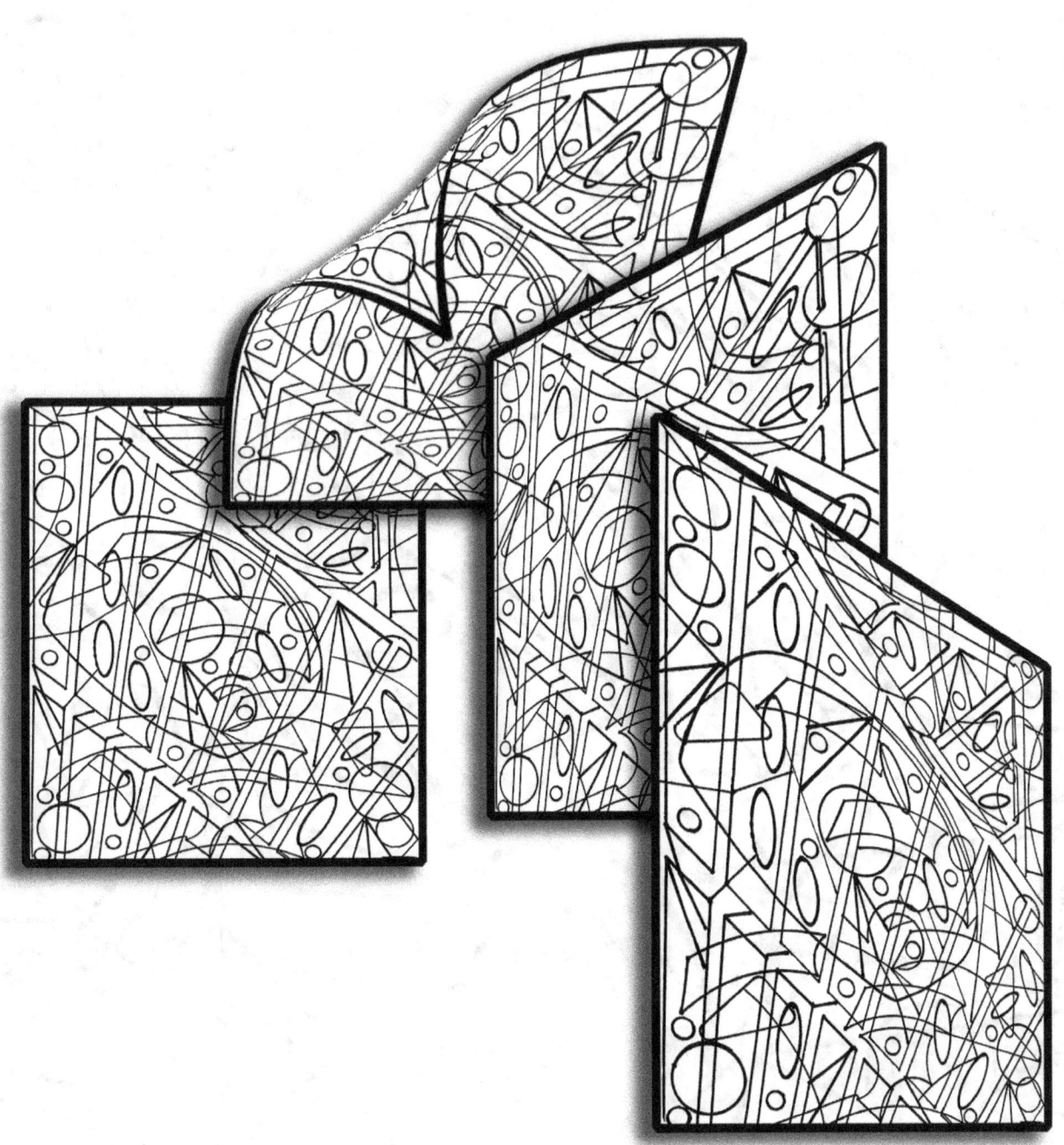

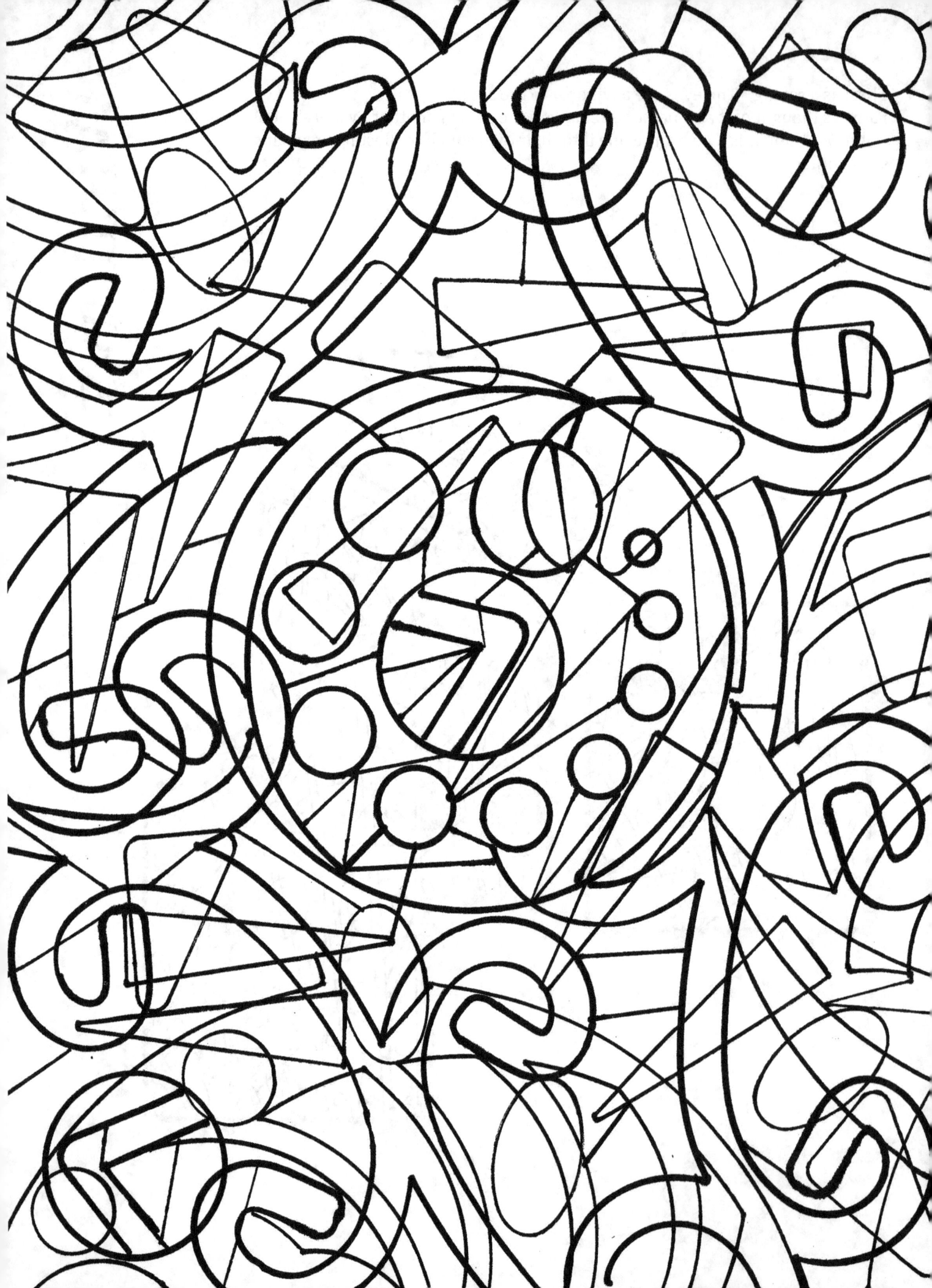

We want others' love and admiration so much that we're willing to sacrifice loyalty to fellow believers—and even God Himself—to get it.

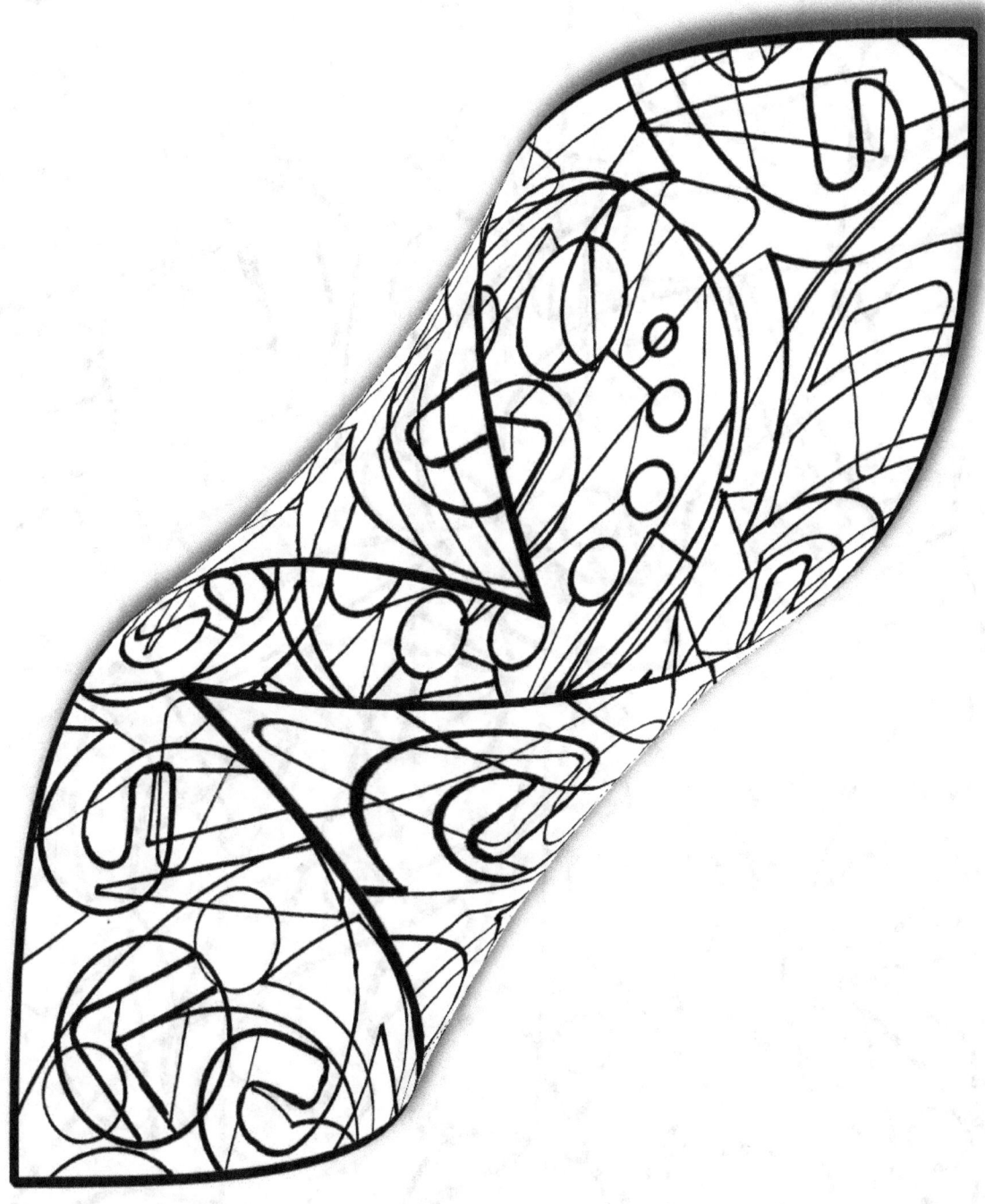

Insecurity.

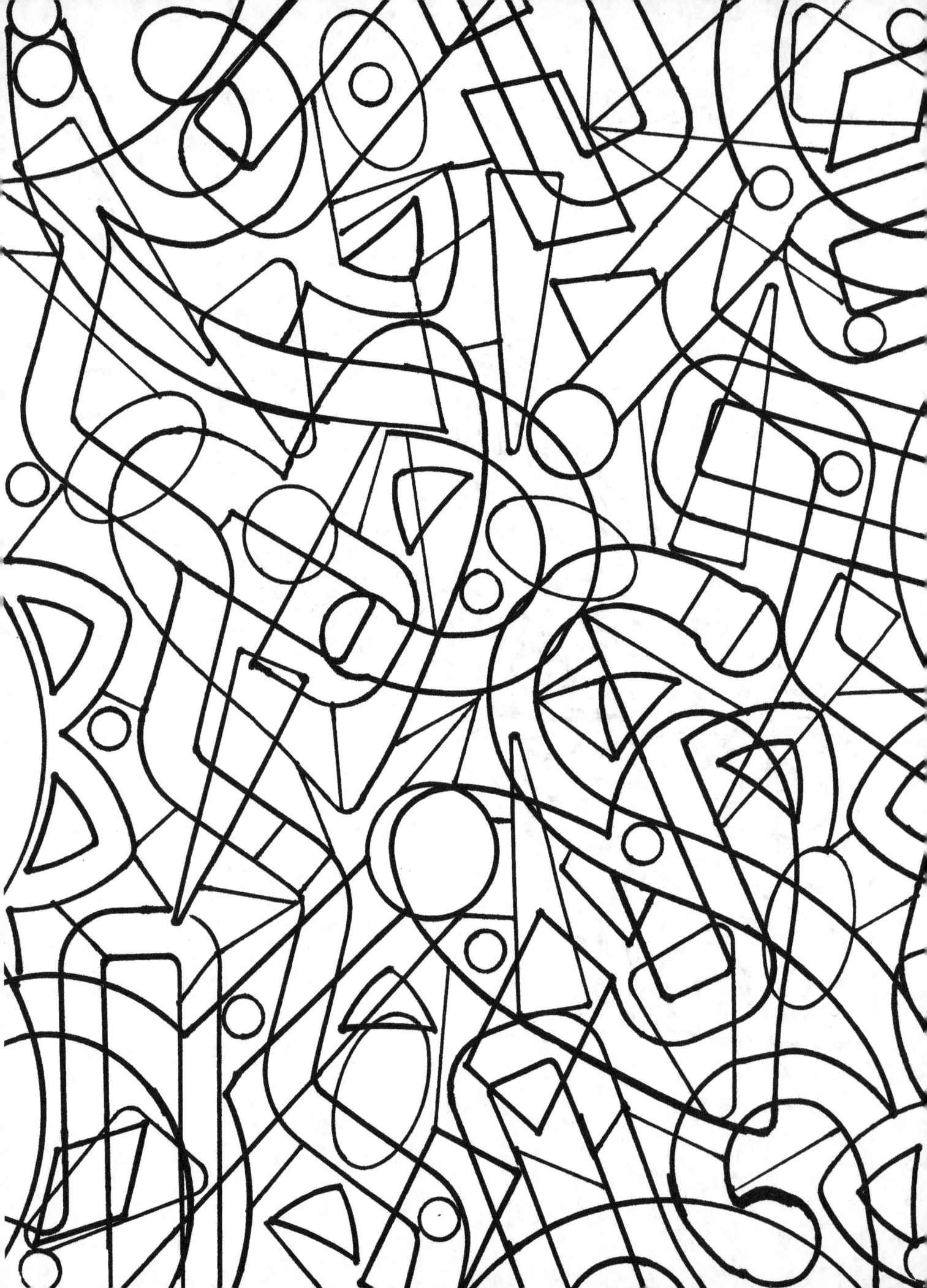

"If you truly cared, you would've never left!" or
"A good friend will always be there, no matter what," we say.
But is it true?
These claims might make us feel self-righteous when loved ones walk away, but in truth, they're self-serving and dishonest.
It's possible that the person left simply because they prioritized their physical, emotional, and spiritual health over our company—no matter how much they loved and cared for us.

We hear a lot about toxic relationships and the importance of letting go, but it's rare that we turn that logic around and take an honest look at ourselves: Yes, it's possible that *you* are toxic to someone you love.

So if they truly care, they'll never leave?
No, this couldn't be further from the truth.
Rather, if they truly care—for their soul—they'll do all they can to protect it, even if it means walking away from someone they love and care for more than life itself.

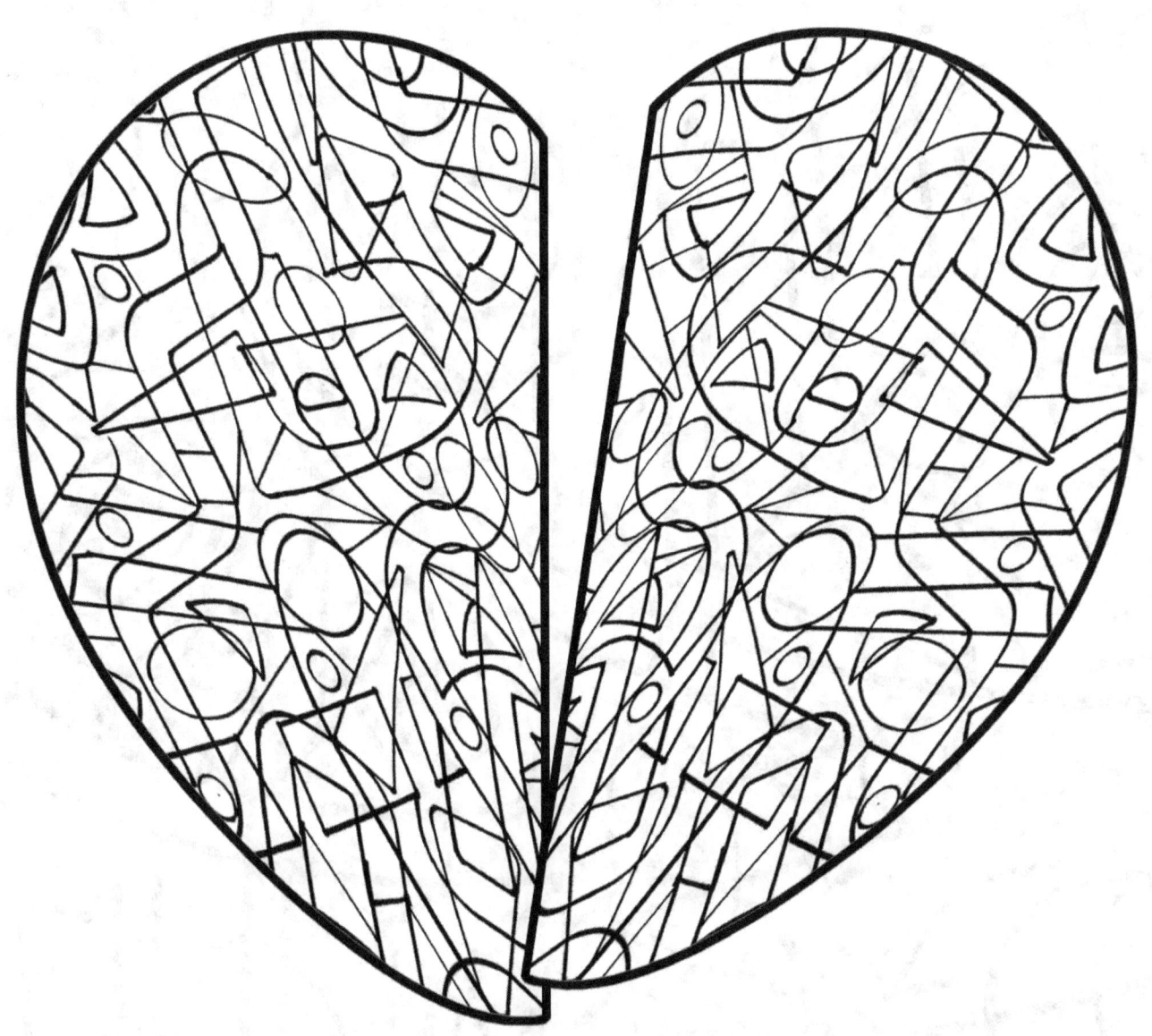

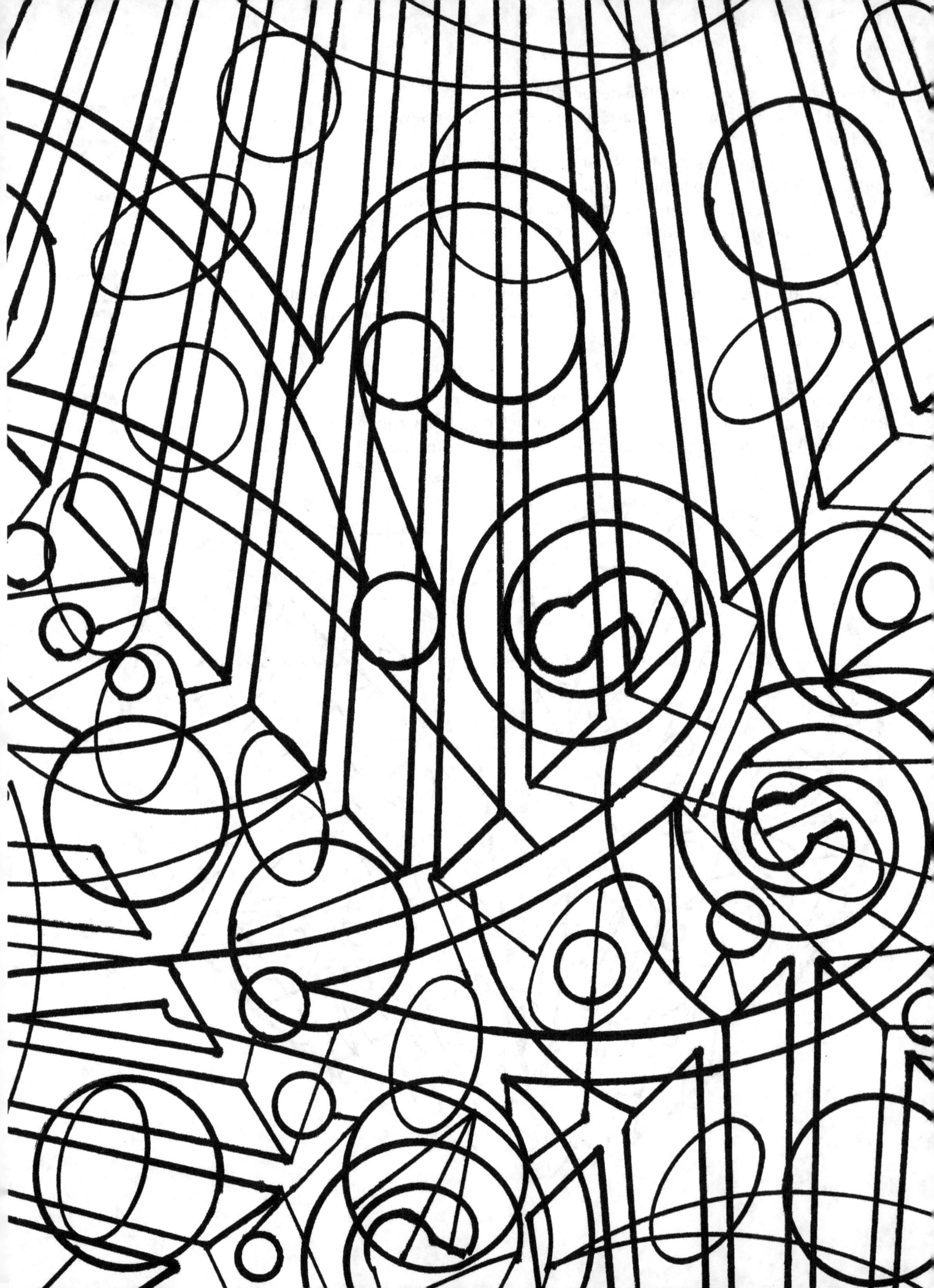

Giving up is worse than sin.
Sinning can inspire repentance, but giving up can inspire disbelief.
And God forgives sins, not disbelief.
So don't despair.
Repent.

Despair.

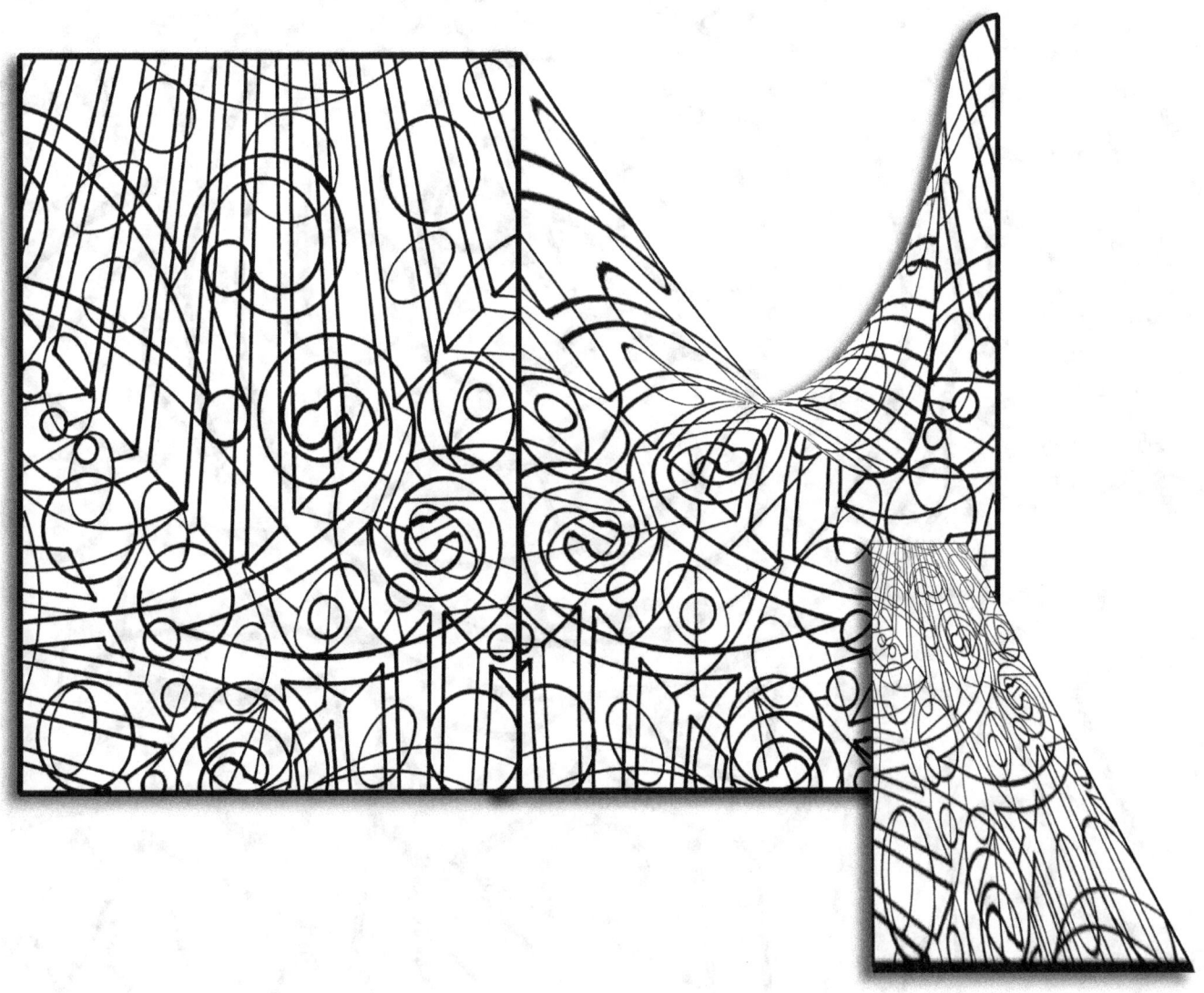

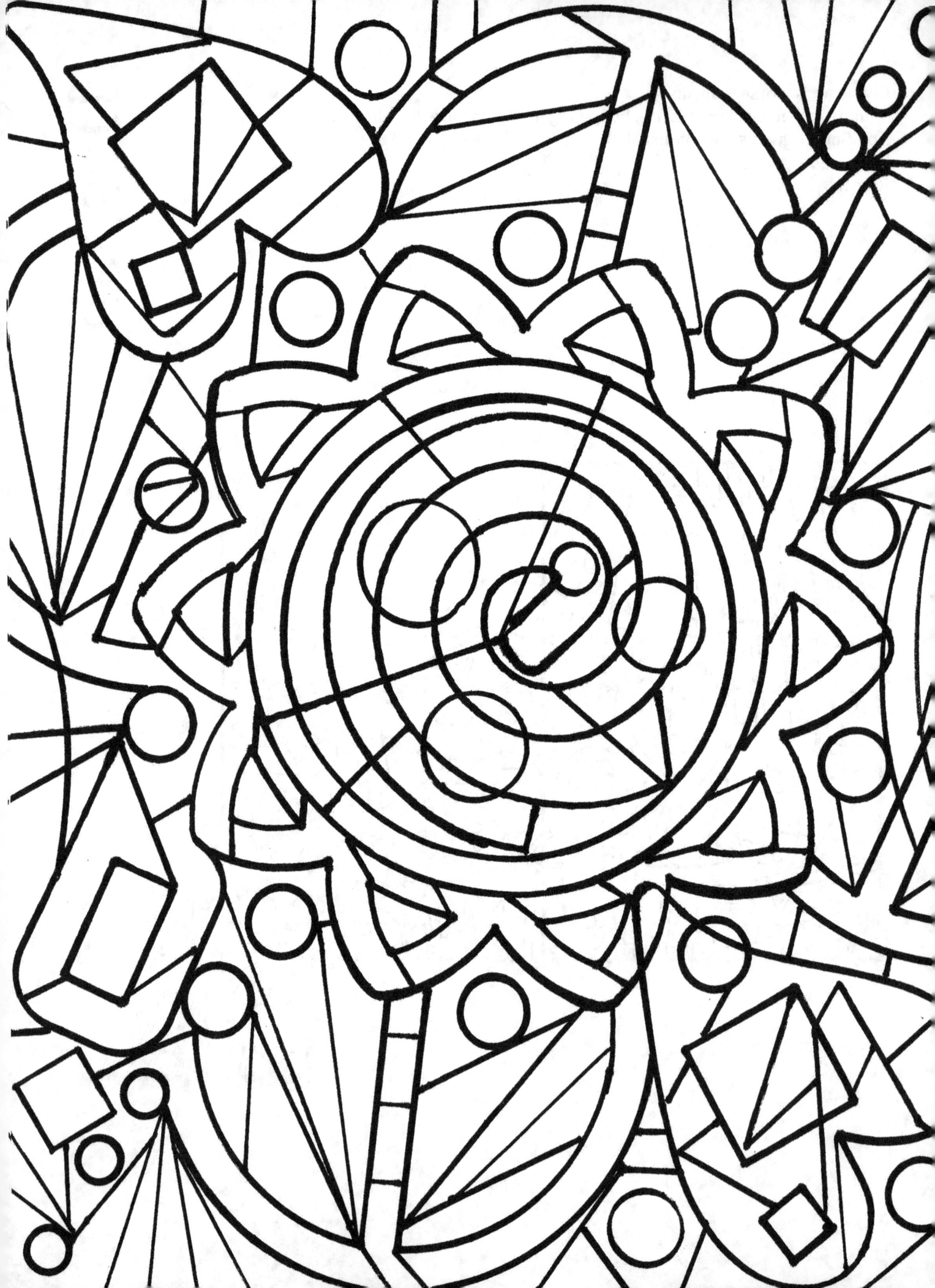

No matter how much you love, admire, or benefit from someone, they will inevitably say or do something that reminds you that they are merely human and all praise and greatness belong to God. Yet even then, some of us miss the lesson entirely, as we try to interpret even their mistakes and wrongdoing as right and good, or we feel betrayed and thus abandon them, saying, "They're not who I thought they were."
Who did you think they were?
From the children of Adam, God created only human beings.

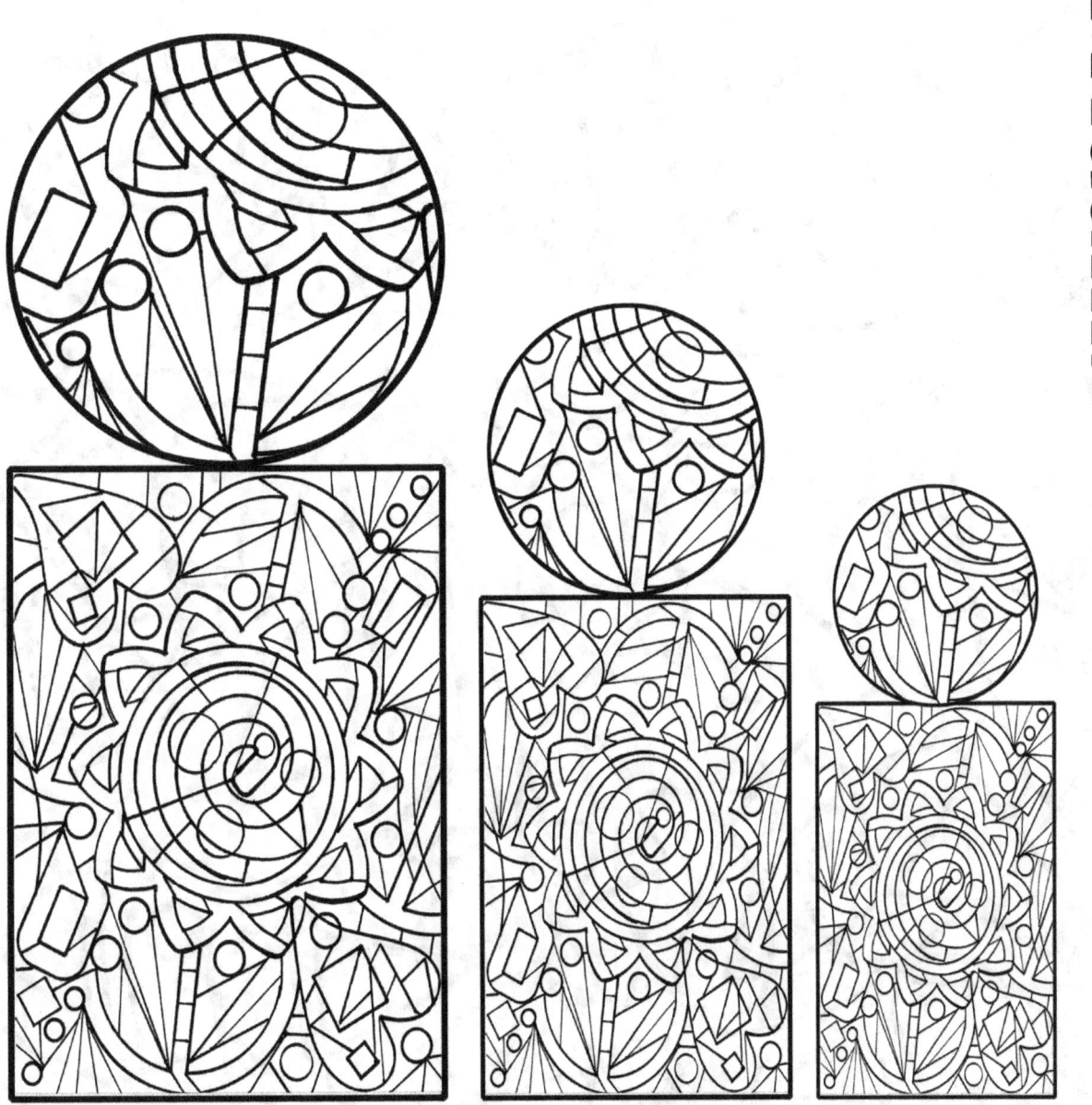

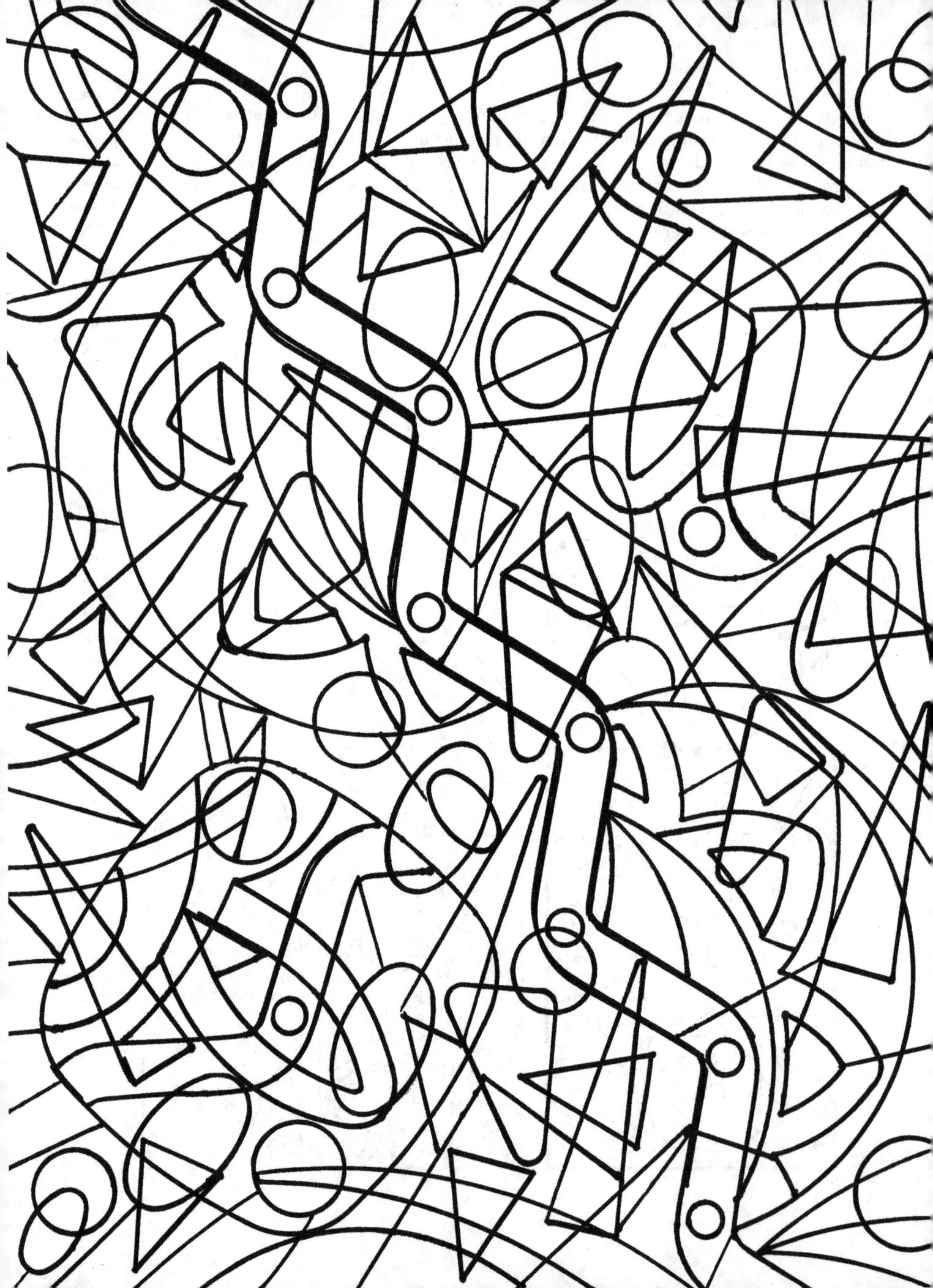

When this world is your Paradise, it only makes sense to believe you should have everything your heart desires and your body craves.
But when this world is merely a brief stop on a longer journey, your heart and body yearn only for home.

Journey.

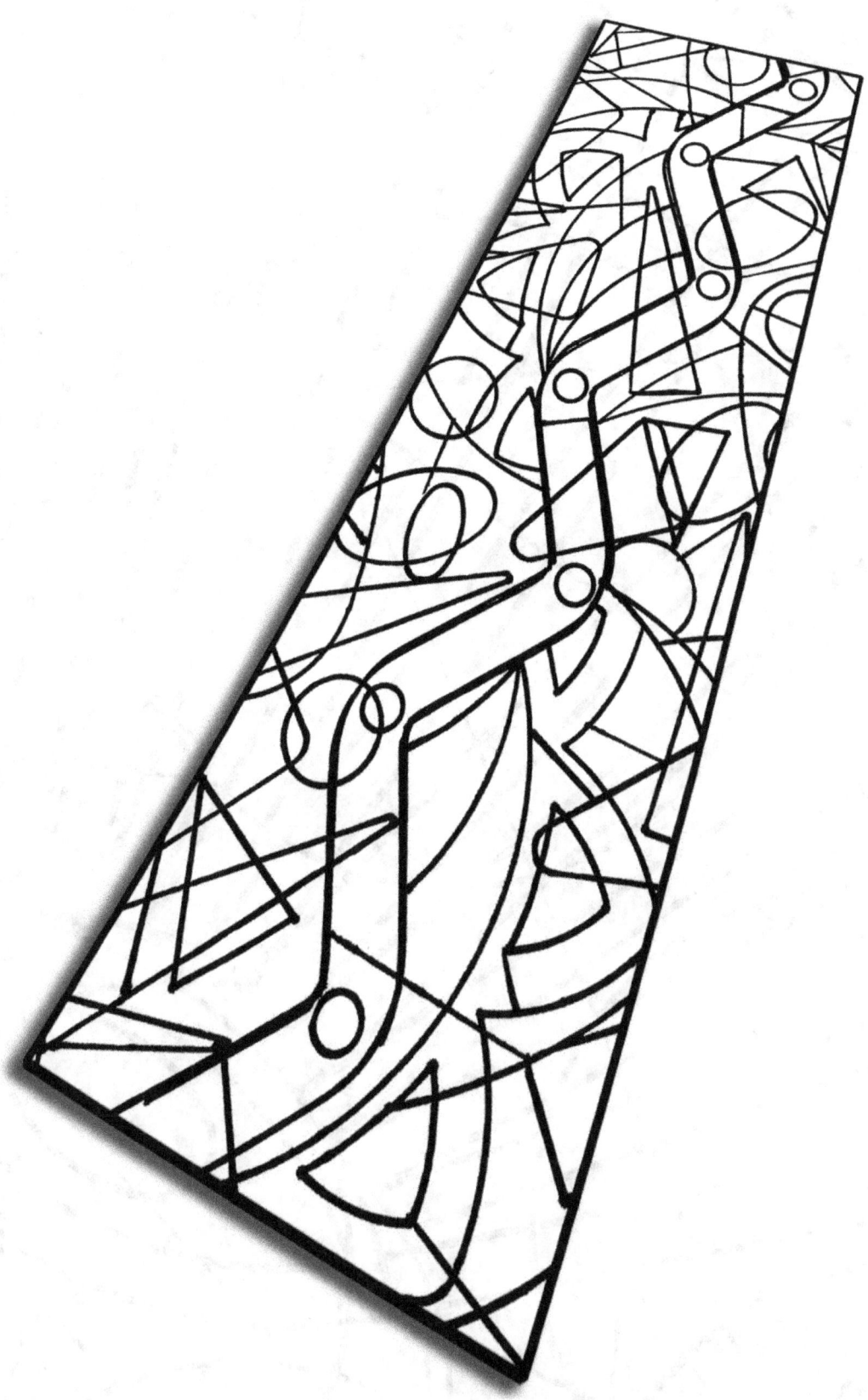

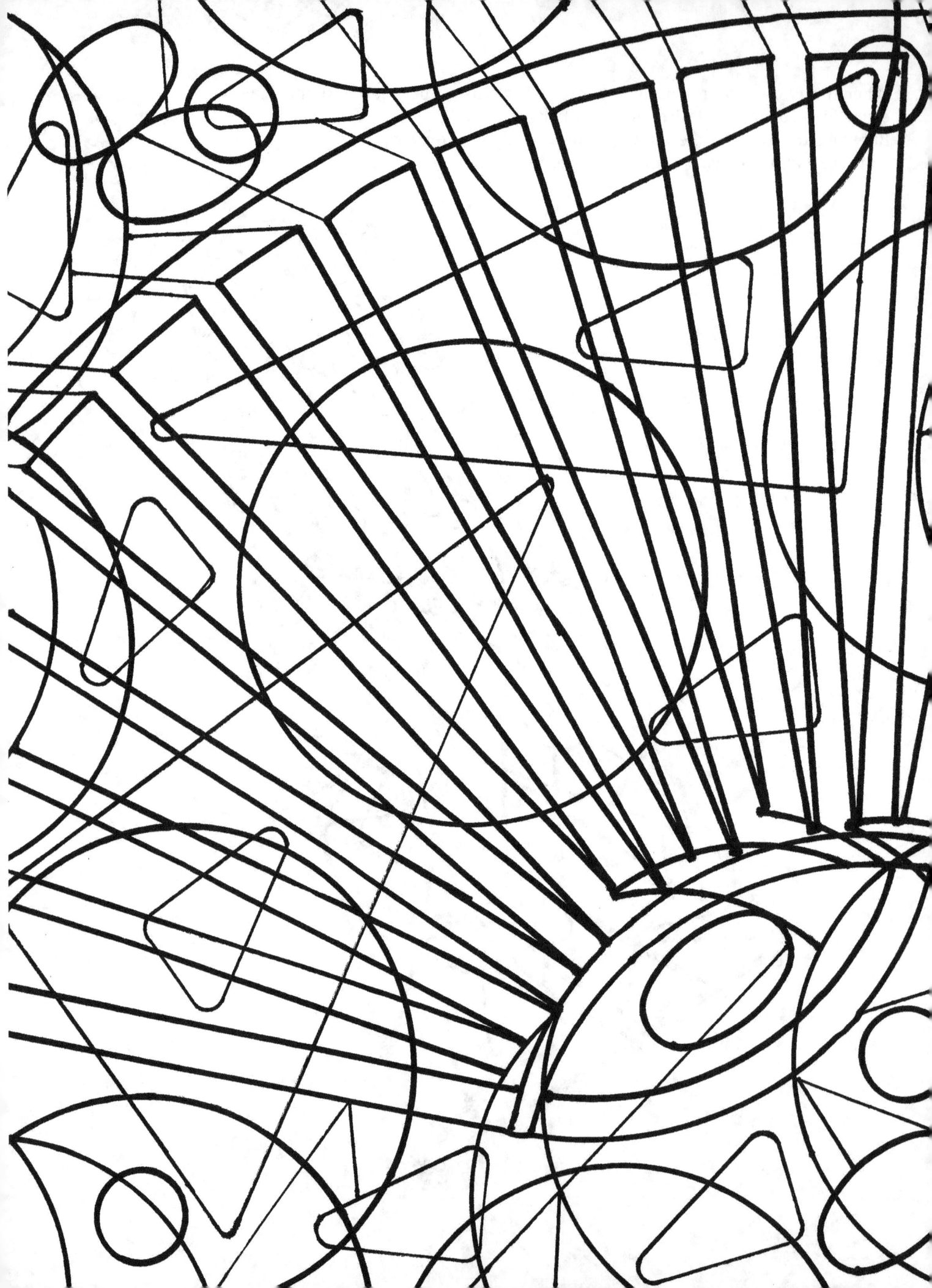

"Anything that's important enough, you make time for!" we say. "No one's too busy!"
But this isn't necessarily true. Anything that's important to you, you'll *want* to make time for even though sometimes you're not able to, no matter how much the sacrifice hurts.

So if you have a friend or loved one who values you and their Lord enough to recognize the existence of an unseen reality they might not be aware of, treasure them.
For most people, if you do anything different from what they want or demand of you, they accuse you of selfishness and not valuing them.
Yet every struggle a person faces in life, whether due to health or personal reasons, isn't something they want to talk about, even to friends and loved ones.'

Time.

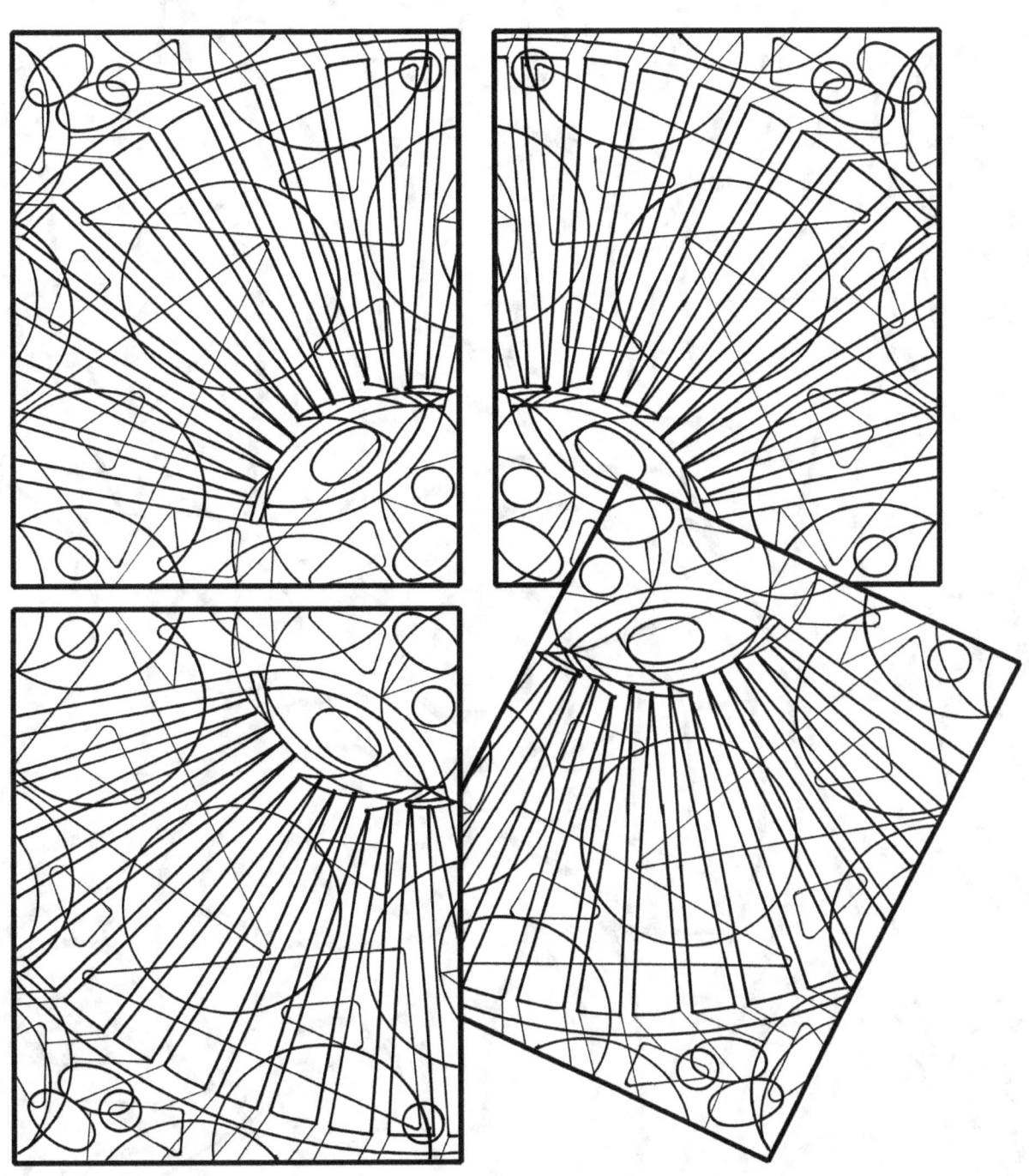

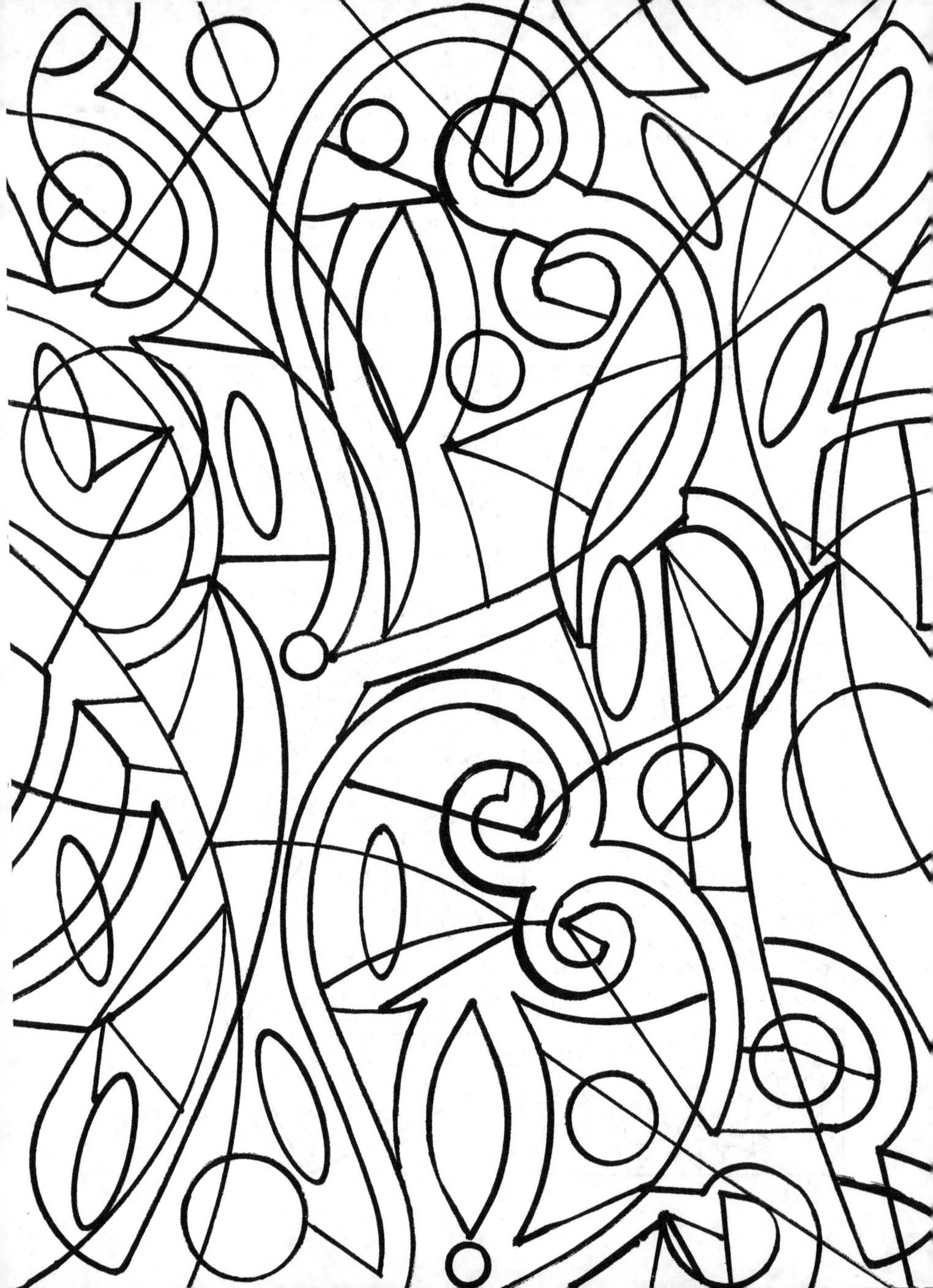

A heart that doesn't soften at the words of God is a hardened heart,
no matter how many tears are evoked by the words of men.

Hearts.

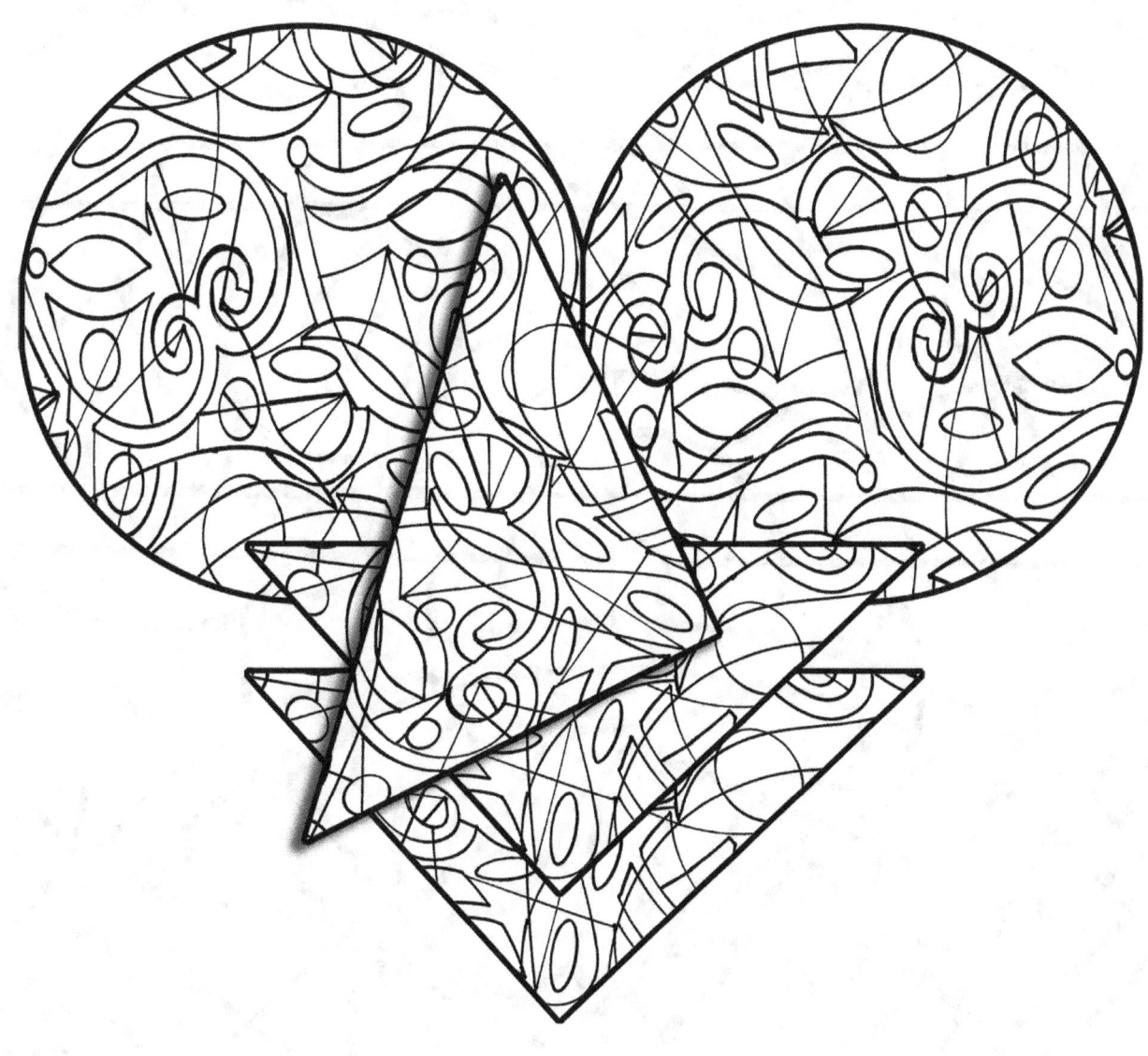

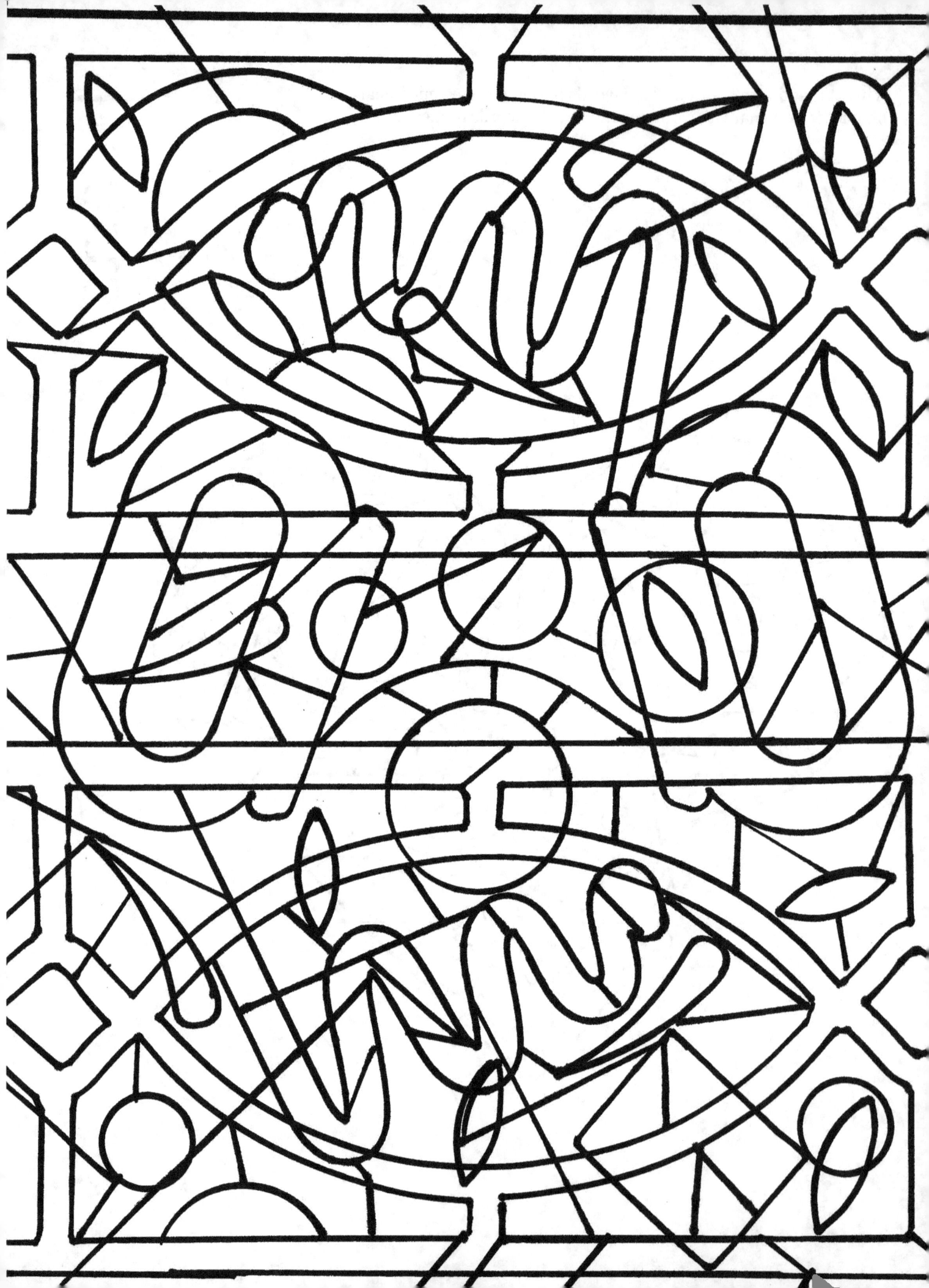

Your soul cries out to you every day. Are you listening?
Guilt is a cry for repentance.
Envy for gratefulness.
Frustration for patience.
Anger for trust in God.
Pride for humility.
And doubt for faith.

cries.

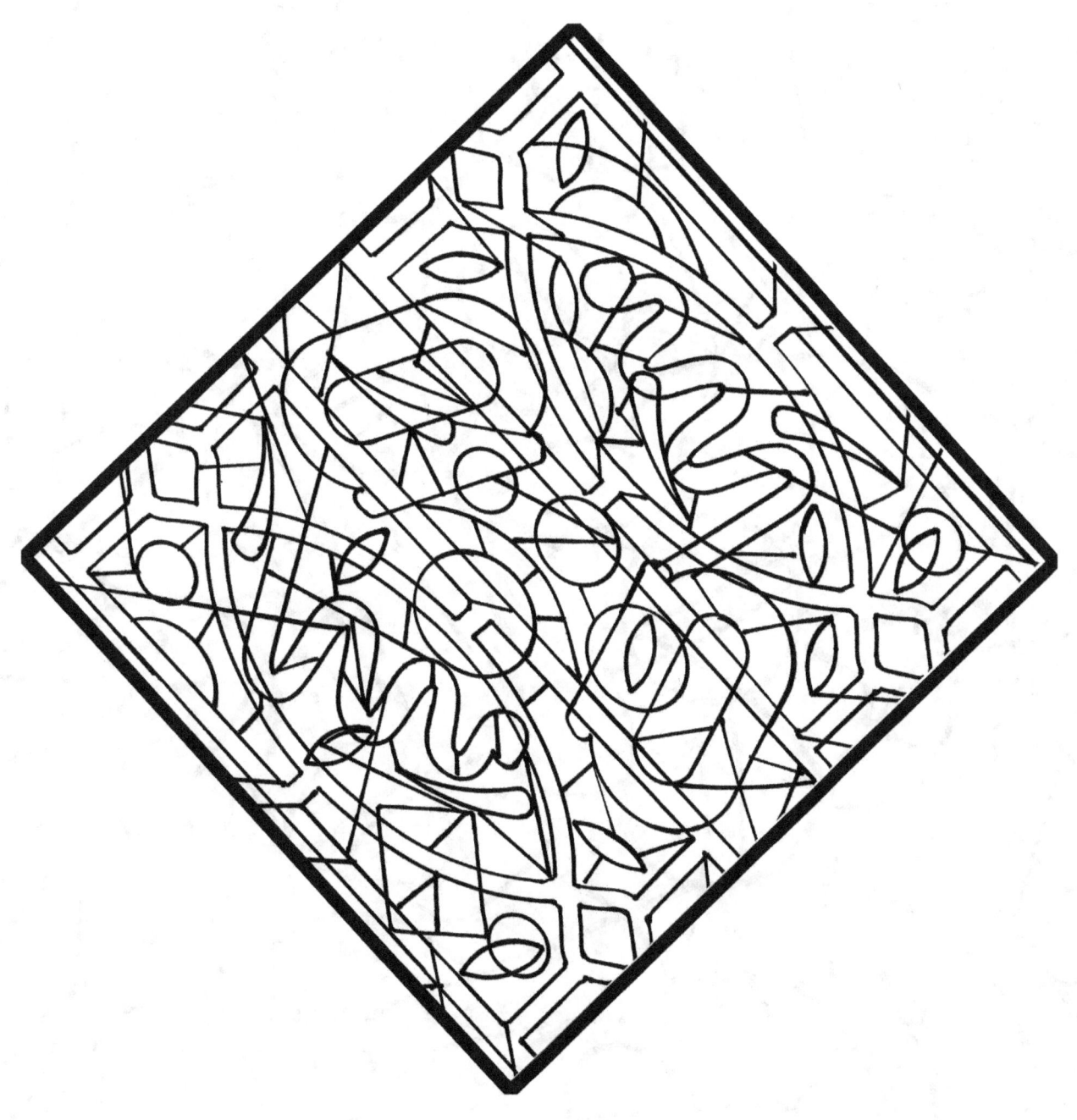

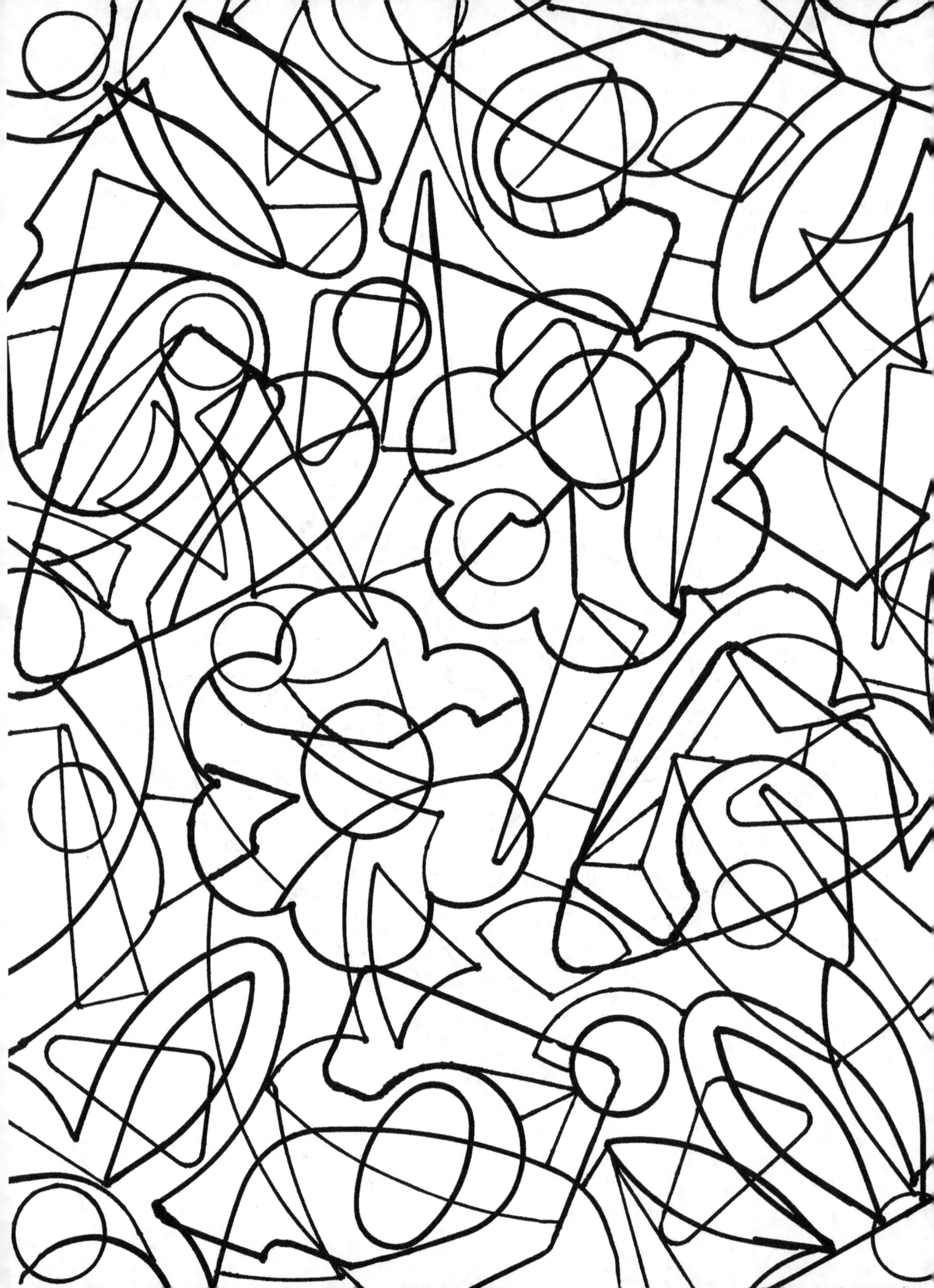

If you want your Lord to speak good words about you above the heavens,
then speak good words about His believers on earth.
If you want your Lord to have mercy on you,
then have mercy on His servants in this world.
If you want His angels to speak your name in their prayers,
then speak the names of fellow believers in yours.
If you want The All-Loving to cover your faults, pardon your errors, and forgive your
sins, then rush to cover, pardon, and forgive your brothers and sisters in this world.

Forgiveness.

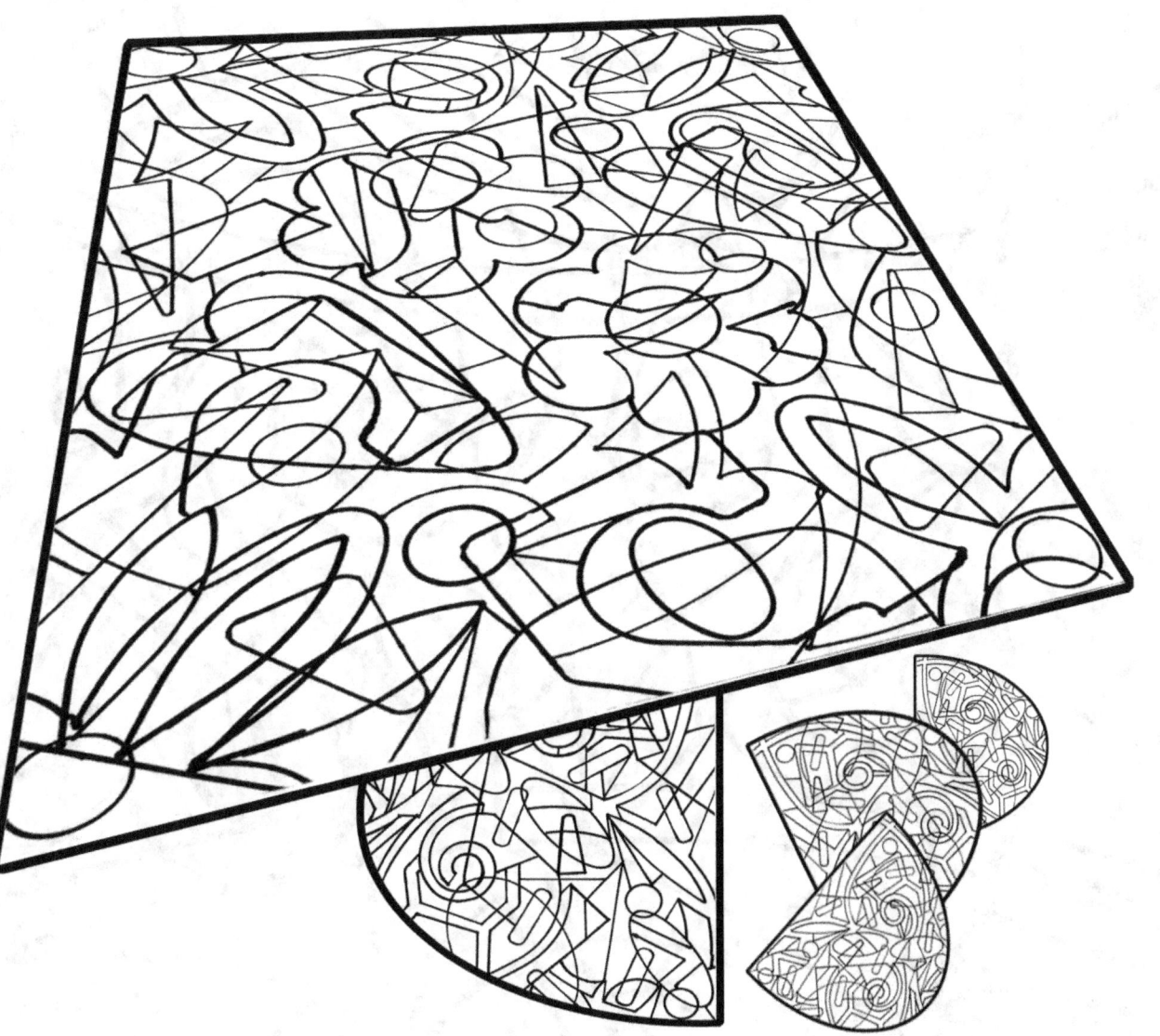

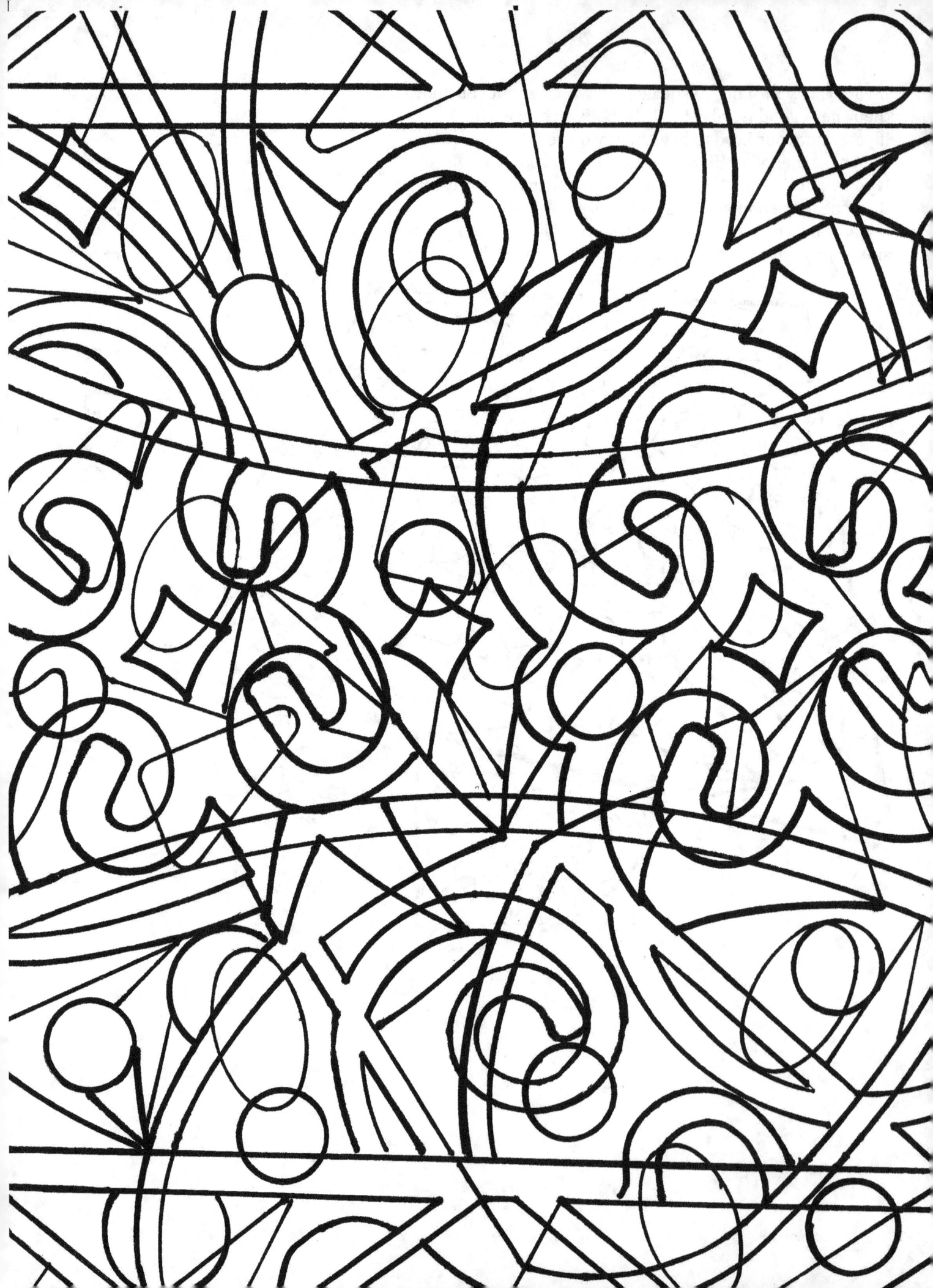

If someone wants to think good of you, they will.
It really is that simple, *bi'idhnillaah*.
It's not upon you to explain yourself to their satisfaction.
It's upon them to make excuses for you to God's satisfaction.

Good.

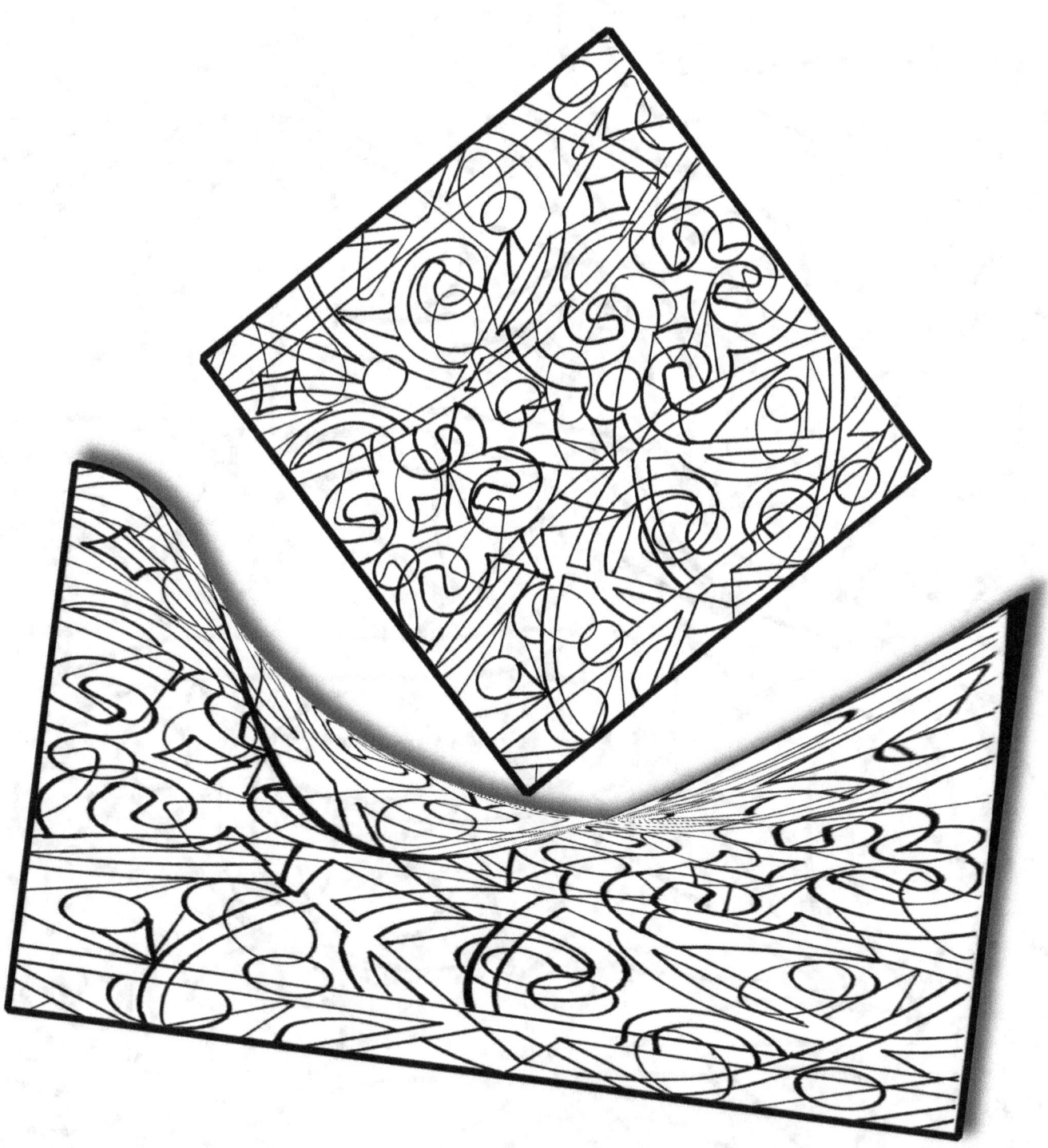

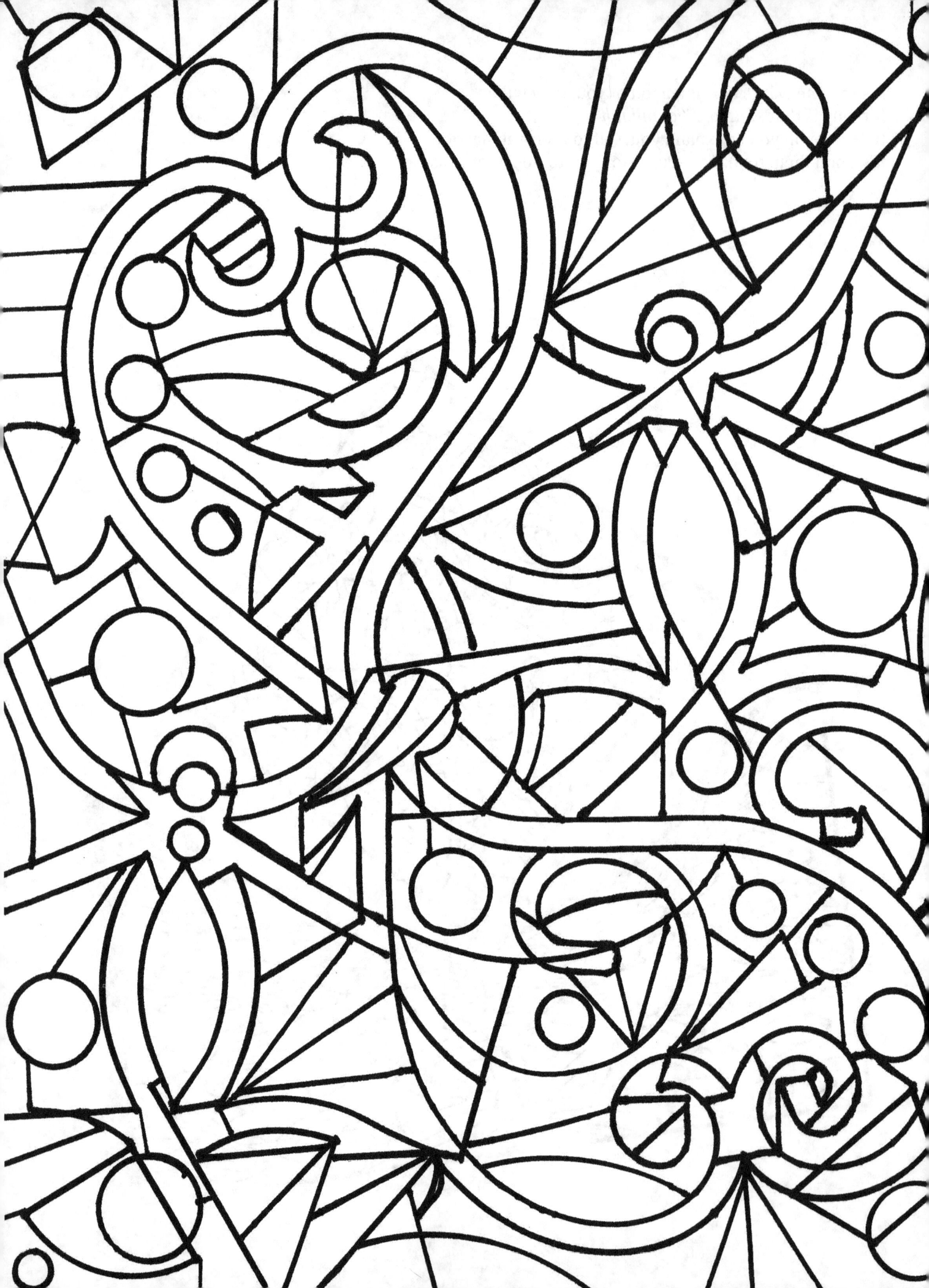

Selfishness and self-care are not the same.
Once you realize this, you free up your mind, body, and spirit to heal emotional
wounds, guilt-free. And you can now draw very clear lines protecting your personal
space from toxic energy—and people—that threaten to disrupt it.

Healing.

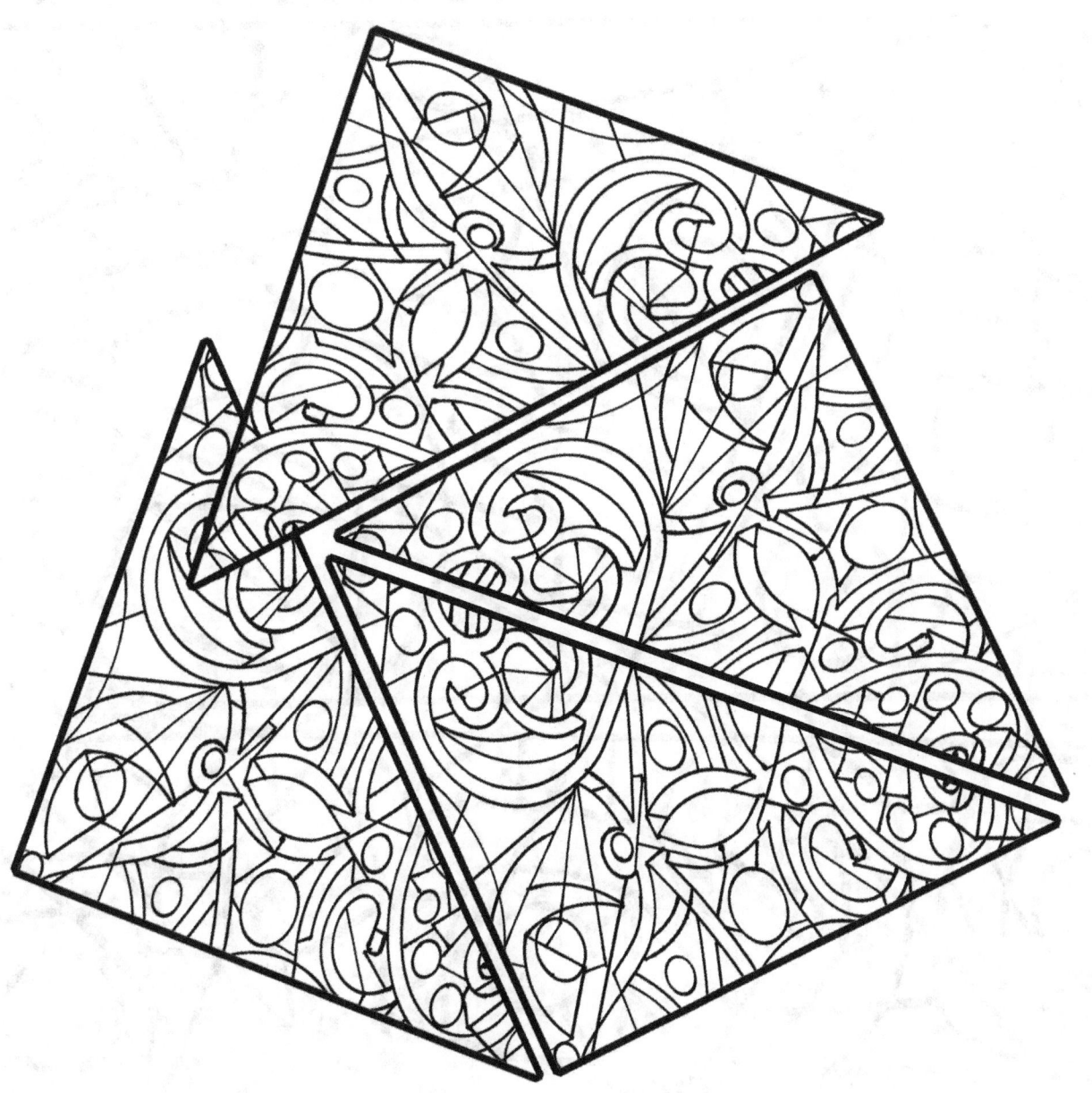

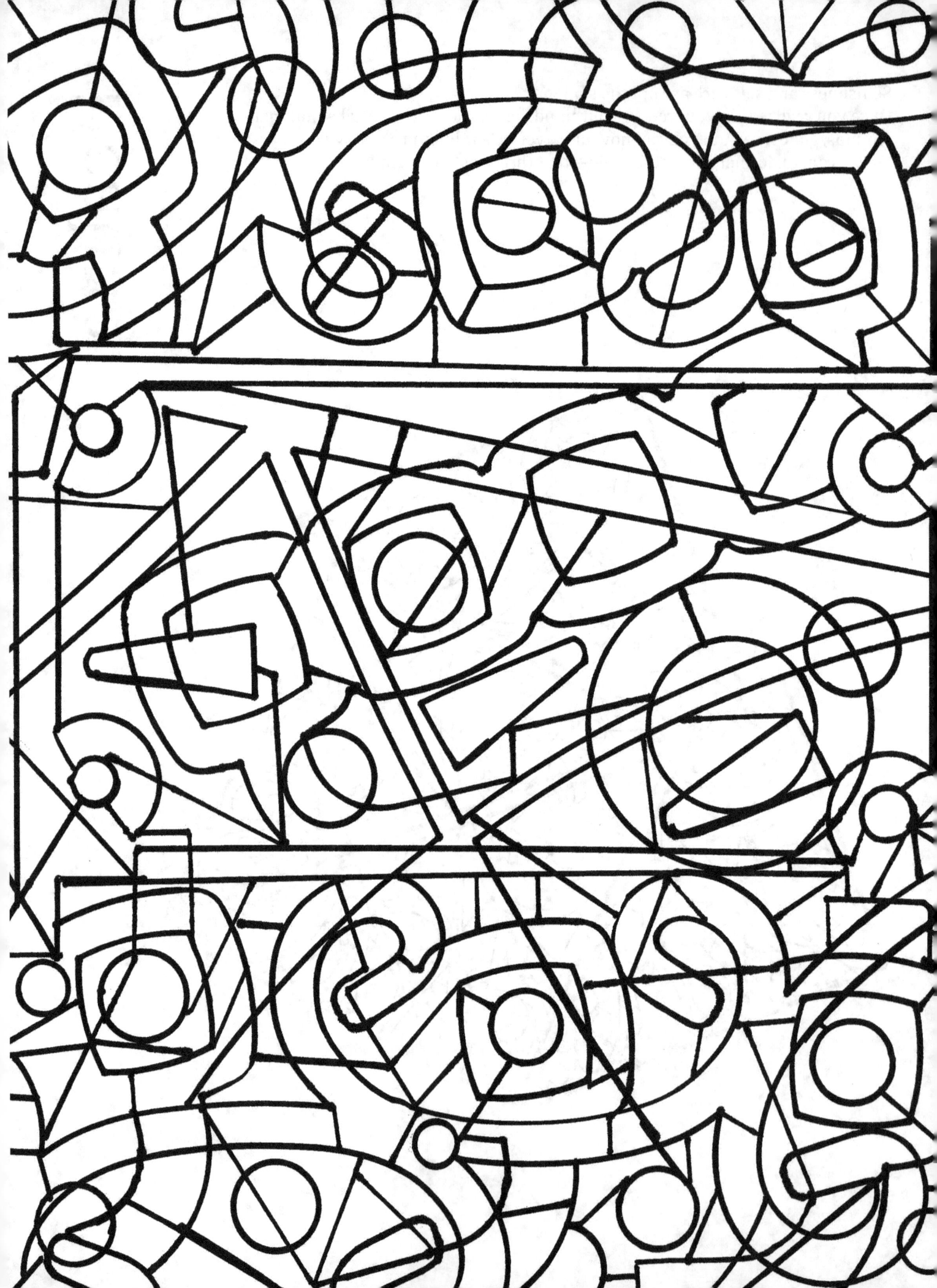

Racial or cultural pride that is not rooted in self-honesty, seeking forgiveness, and serving God is merely self-deception and laying our own path to spiritual destruction in this life and in the Hereafter.

~

We love speaking highly of ourselves and our achievements.
However, true pride in oneself starts with self-honesty.
No group of people is perfect, and if we want to pride ourselves based on traits that make others think highly of us, then let us also be honest about the areas we need to work on, especially regarding our spiritual health and improvement.
Whenever our pride overcomes our humility, we are in trouble spiritually.

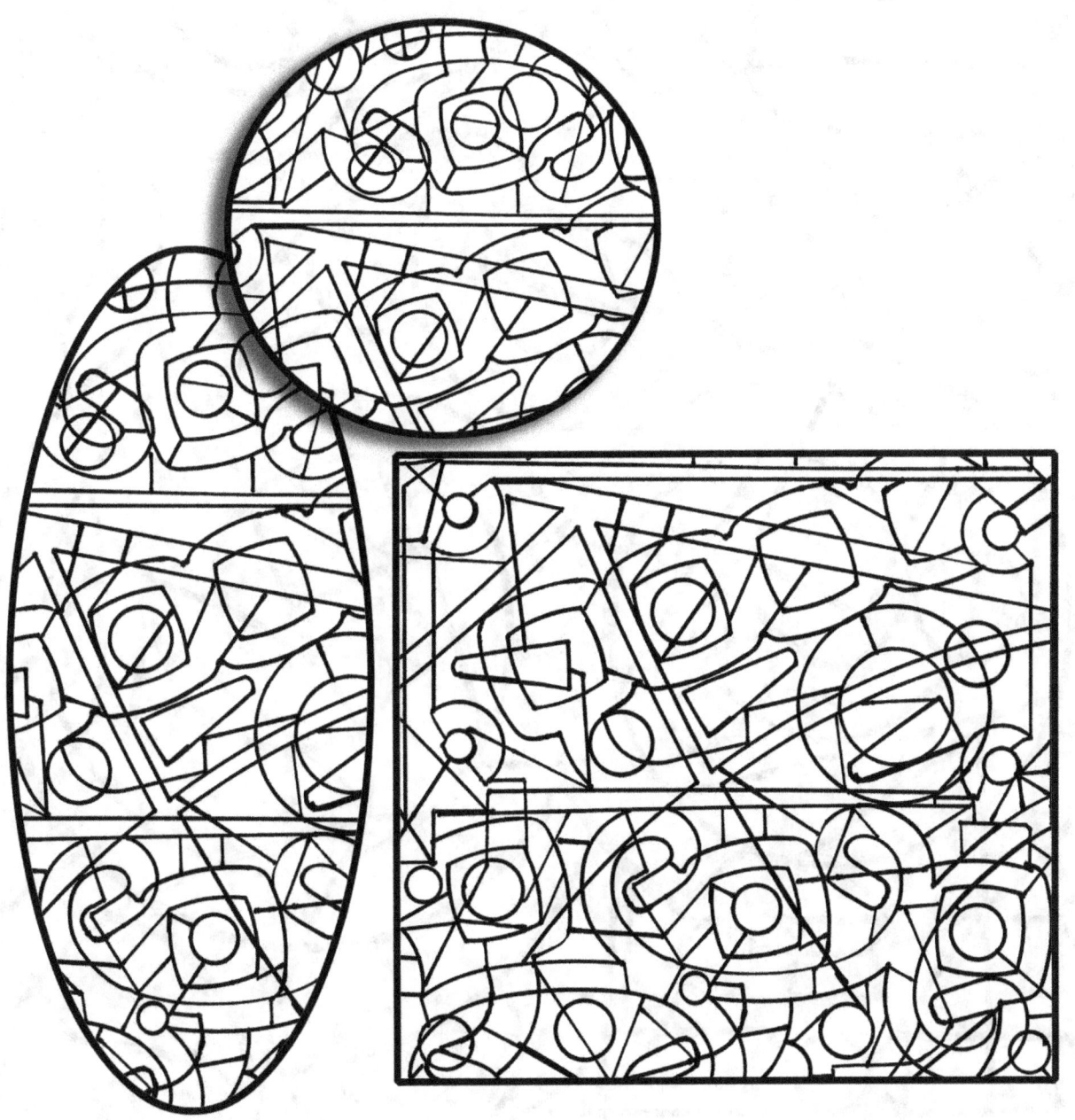

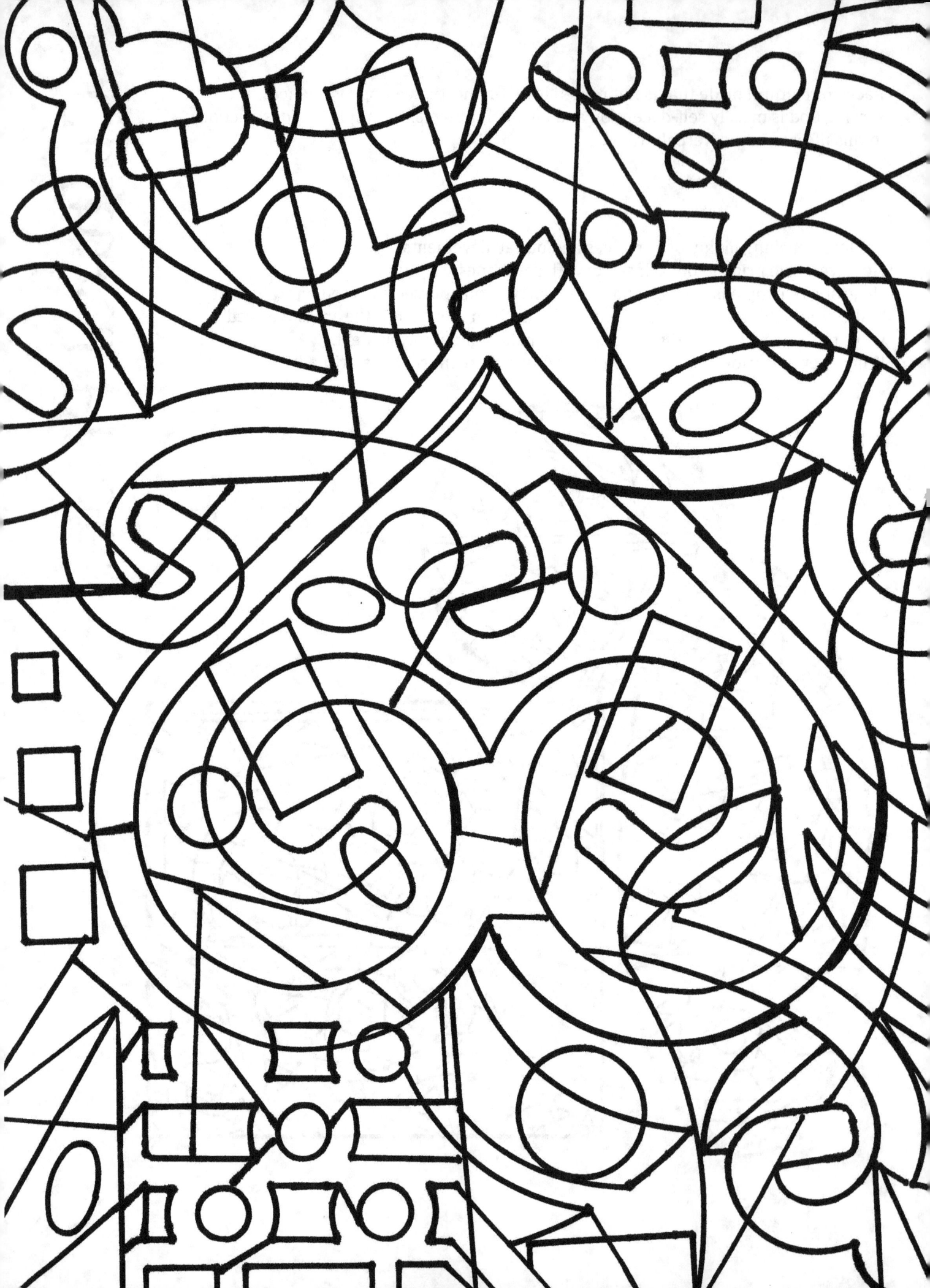

Understanding criticism is easy.
But understanding *each other*...
That's where the real work begins.

work.

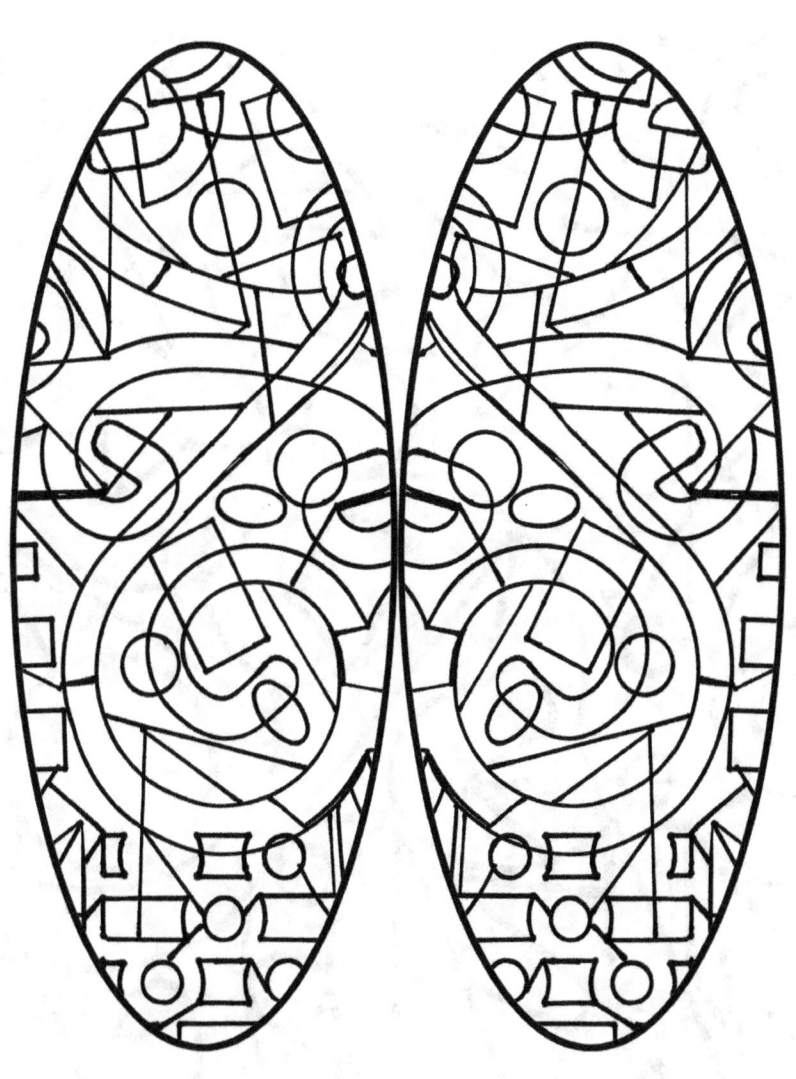
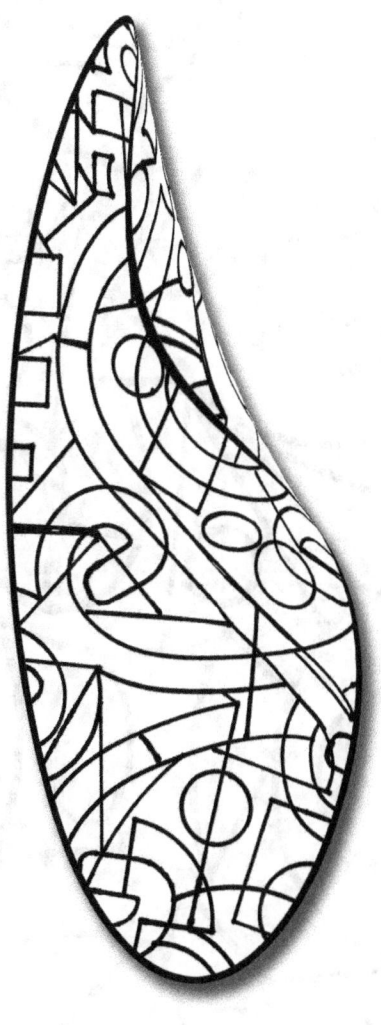

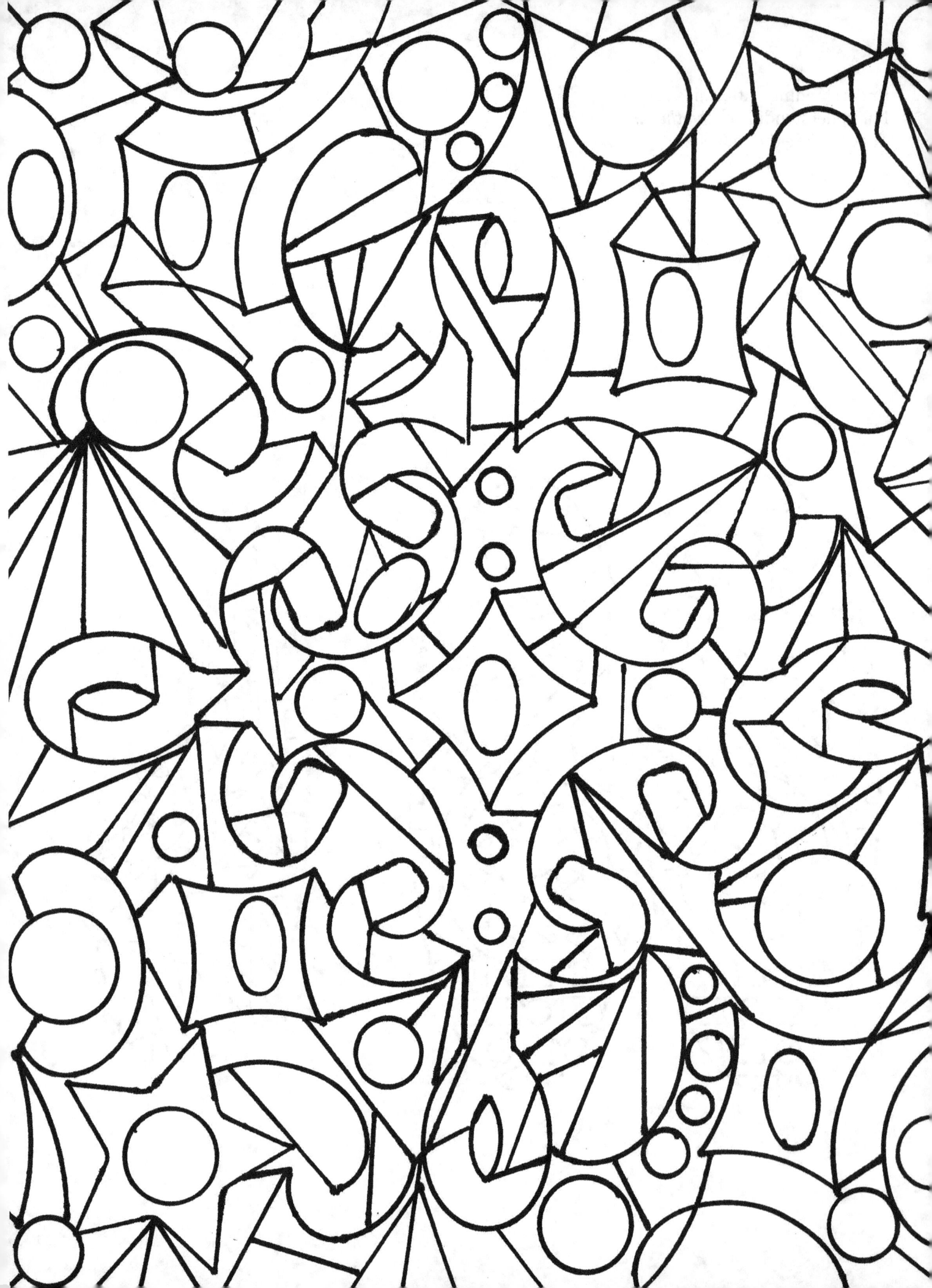

Wanting more than you have is not ungratefulness.
Feeling you *deserve* more than you have is ungratefulness.

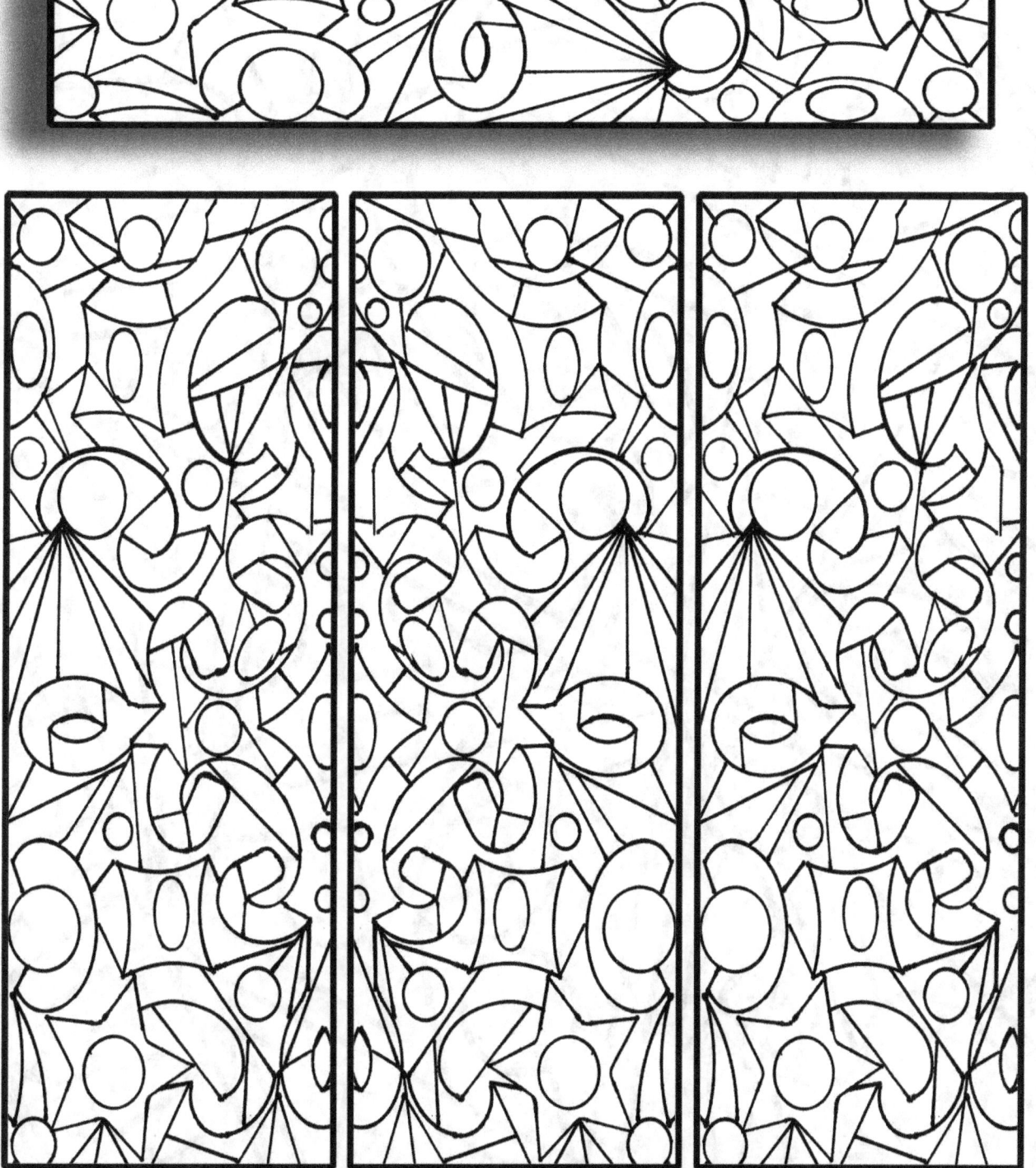

59

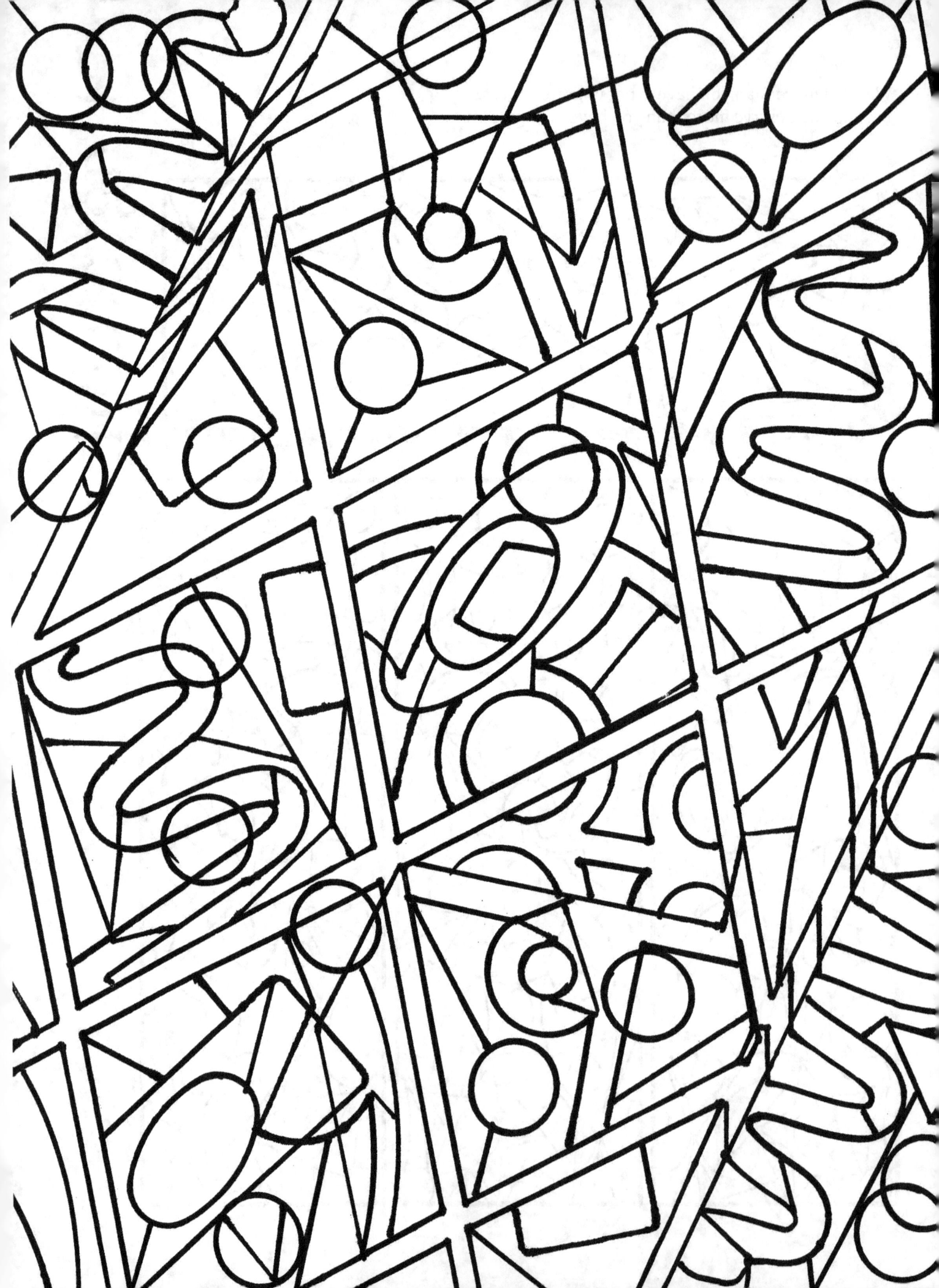

Just as our fancy cars, big houses, or sexual desires can direct us toward good or evil; our marriages, families, and religious communities and leaders can direct us toward good or evil.

These are all ropes that can pull us either toward God or away from Him.

Thus, it's helpful to remember that all of these things are part of this "worldly life."

So when God cautions us not to allow this worldly life to distract from worshipping Him, let us look beyond our material possessions and carnal desires.

This worldly life comprises so much more than that.

And if our apparently good marriages and successful families, or our strong religious communities and inspirational spiritual teachers, are making us feel emboldened to criticize or look down on those who don't seem to have what we have—or to dictate how someone else's marriage, family, or relationship with God must look— then most likely, we are using these blessings as ropes to harm, not purify, our souls.

Ropes.

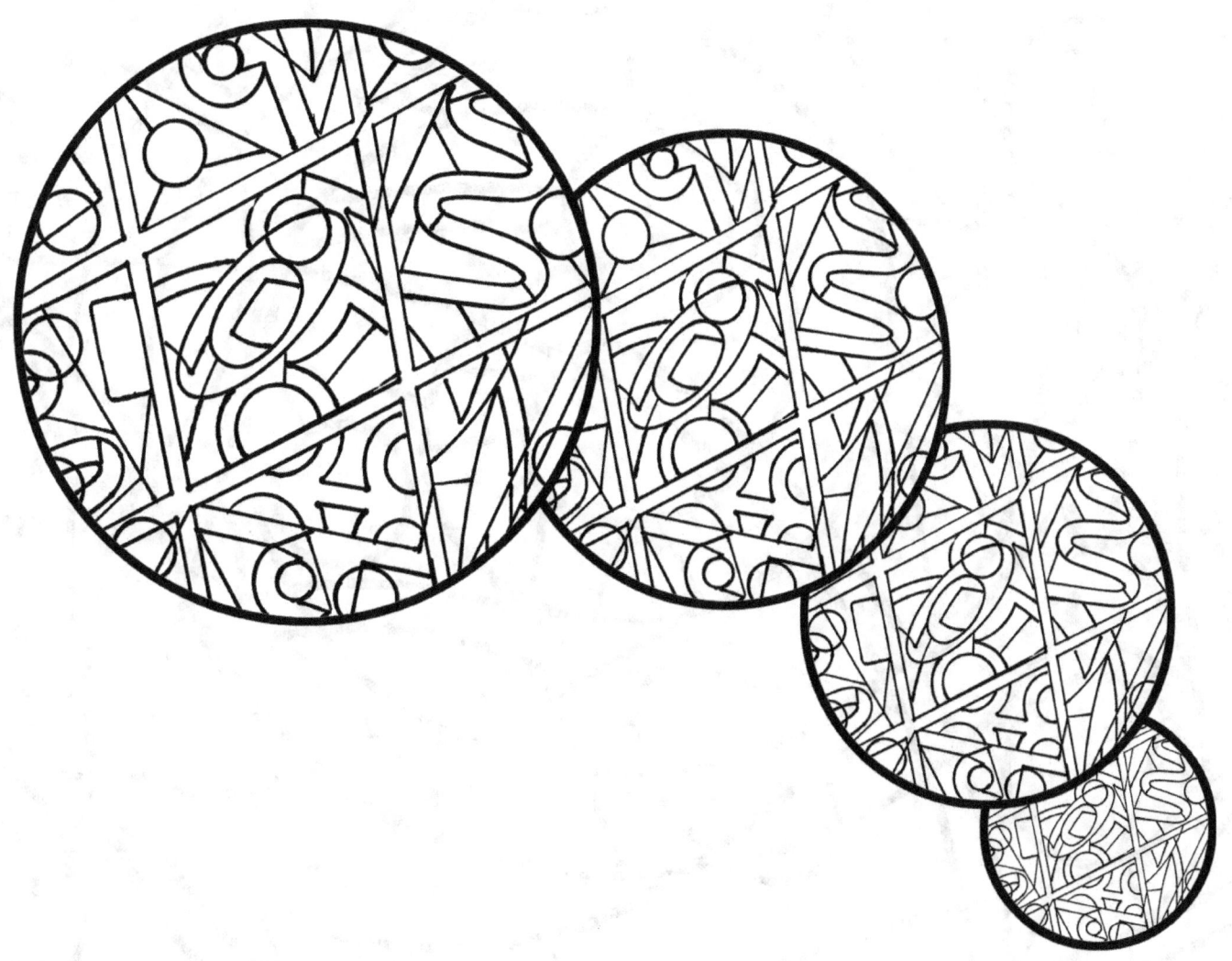

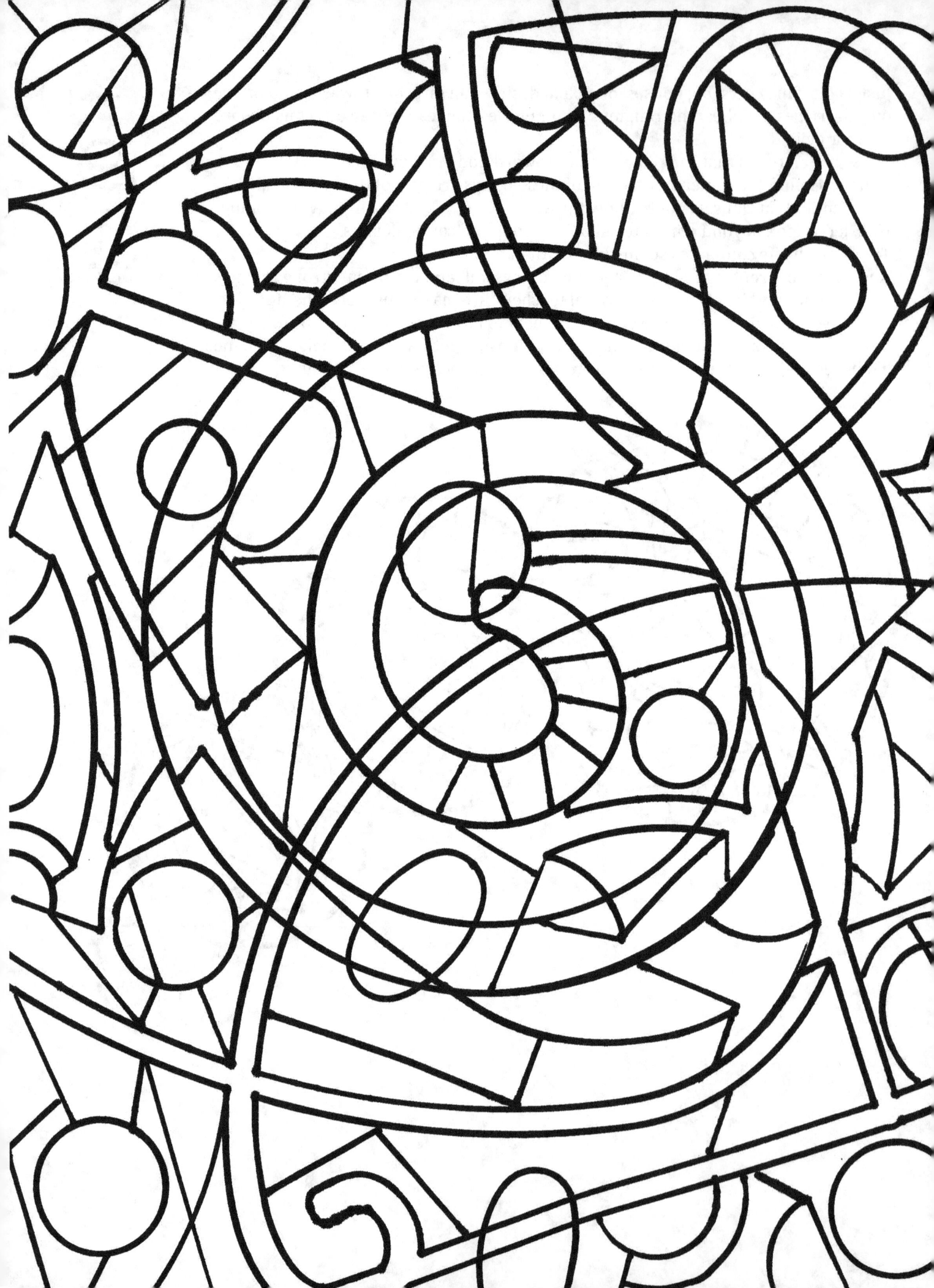

Truth and compassion should almost never be at odds.
If they are, most likely you're misunderstanding the meaning of one or both.
Nevertheless, truth—if it is indeed truth and not your personal opinion or emotions—almost always takes precedence.
And truth *is* compassion.
Even if it hurts.

~

Demanding that others never hurt your feelings is not asking for compassion.
It's assigning yourself as the only person who matters.
Otherwise, you'd realize that others have feelings too—and you may have hurt *theirs* while demanding they cater to yours.

Compassion.

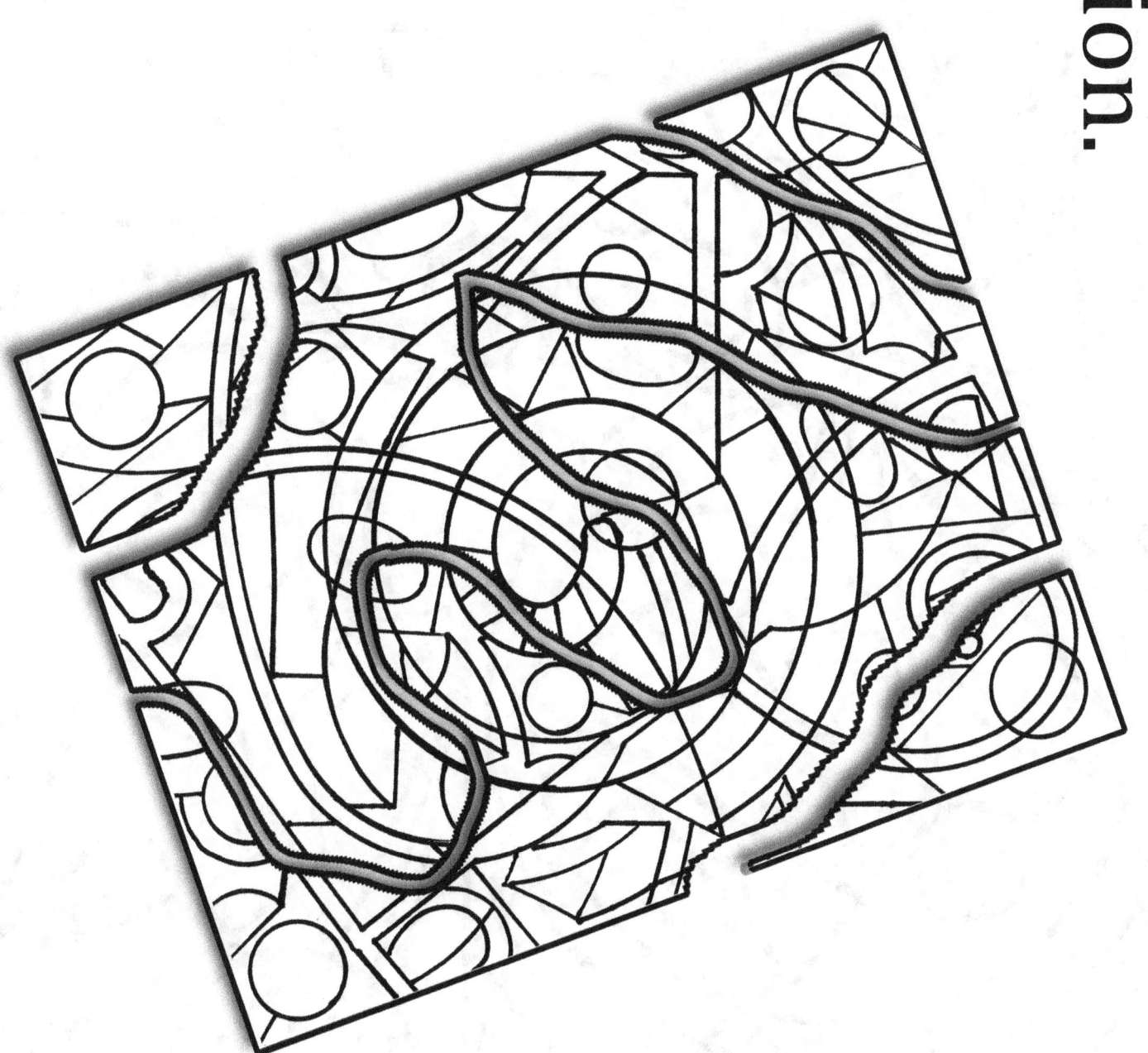

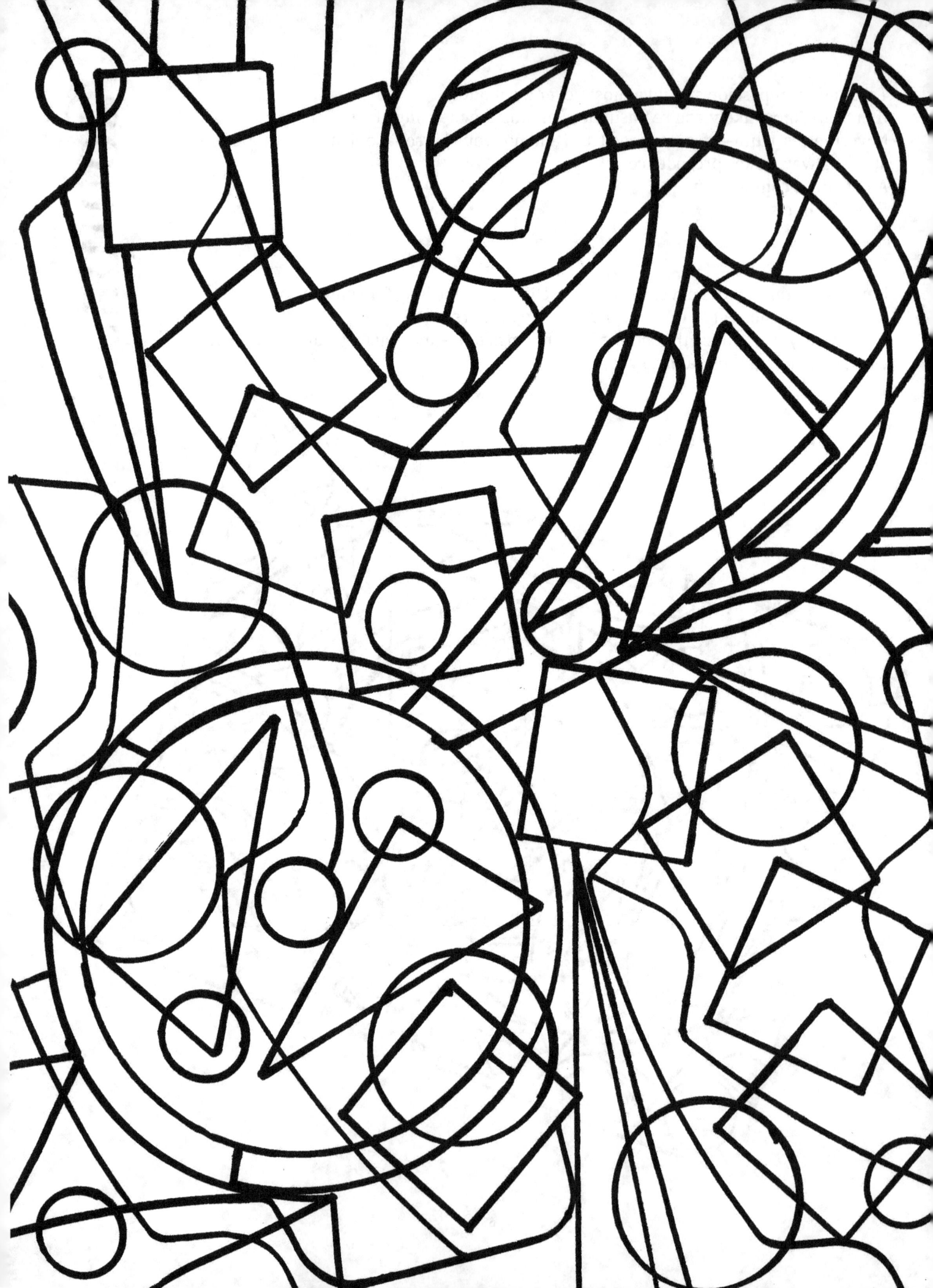

Peace and harmony is a beautiful thing.
But so is justice and remaining firm in your position against open wrong.
If we can find a way to have both, this is the most beautiful of all.

Beauty.

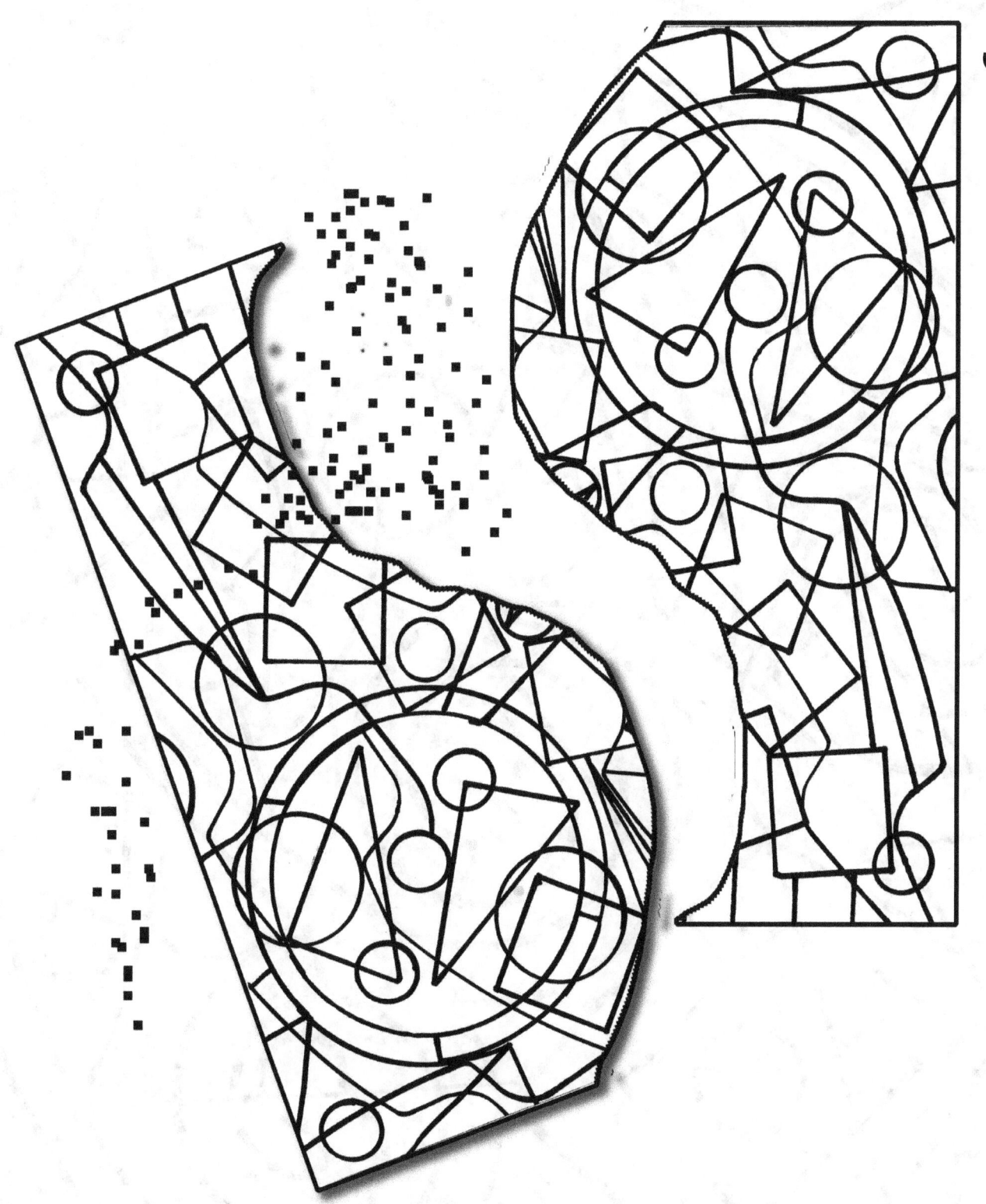

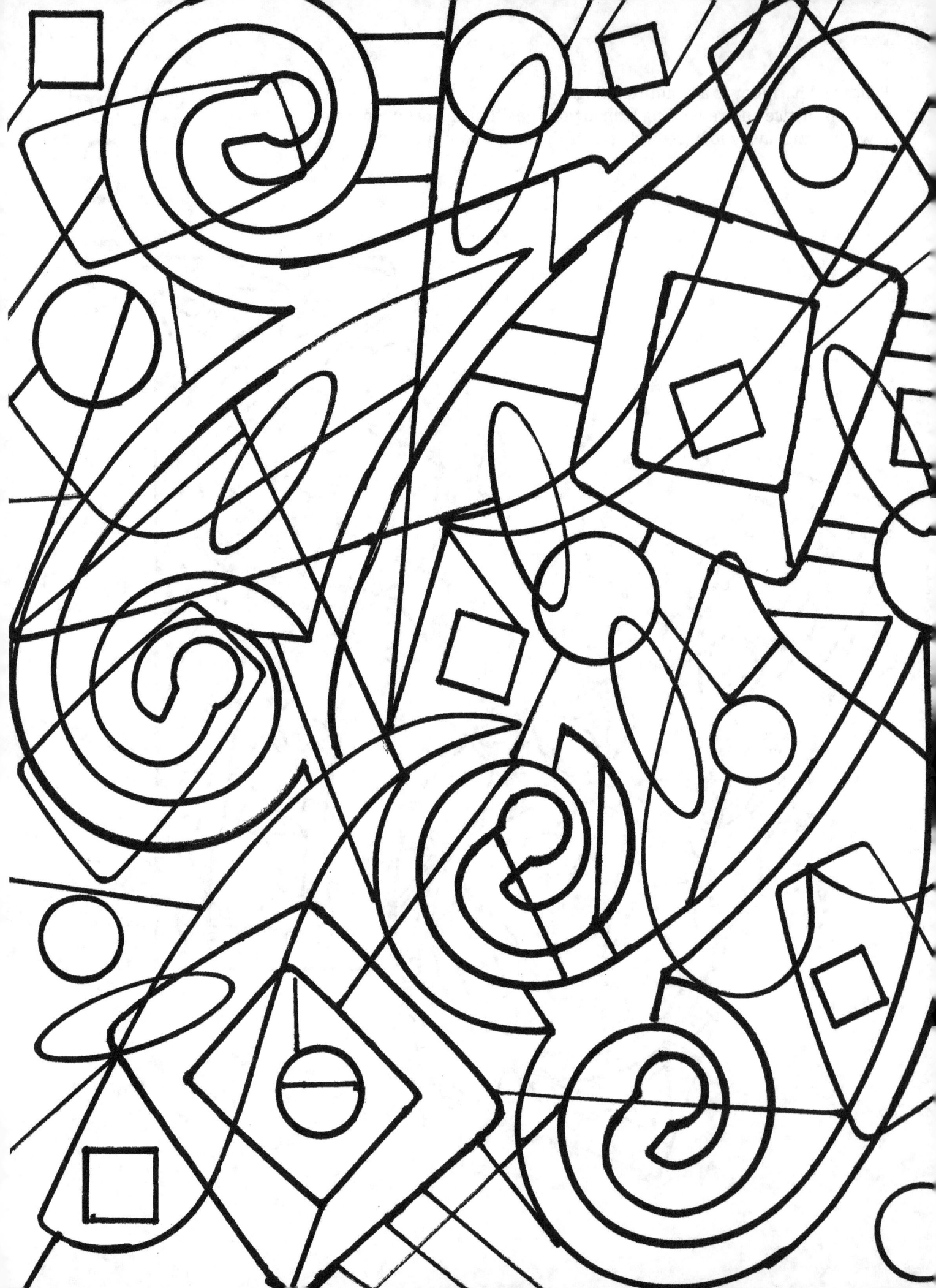

There are no shortcuts to purifying the heart.
There are no shortcuts to patience.
And there are no shortcuts to Paradise.
Do the work, and embrace the daily, harrowing struggle of living upon
the Straight Path.

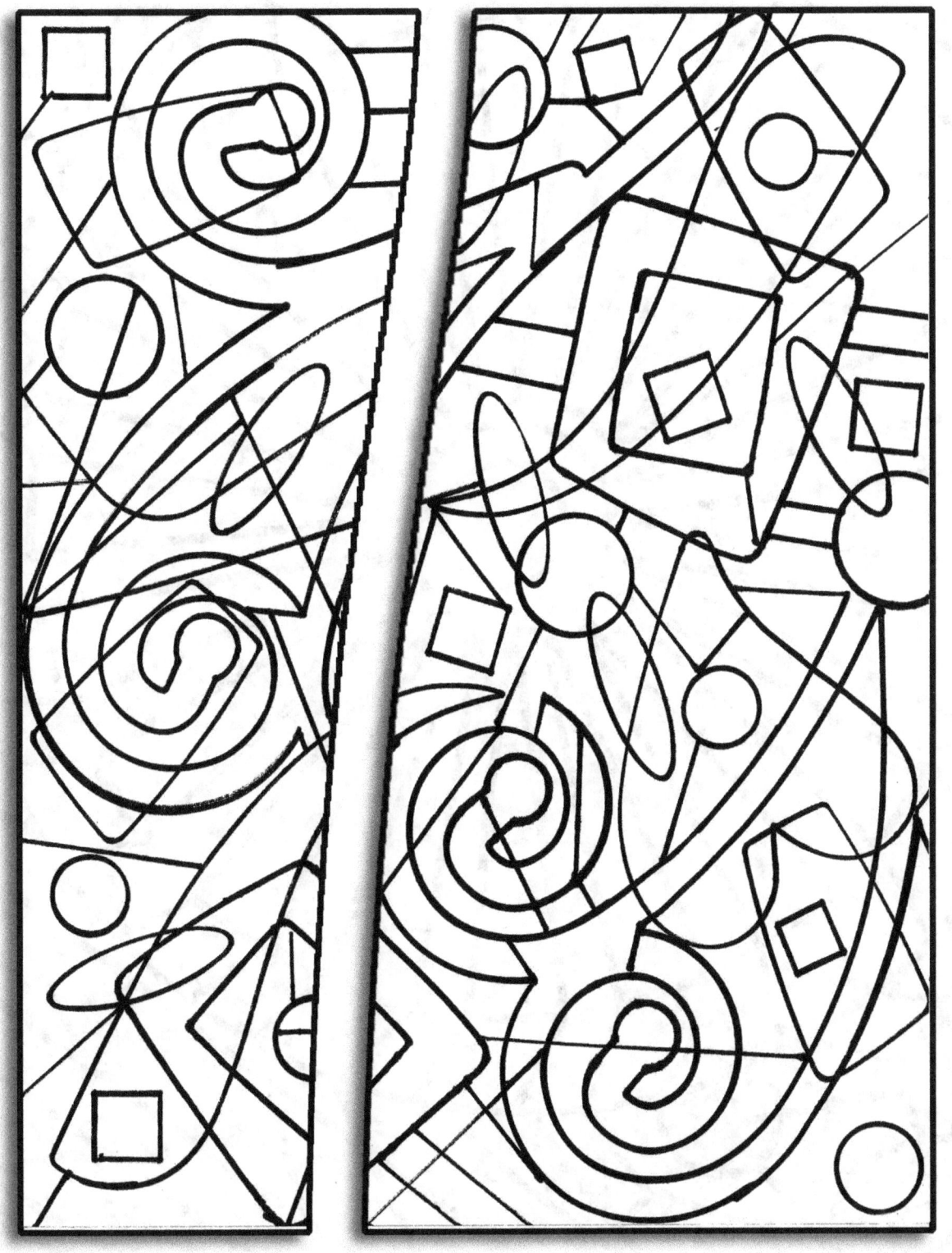

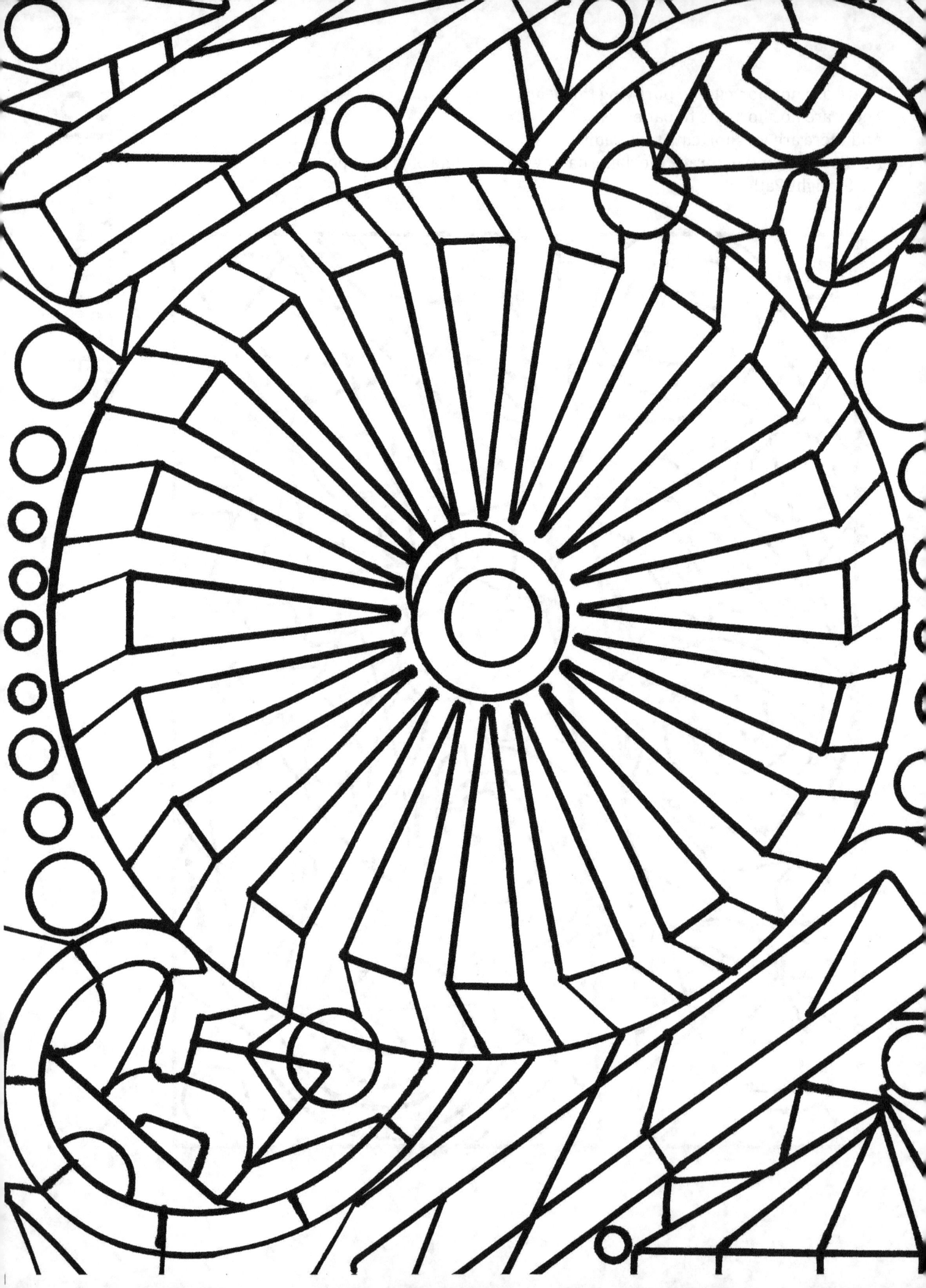

Topics are only secular when the spiritual element is forcibly removed from them. There is nothing on this earth that doesn't belong to the Creator.

Dominion.

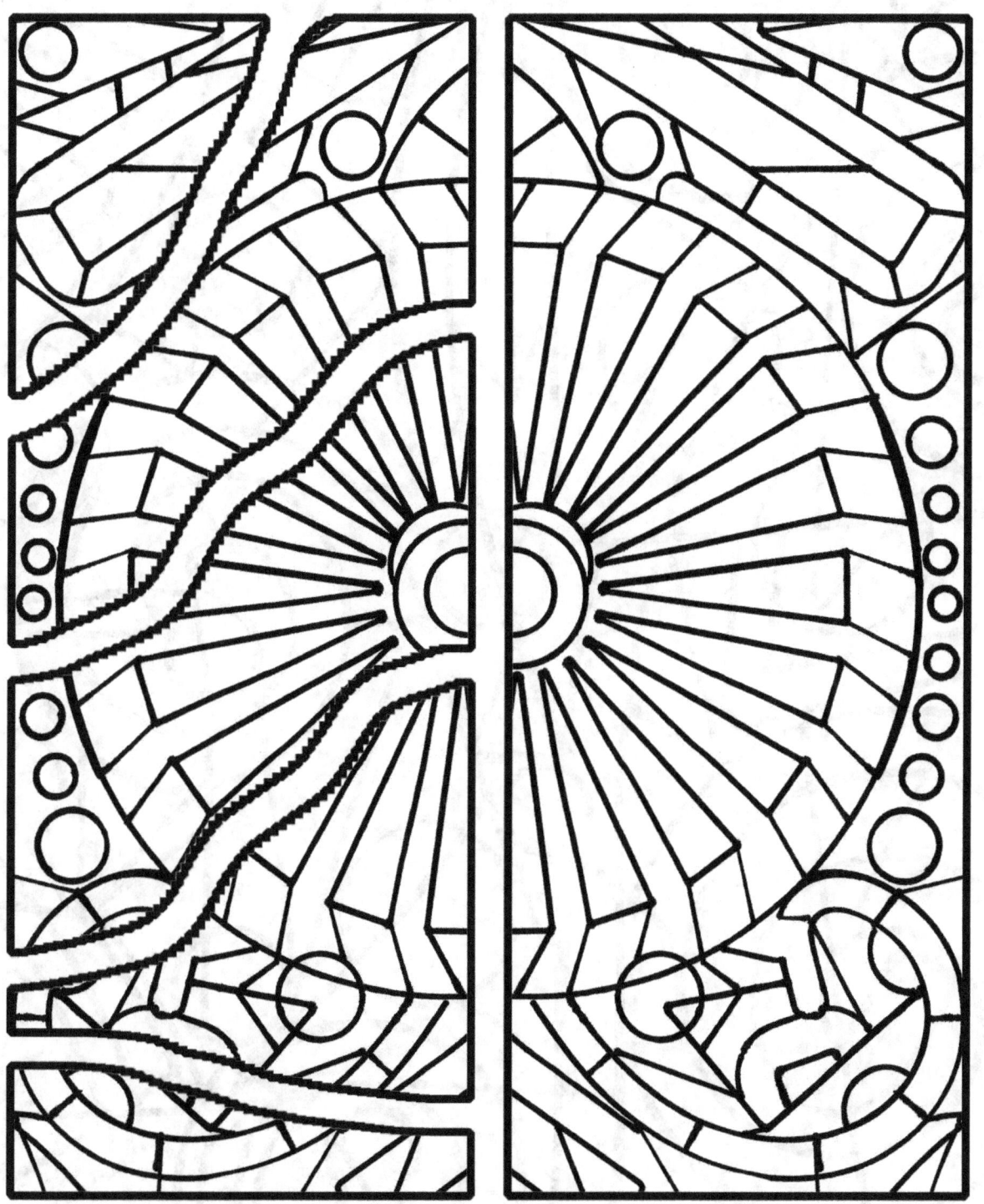

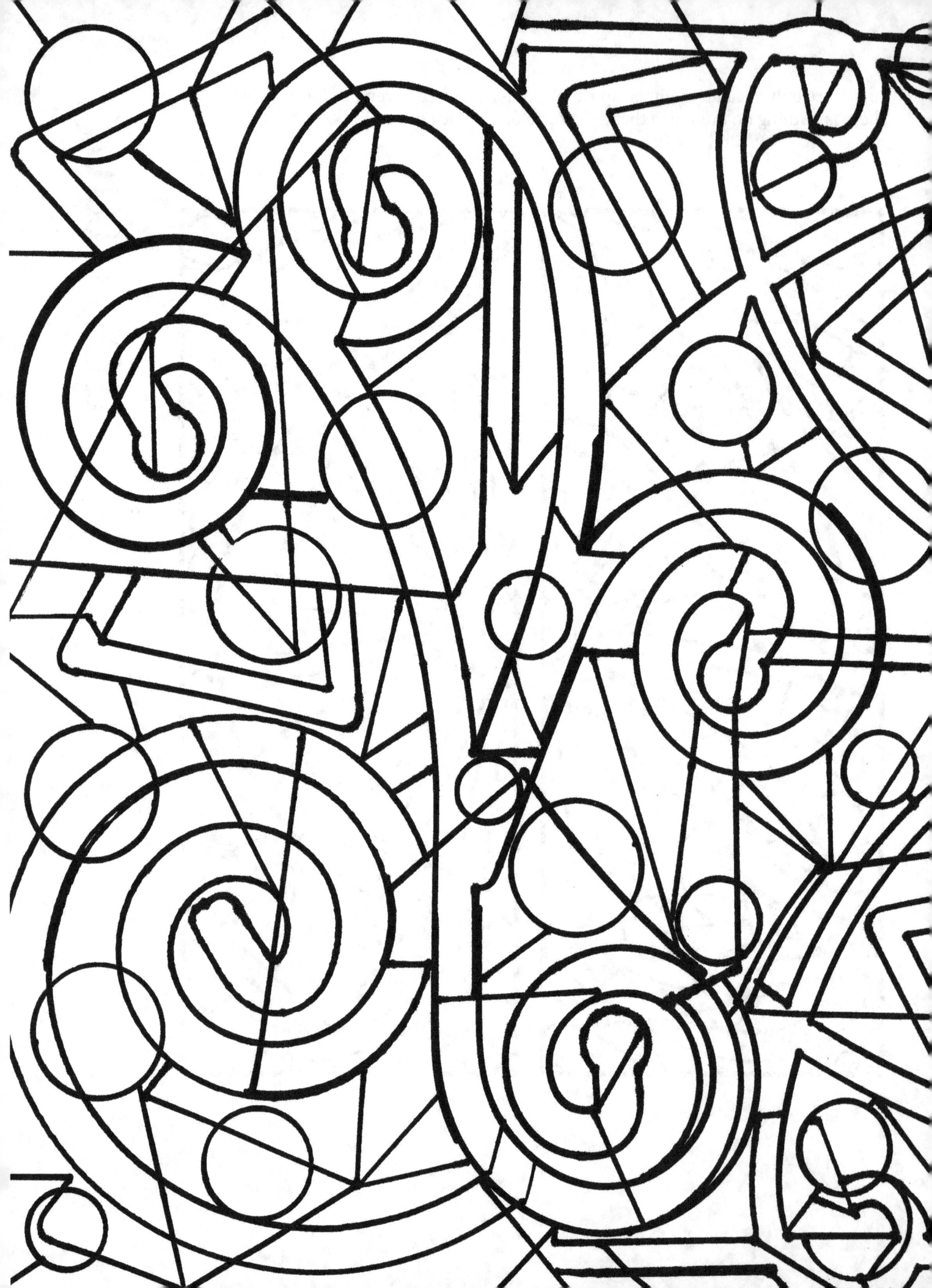

Know your place. You have not always earned the right to be someone's advisor.
So give your support publicly and your suggestions privately.
This is a good rule of thumb whenever someone is striving to save their soul and do the right thing in front of God.
If you do not know the person in real life, then as a general rule,
your *only* role is to show support—publicly and privately.
Or keep silent.
You do not know their circumstances.
Therefore, you wouldn't even know where to *begin* offering advice.
The best person to determine what to do in a situation is the person *in* the situation.
Or someone personally familiar with the details of their life.
If that's not you, then keep your "suggestions" and "disagreements" to yourself.

Advice.

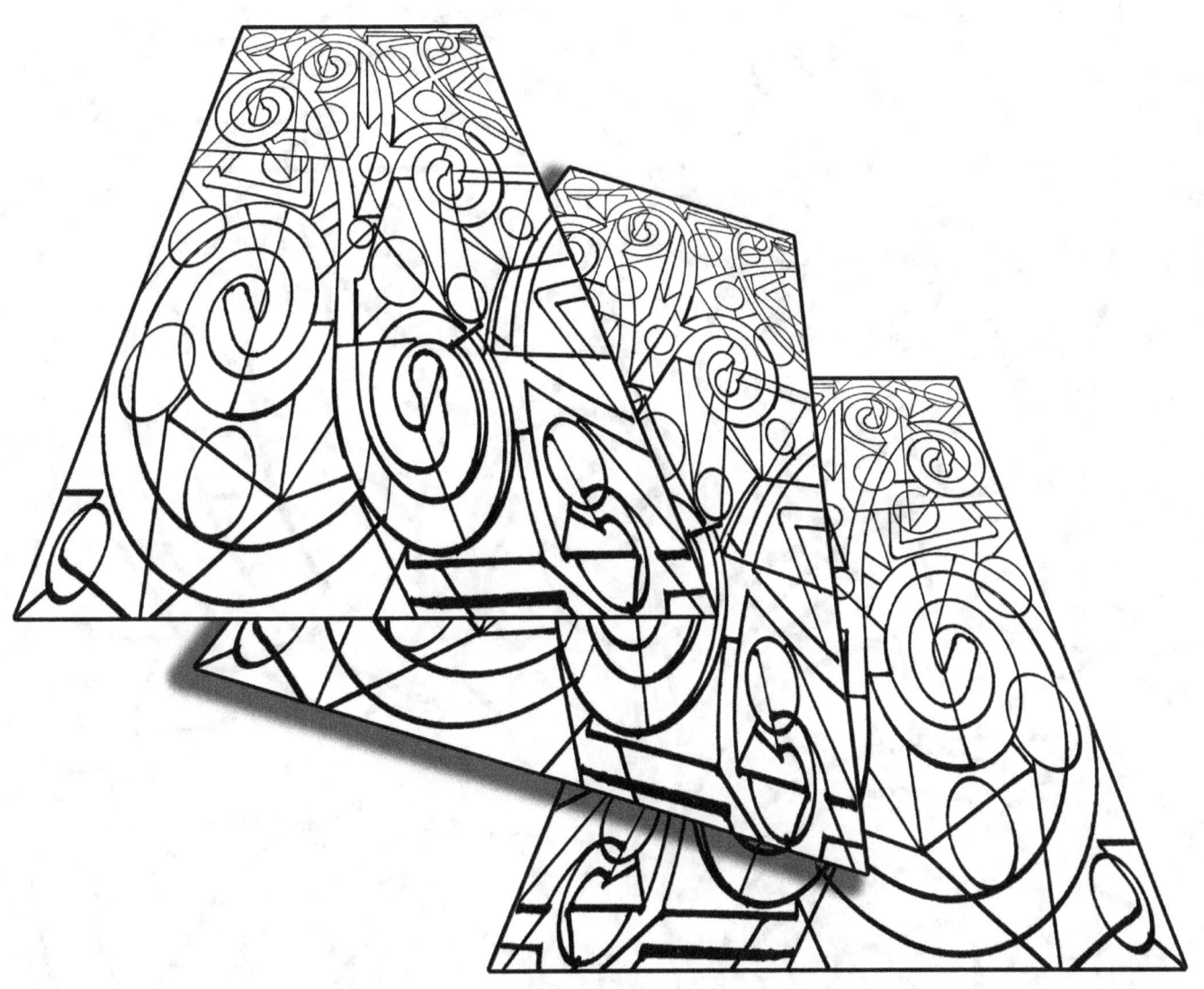

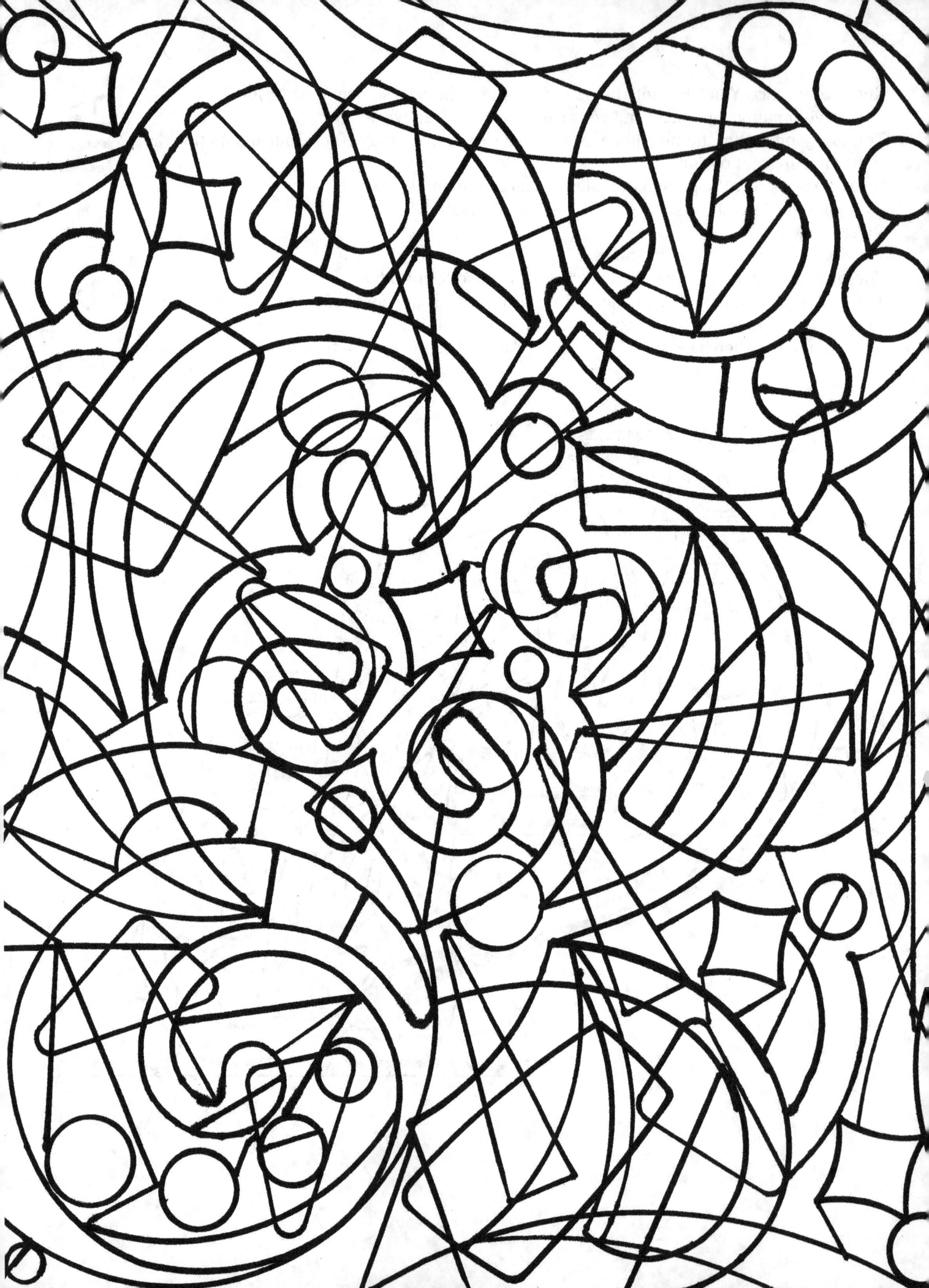

Natural or innate love, like that between a mother and child, is not the same as unconditional love. Natural love is like a seed lying in fertile ground with no prior effort on your part. However, for that seed to blossom into a fragrant flower or delectable fruit, it requires daily nurturing and care. Otherwise, it dies. Similarly, all love—whether innate or romantic—is conditional upon some level of effort and dedication if it is to remain alive.

Effort.

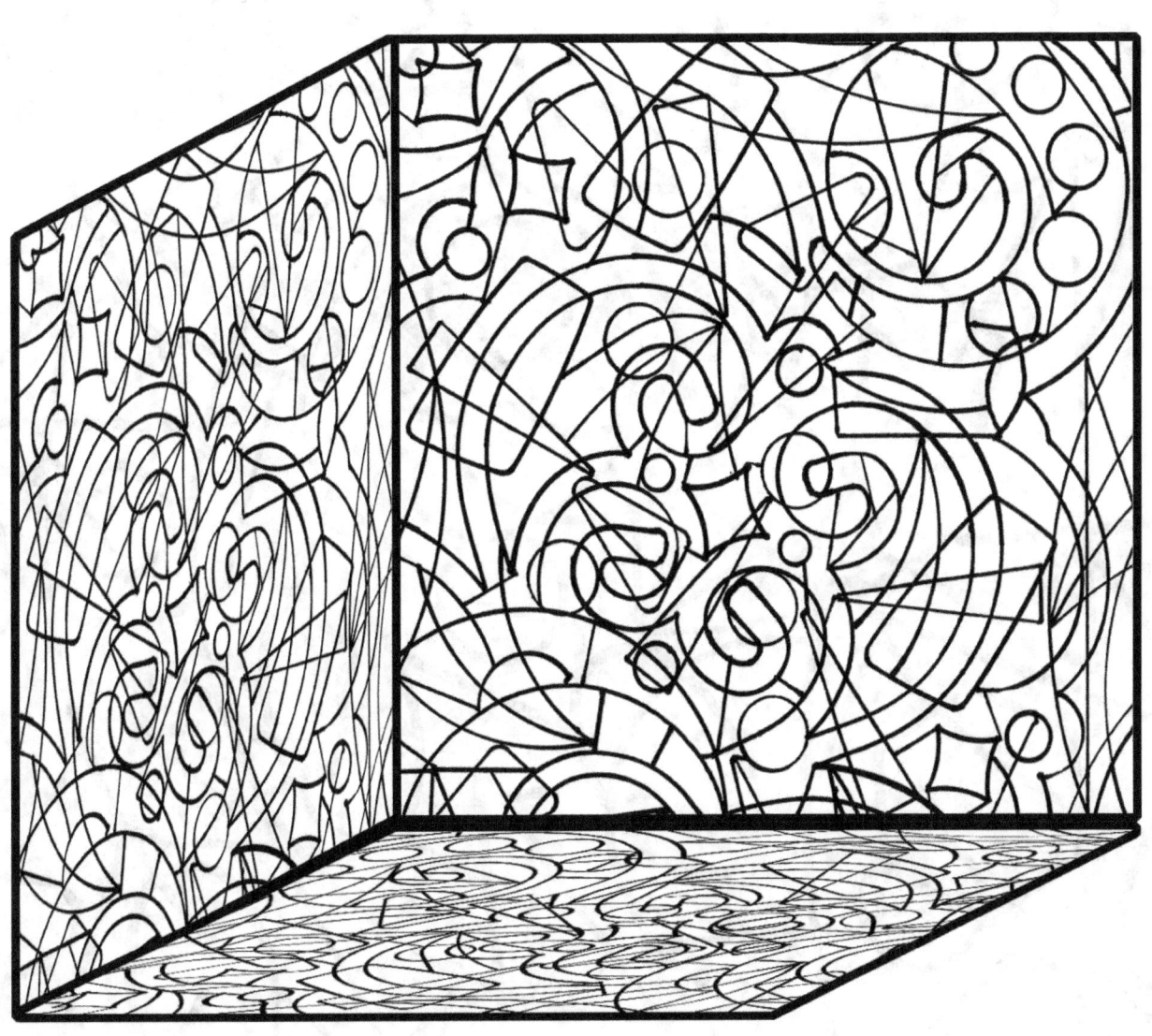

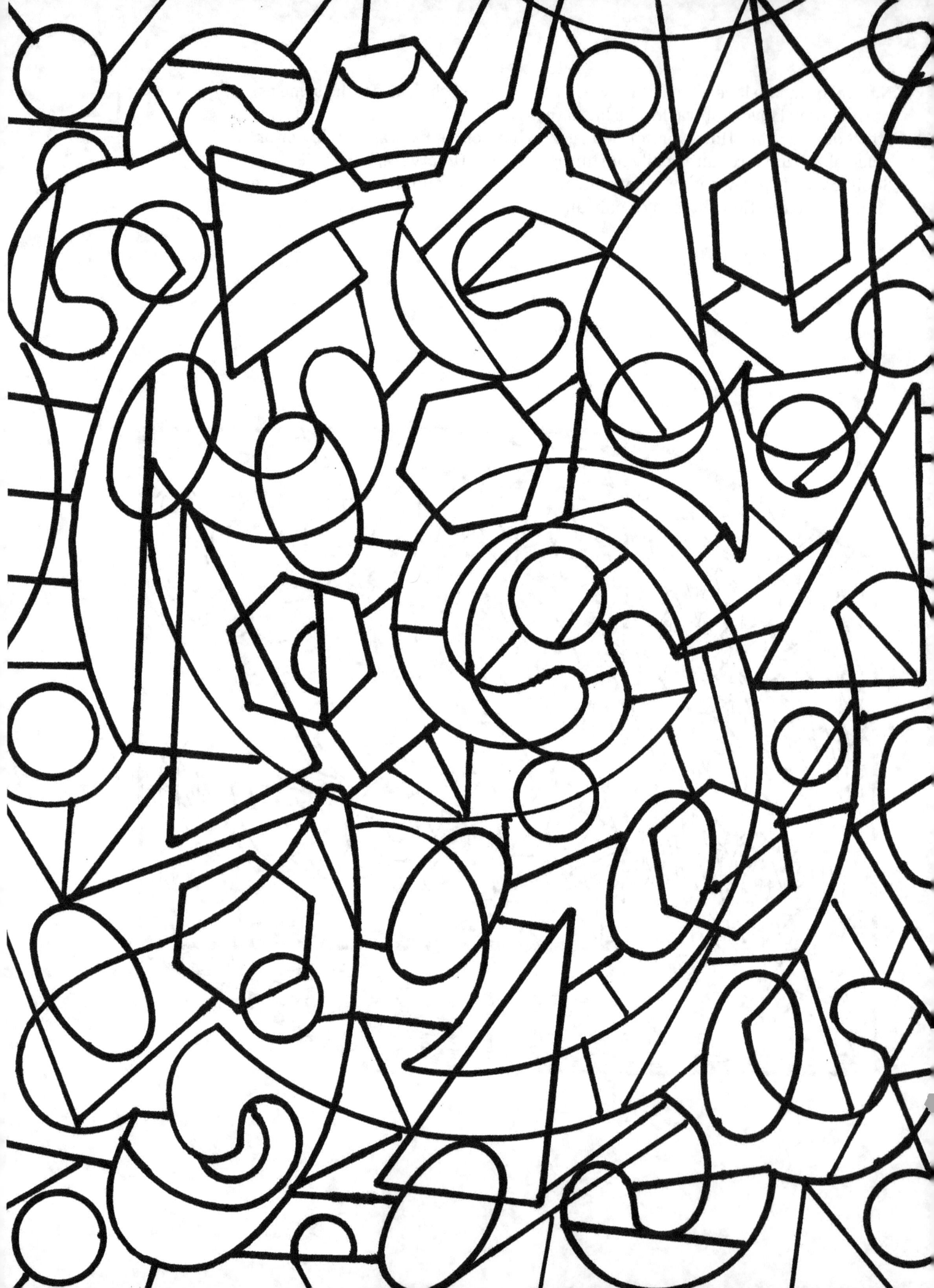

A good relationship and a lasting relationship are not synonyms.
Just because you have one doesn't mean you automatically have the other.
Some people hold on to toxic friendships, marriages, and religious acquaintances because they're afraid to let go.
They don't trust themselves, and they don't trust God.

Letting Go.

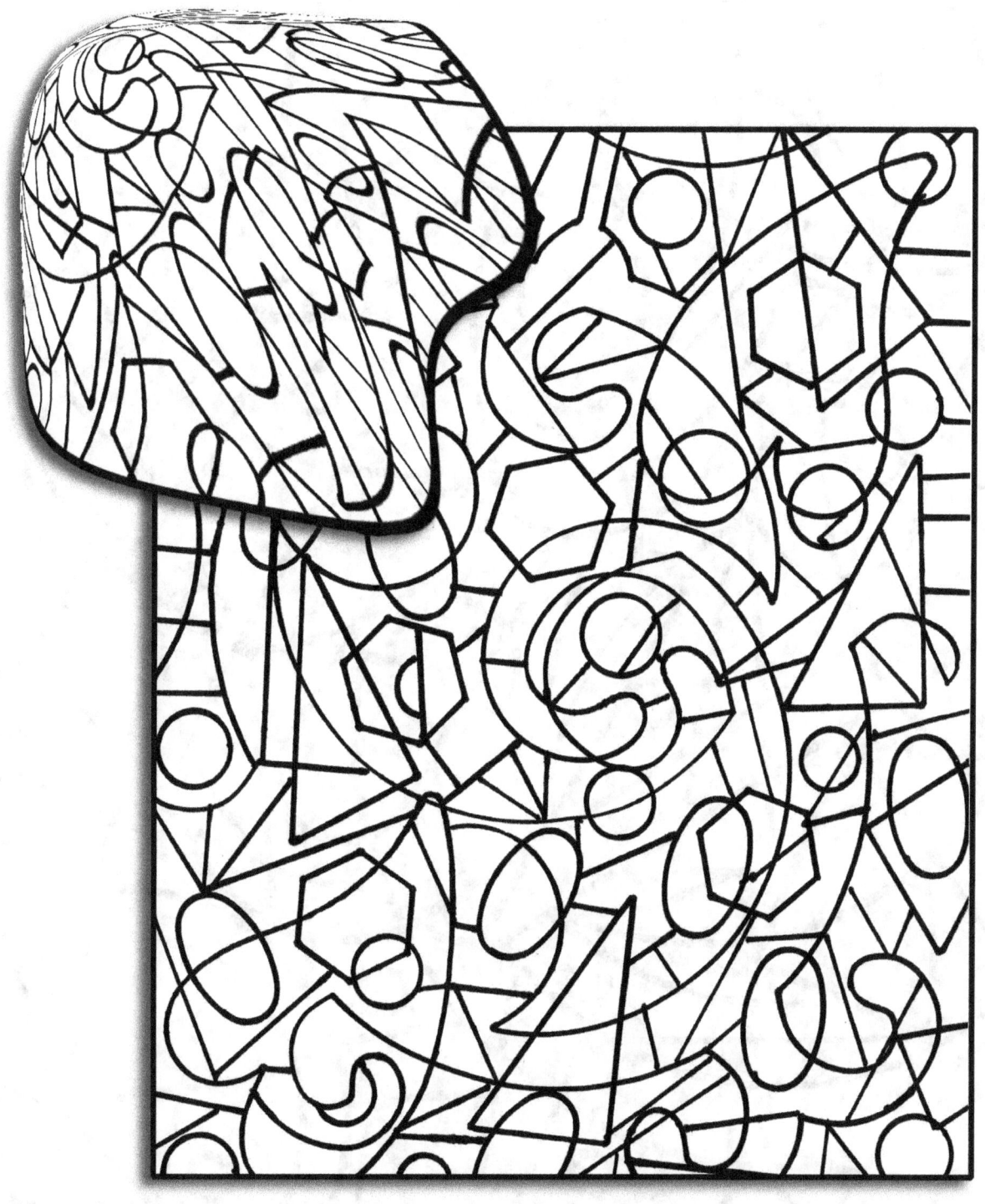

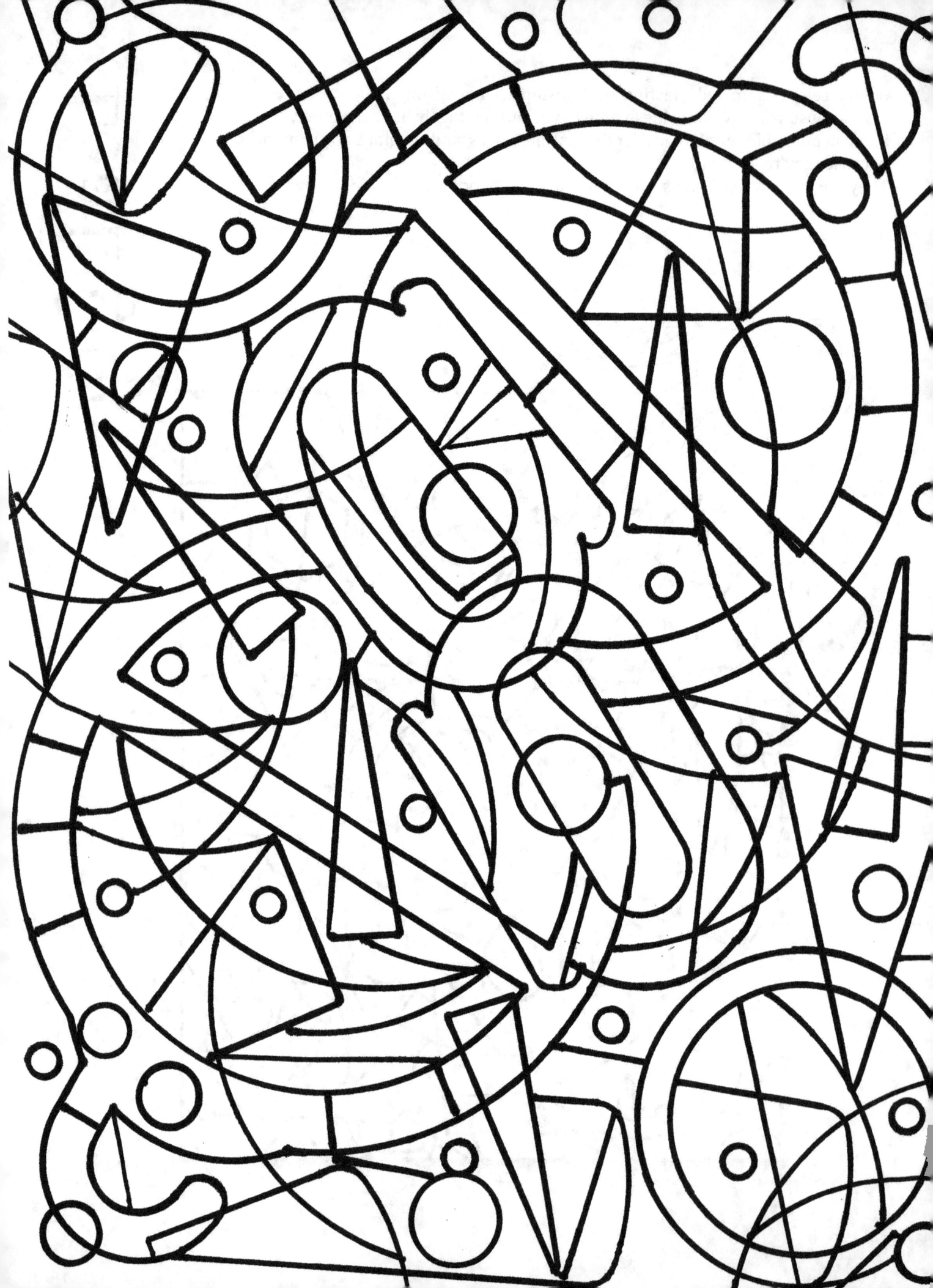

Every bad relationship doesn't include a bad person.
So let's stop insisting on casting blame when things fall apart.
Like constructing a high rise while using the foundation meant for a small family home, sometimes things fall apart because they were never meant to be together.
So make your peace with this natural reality, then move on and construct your foundation where it belongs.

Foundations.

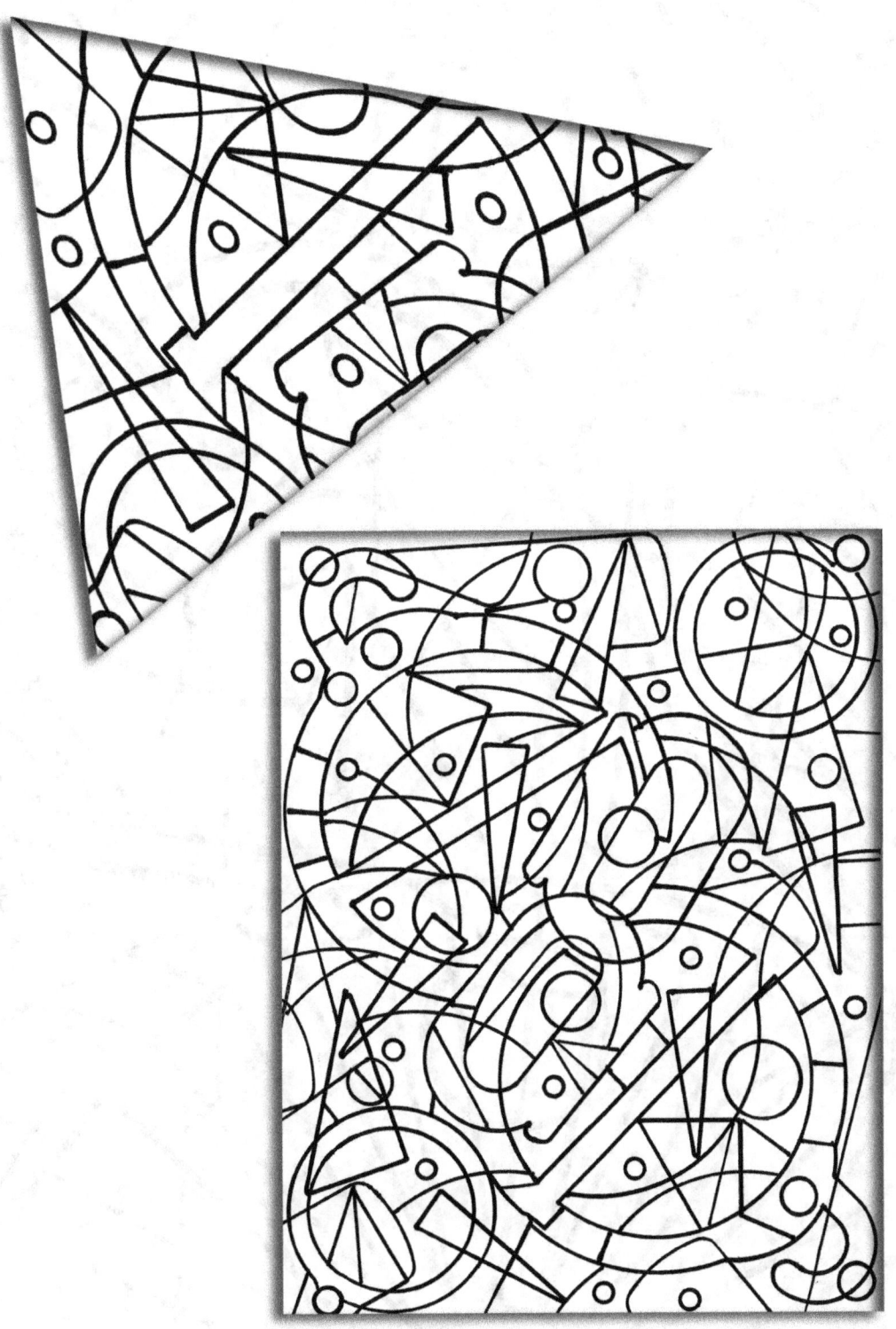

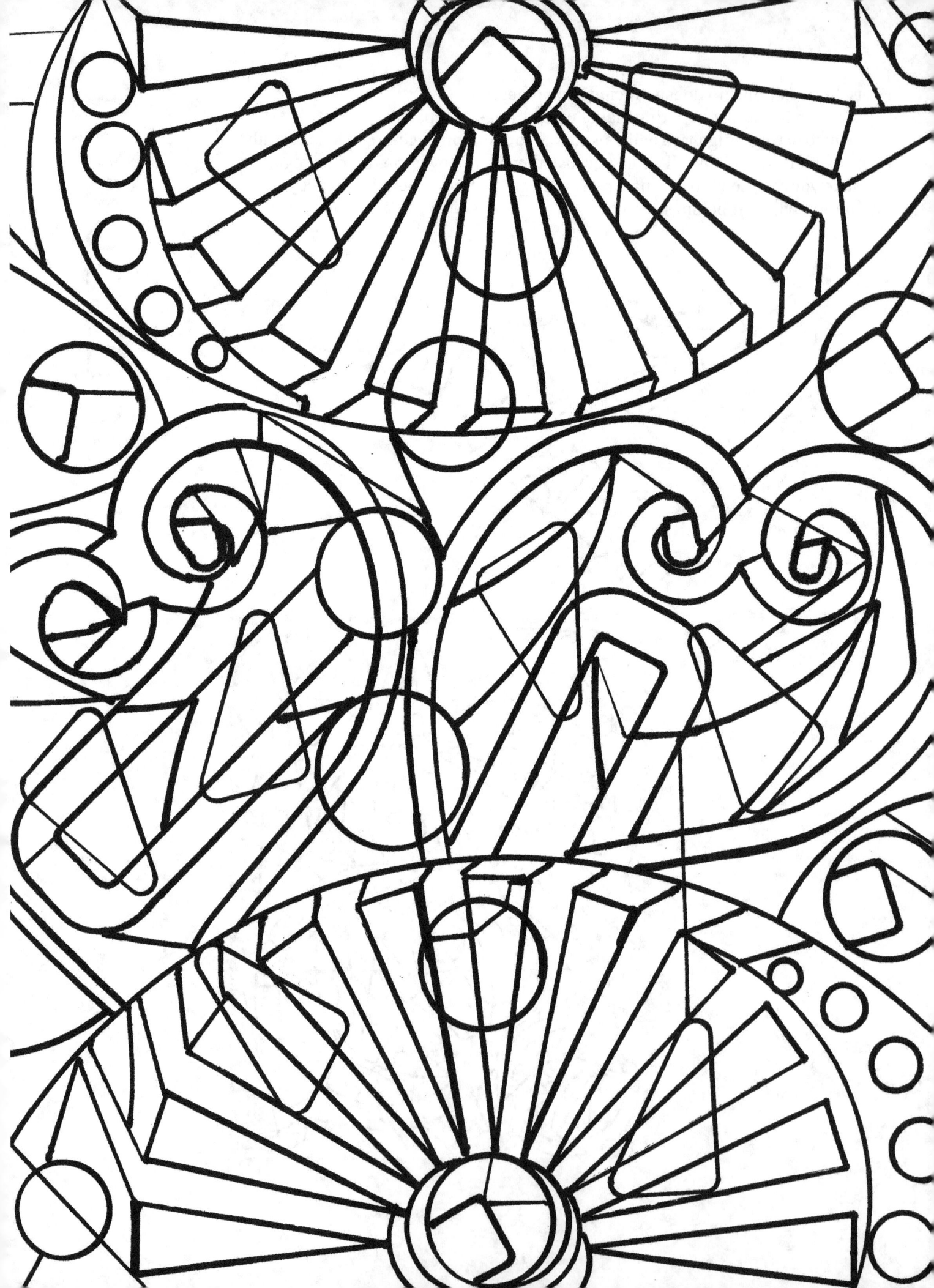

The angels do not stop writing for us just because the topic we're discussing isn't inherently "religious." In truth, there is no subject in this world that isn't intimately connected to our souls in some way.

If you have difficulty comprehending this obvious reality now, then know, dear soul, you'll have no such difficulty when standing before the Creator on the Day of Judgment—and you answer for every word spoken, every opinion shared, and every cause you stood for.

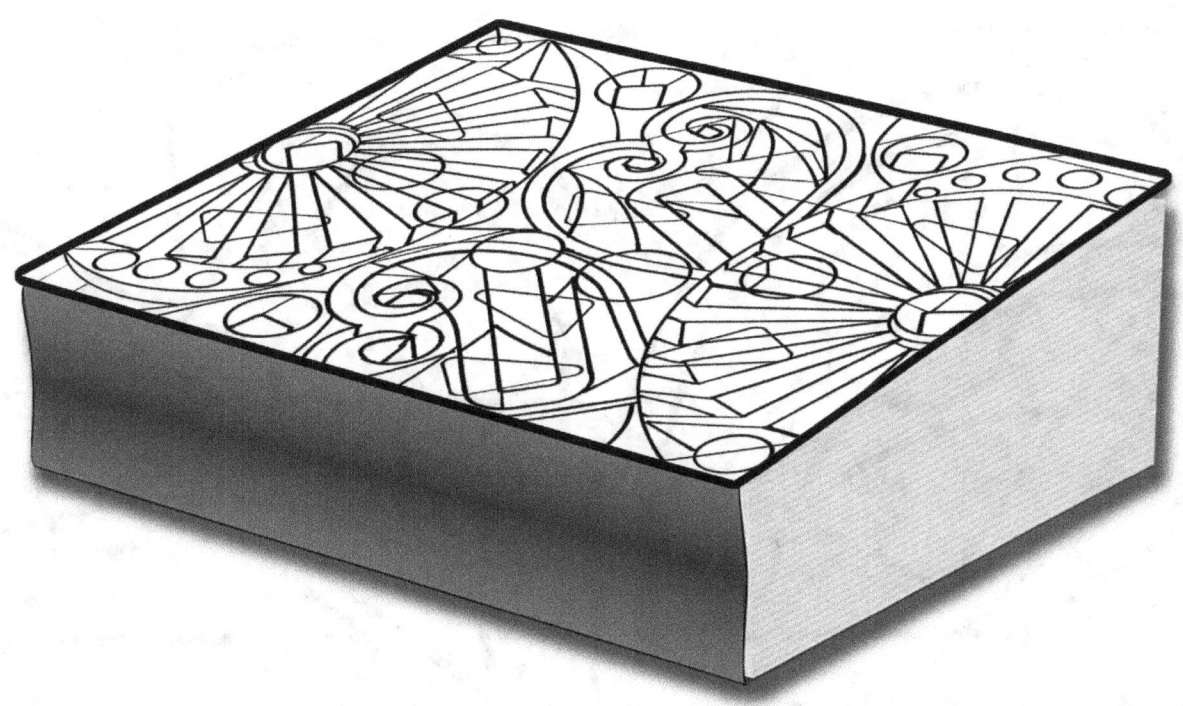

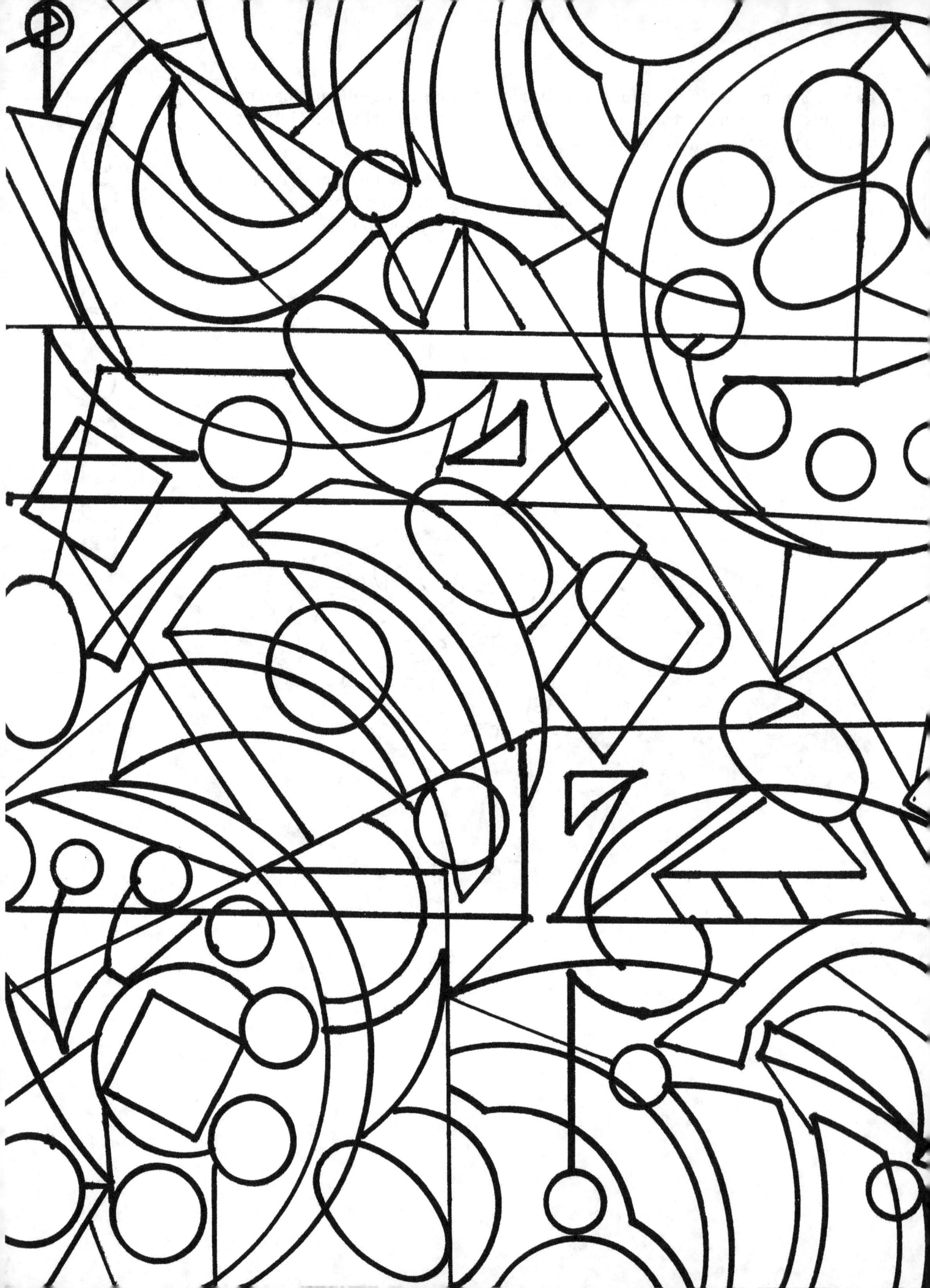

If reminders about our souls and the Hereafter do not still our tongues,
then by God, I have no idea what will.
Perhaps, our tongues must grow limp and useless upon illness or death before we
comprehend the enormity of using them so carelessly during wellness and life.

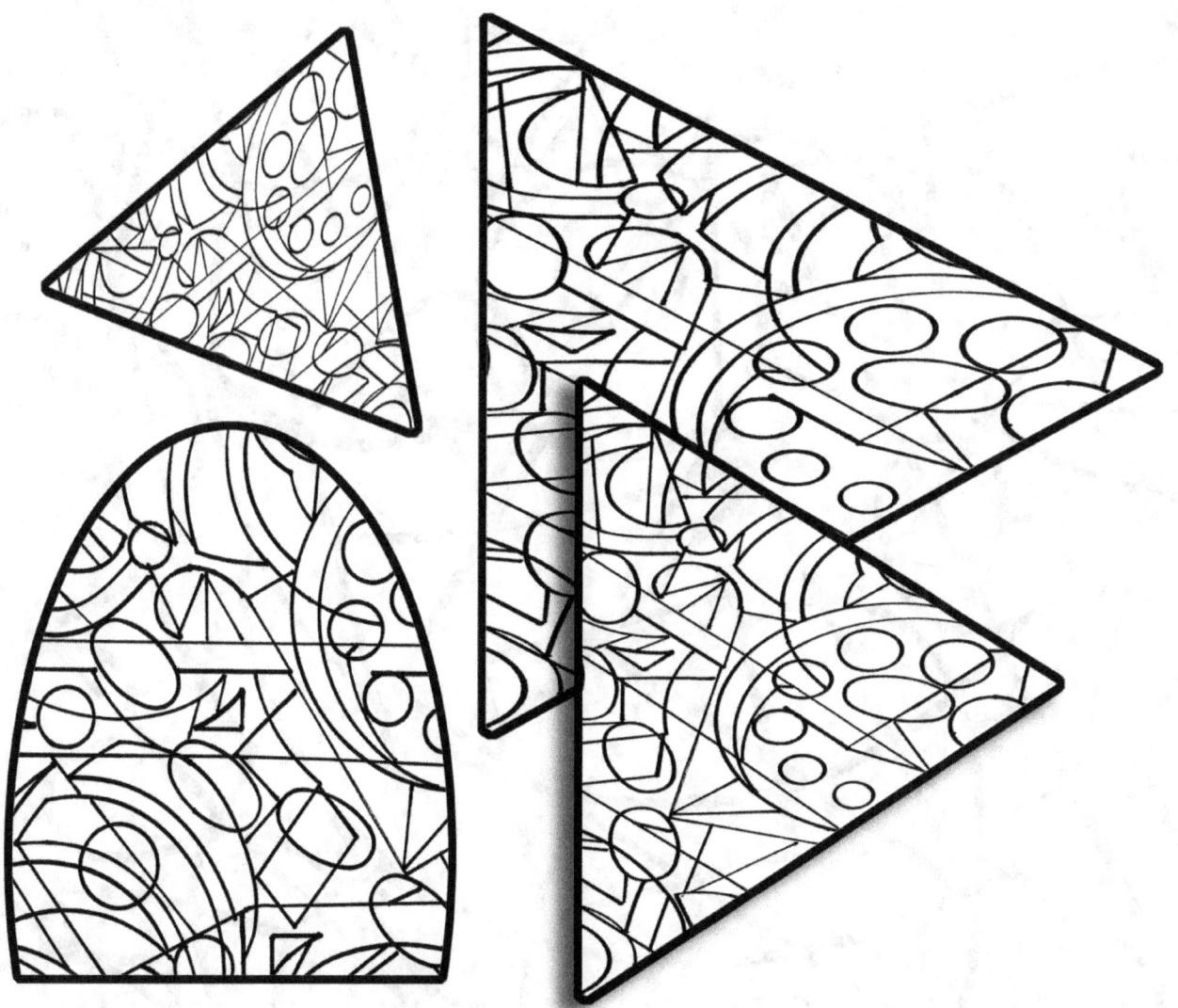

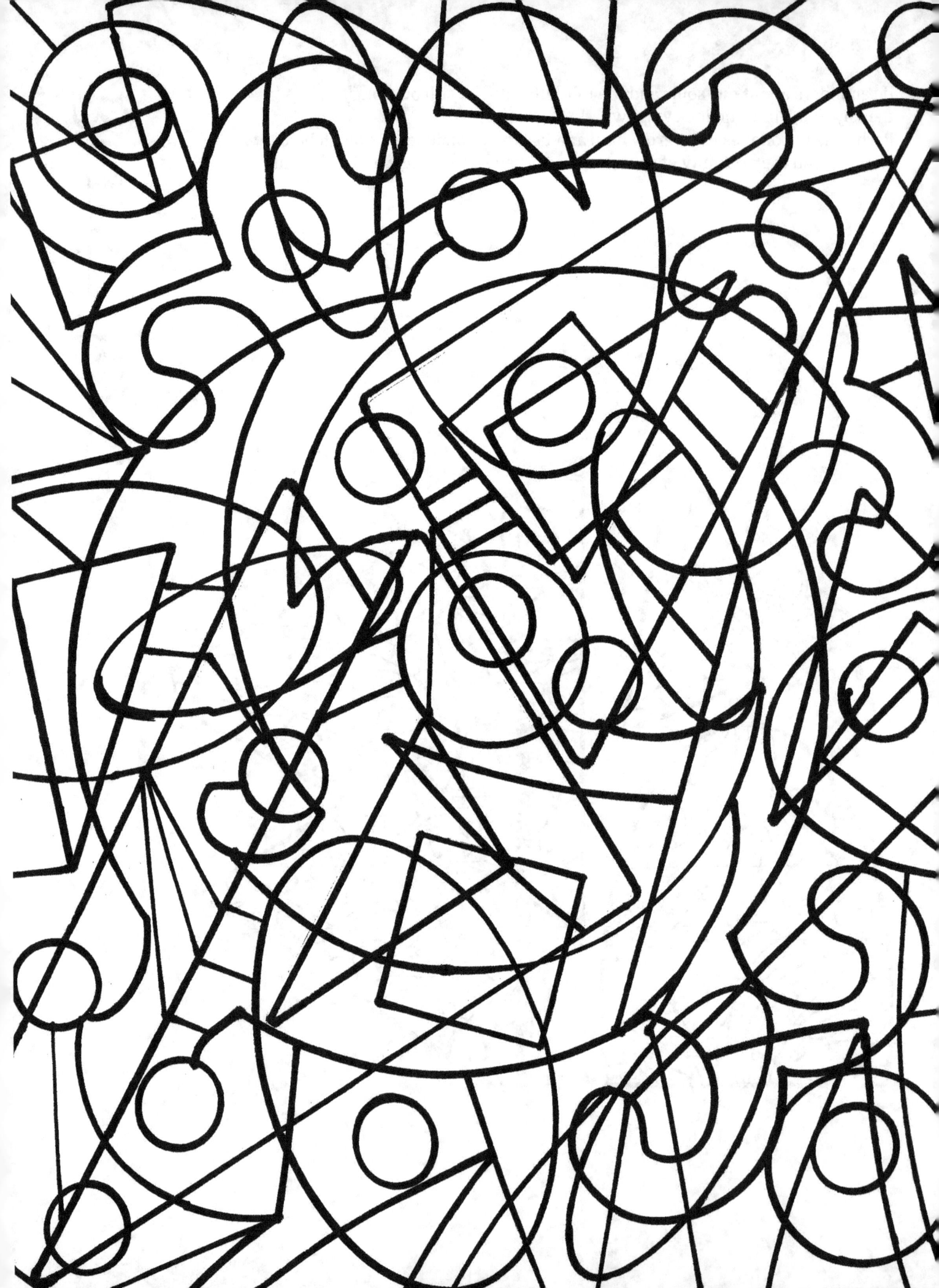

In the end, everything boils down to what your heart covets most.

Worldly circumstances and experiences only bring to surface who you already are deep inside. This is why relatively identical trials—whether of prosperity or adversity—bring out the good in some and the evil in others...and why some of us become more humble with time and why some of us become more arrogant.

Yes, we all have very rational reasons for why we view ourselves and the world through a certain lens, but rarely do we ponder the deeper reasons for our conclusions.

The truth is, when it comes to our spiritual outlook—whether we believe adhering to God's laws leads to the solution or to further problems upon earth—our conclusion has more to do with our hearts than with any "proven" worldly reality.

The humble heart has faith in God's wisdom and guidance, fully aware that it doesn't have the capacity to effect ultimate good or bad upon earth, while the arrogant heart actually believes it can not only effect ultimate good or bad upon earth, but that it also has the capacity to accurately analyze and measure the root of all righteousness and evil in this world.

The irony is, in the end, the earth will never see "ultimate good" no matter what worldly system you value, religious or secular.

So whether we ascribe to God's laws or to secular legislation, evil will still remain— because the source of evil is in the human heart, not in any ostensible worldly system. And the system we prefer is ultimately due to the state of our hearts, not to the state of the world.

Humble people tend to have faith in God and what He decrees—because ultimately their hearts covet the everlasting good in the Hereafter, so it matters little what good or bad they experience on earth.

And arrogant people tend to have faith in only what they and others humans decree— because their hearts covet the transient, fleeting good of this world, as they believe their entire purpose rests in the good or bad they experience on earth.

Yet, ironically, it is only the people who are humble believers in God who will taste both the good of this world and the good of the Hereafter—and who will effect the highest possible good on earth. Meanwhile, arrogant people (who will effect the worst possible evil on earth) will remain restless, bitter and discontent, no matter how much good they experience, because their arrogant hearts make them distrust the only One who can provide the worldly good they covet most.

Perception.

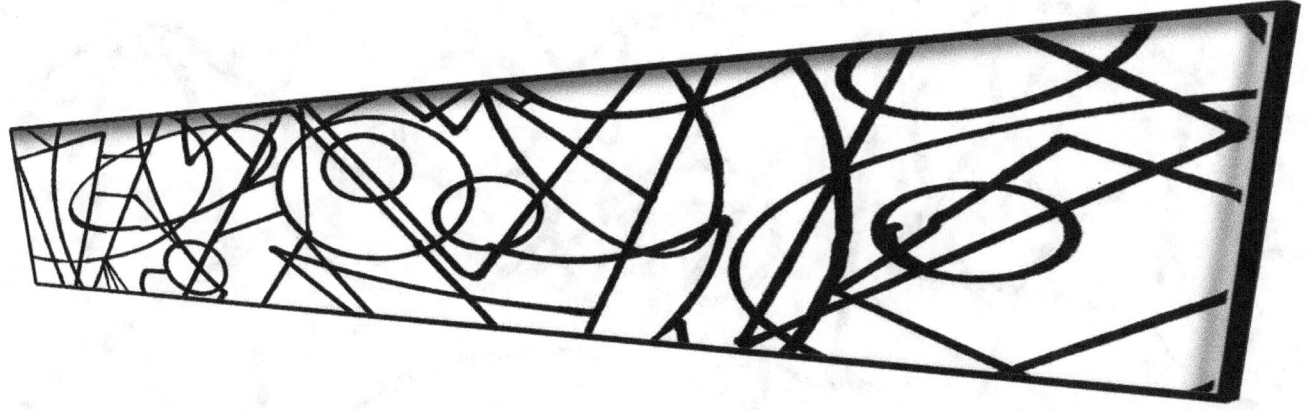

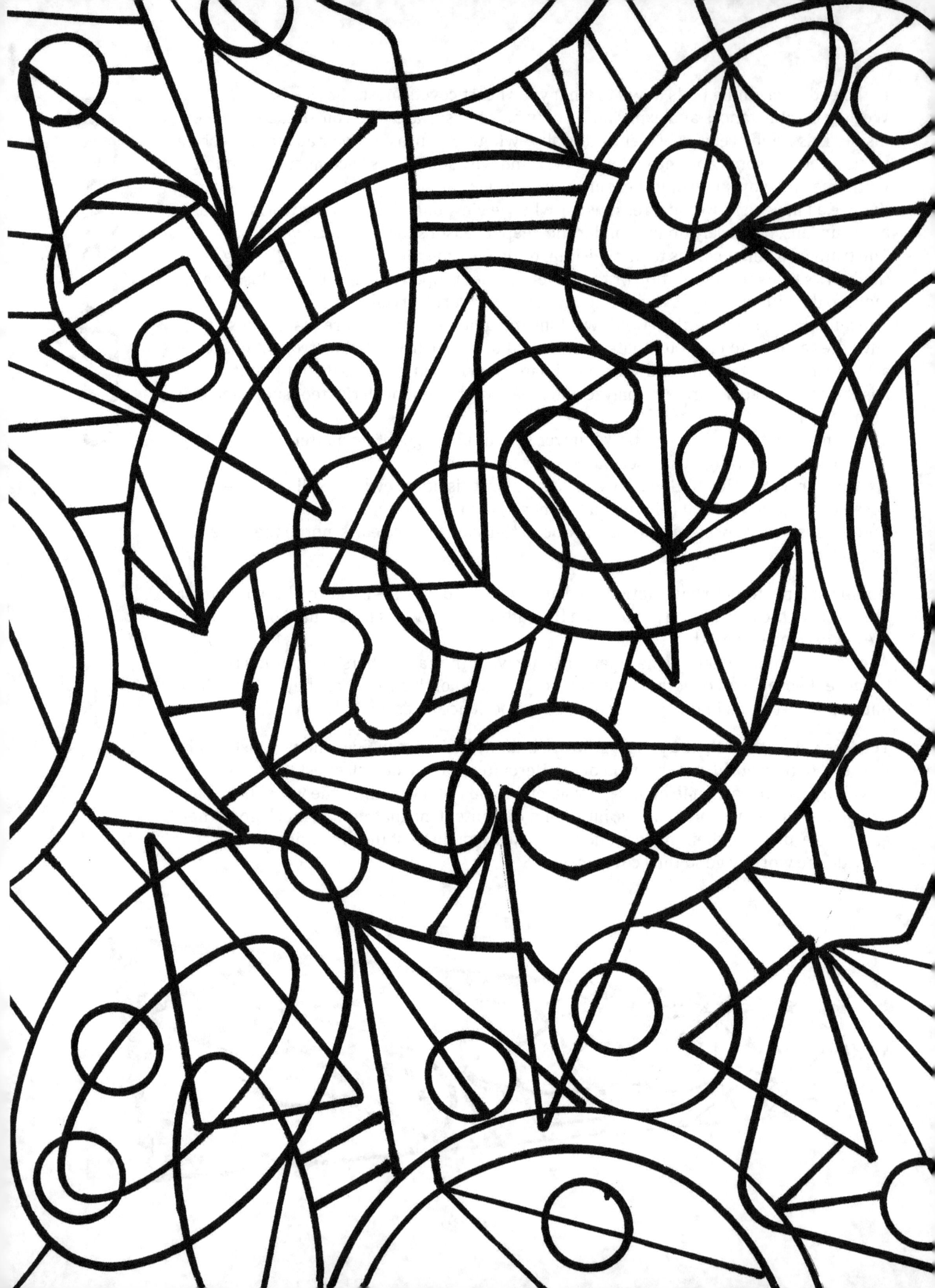

Truth is only hard to swallow if pride is stuck in your throat.

~

When religious truth is told in a powerful, soul-touching manner, there is usually one of two reactions: sincere reflection, or indignant rage.
And each represents not the details of the reminder,
but the spiritual state of the heart receiving it.

Truth.

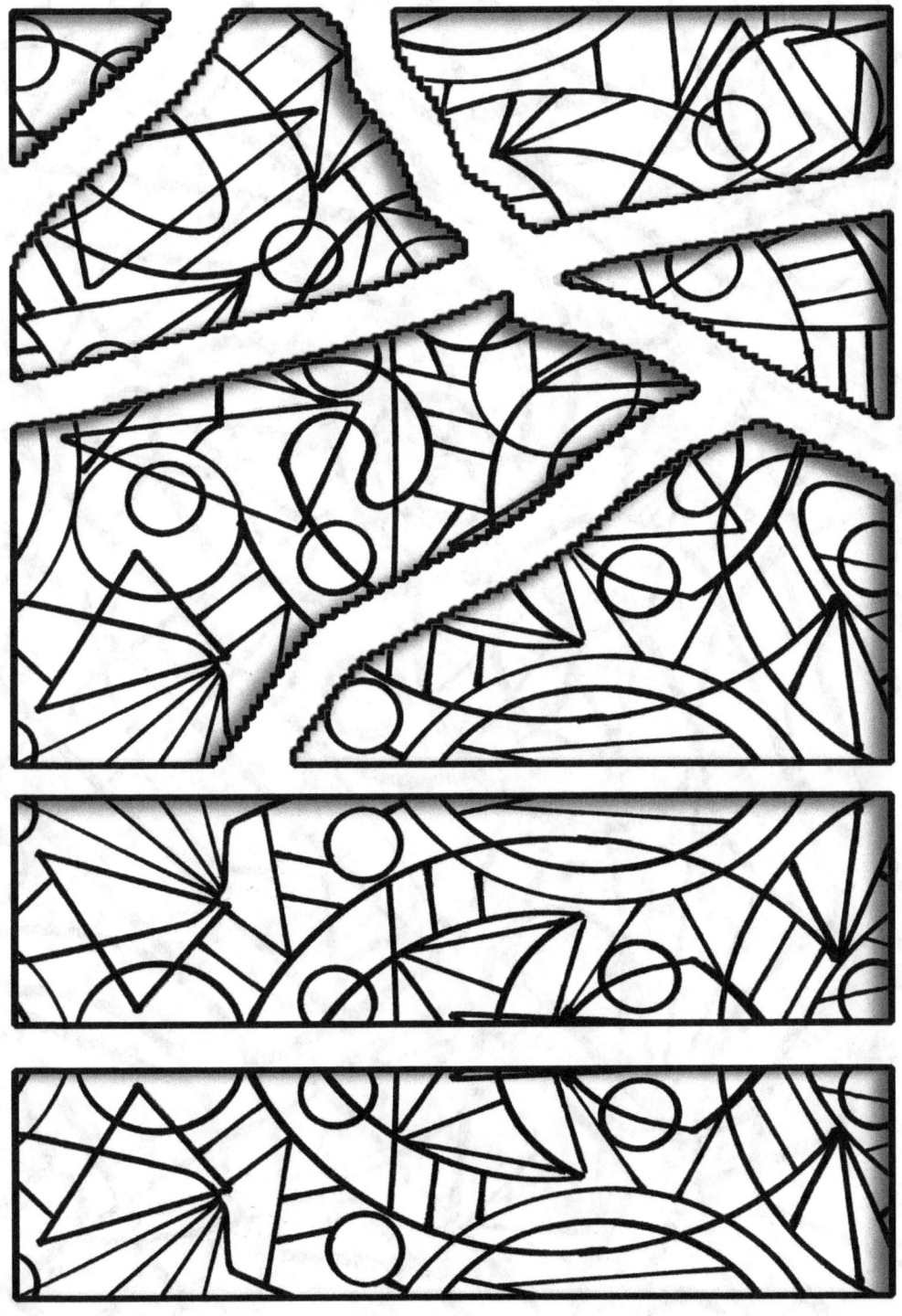

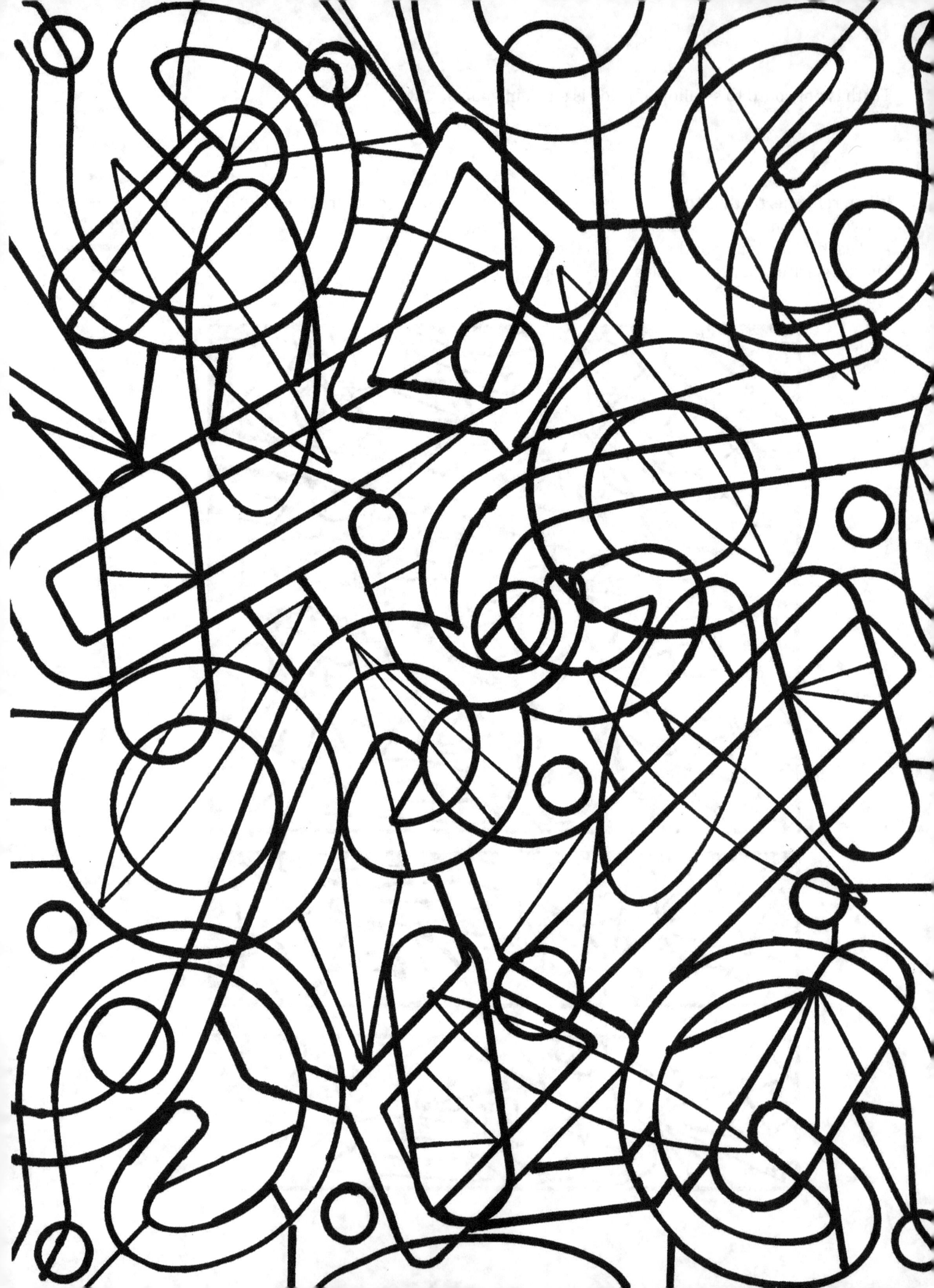

There are some things only God can teach us.
So He brings into our lives the perfect storm, tearing through our desires and convictions, and uprooting the pride and self-deception that entangle our hearts.

Storms.

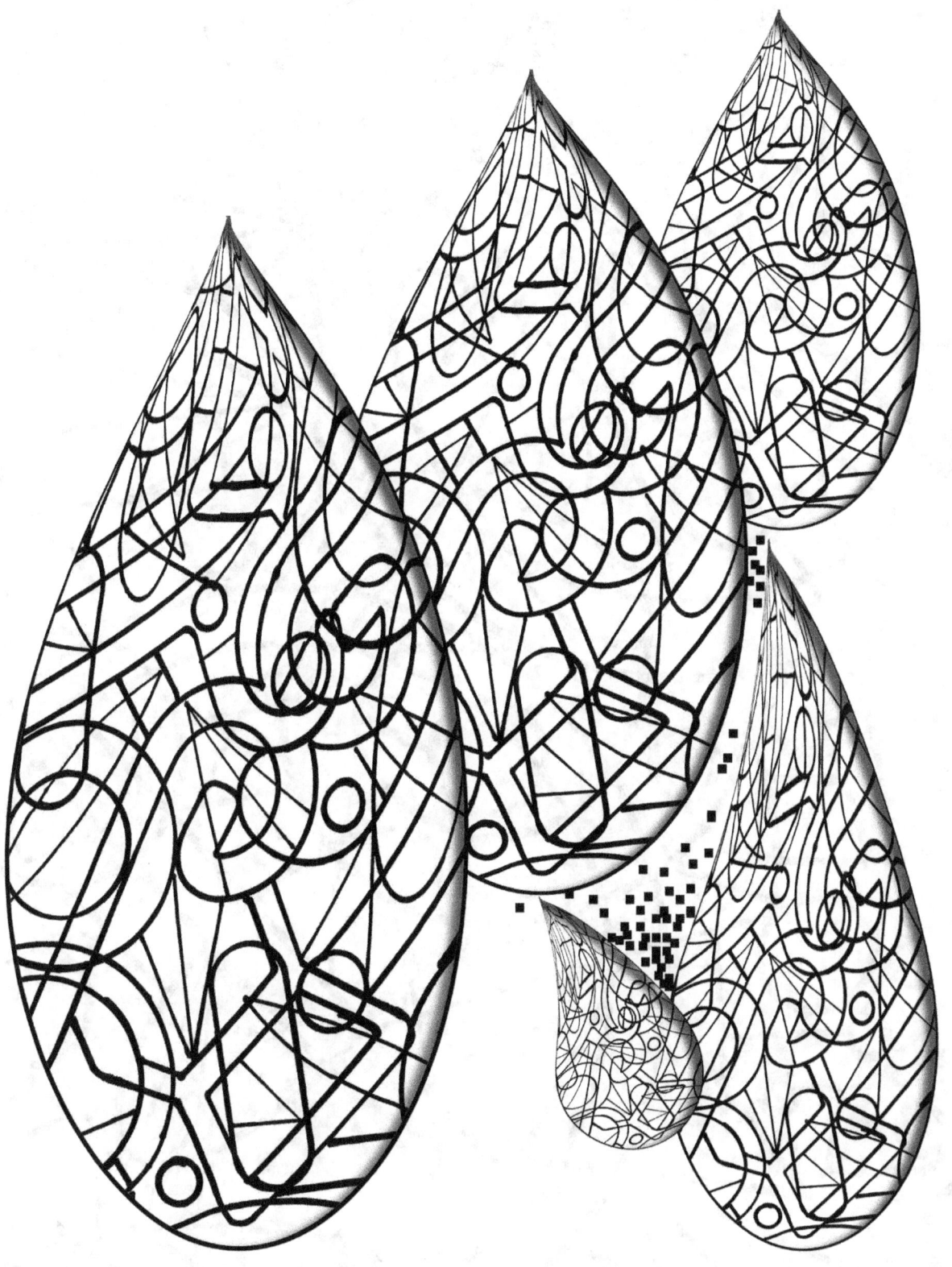

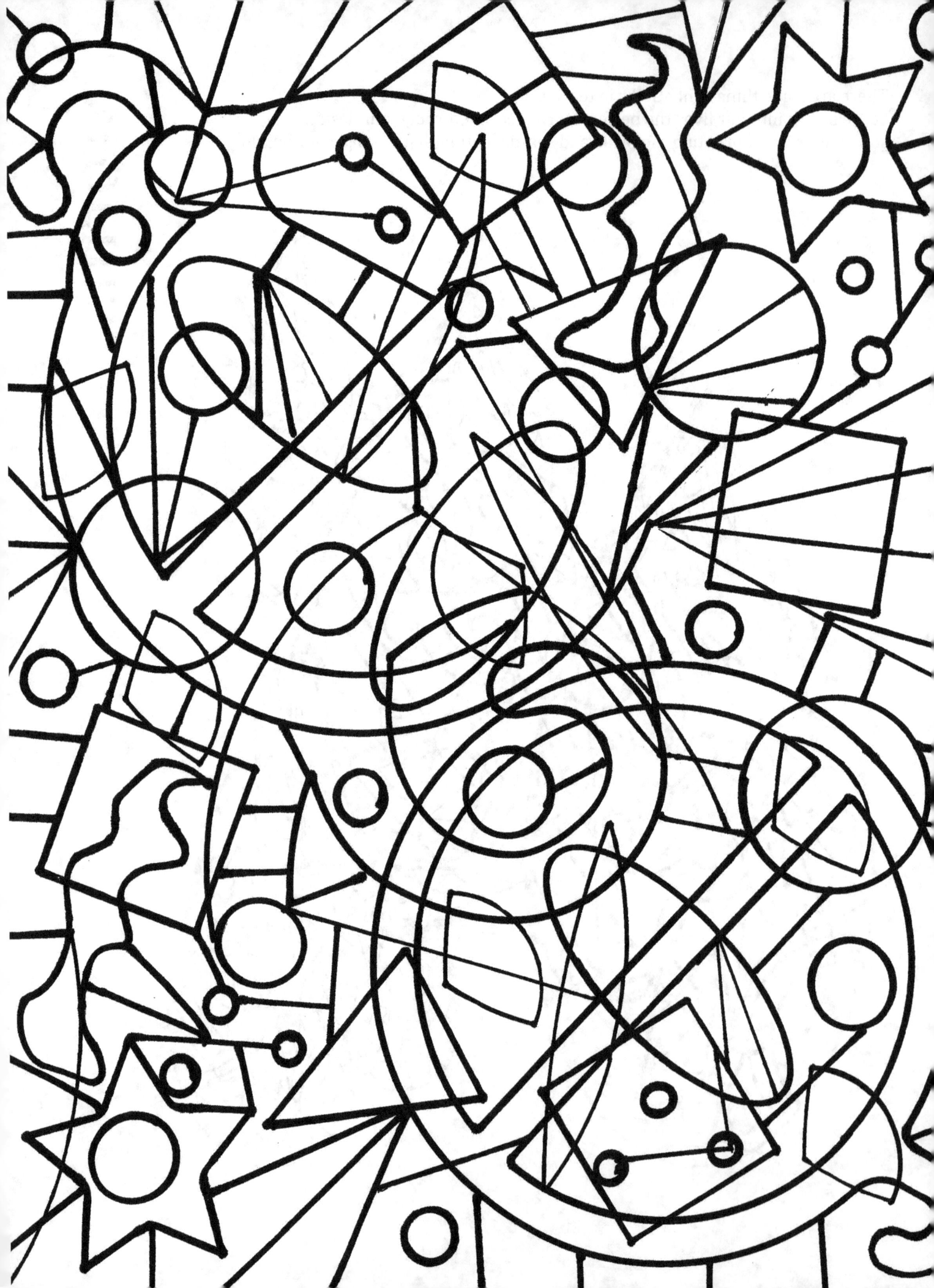

Oh how deceptive the impure heart is!
It makes endless excuses for itself, even in the face of obvious evil—and endless
accusations for anyone it dislikes, even in the face of obvious good.

Deception.

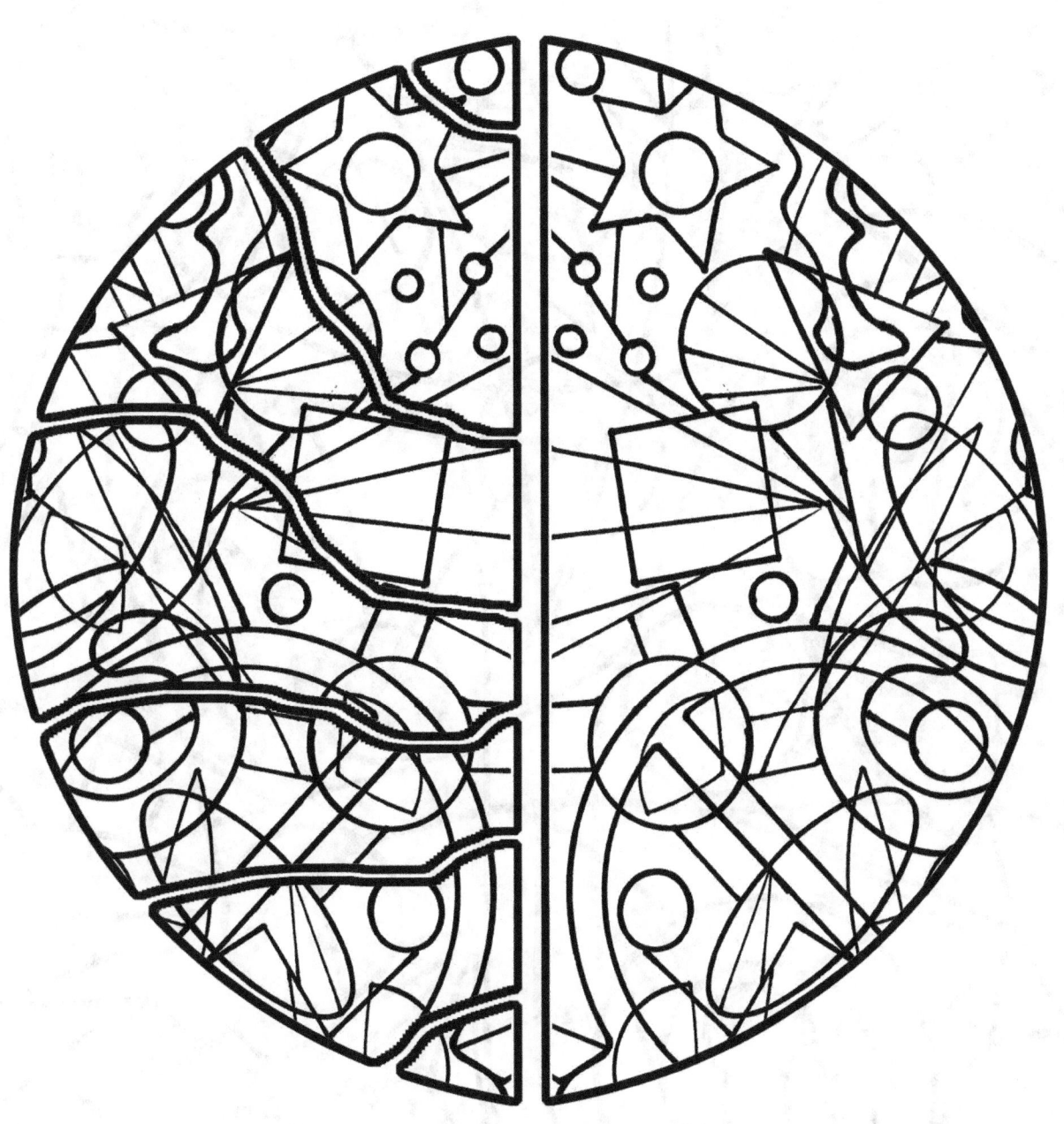

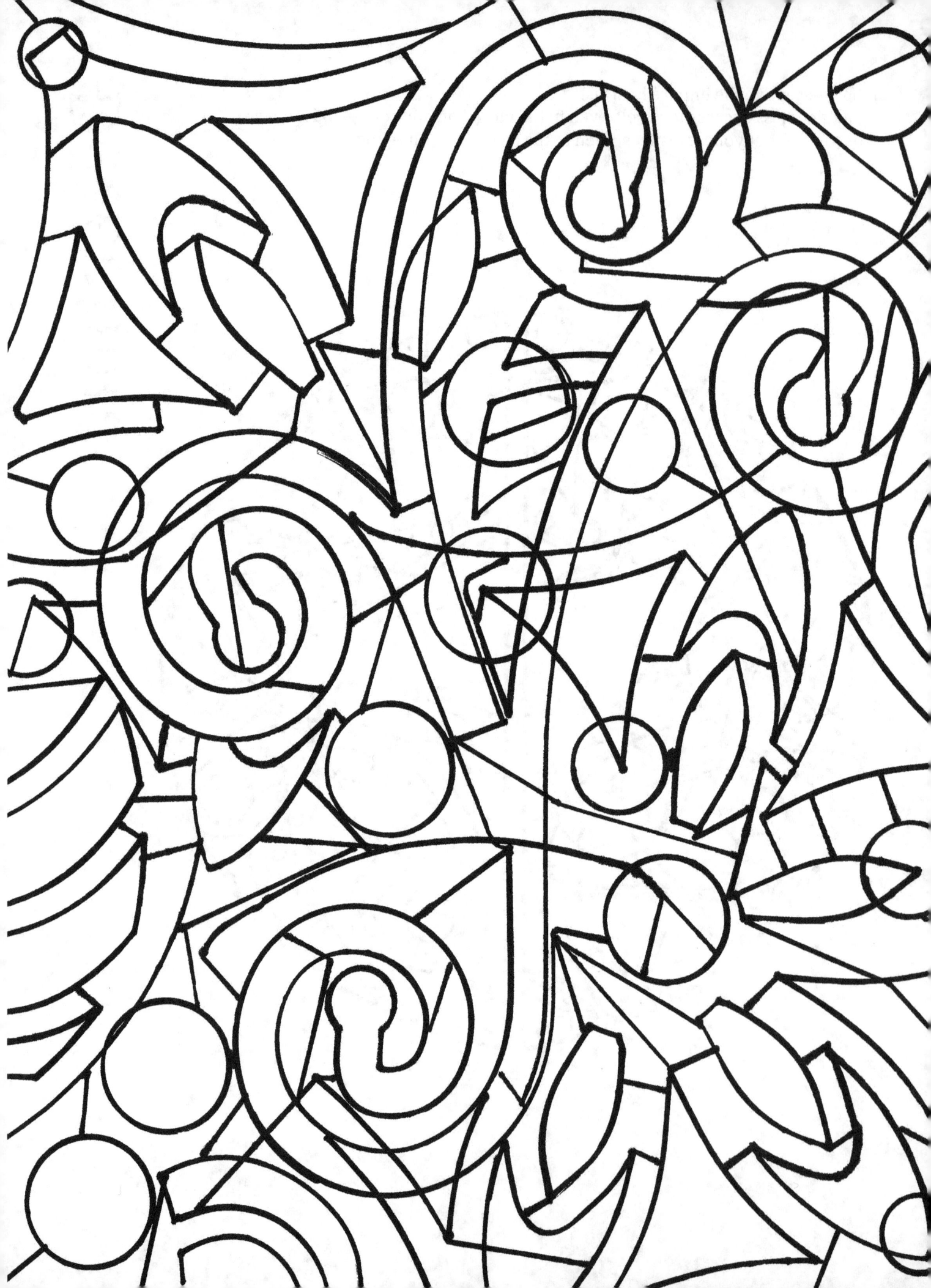

What's the fastest way to destroy your blessings and have them taken from you?
Filling your heart with pride by imagining that you were granted this good because of some greatness in you, or because of your hard work alone.
And by becoming lazy in your worship because the numerous blessings you enjoy have made you "too busy" or "too tired" to humbly and sincerely stand in prayer before the One who granted them to you.
Be careful...

Destruction.

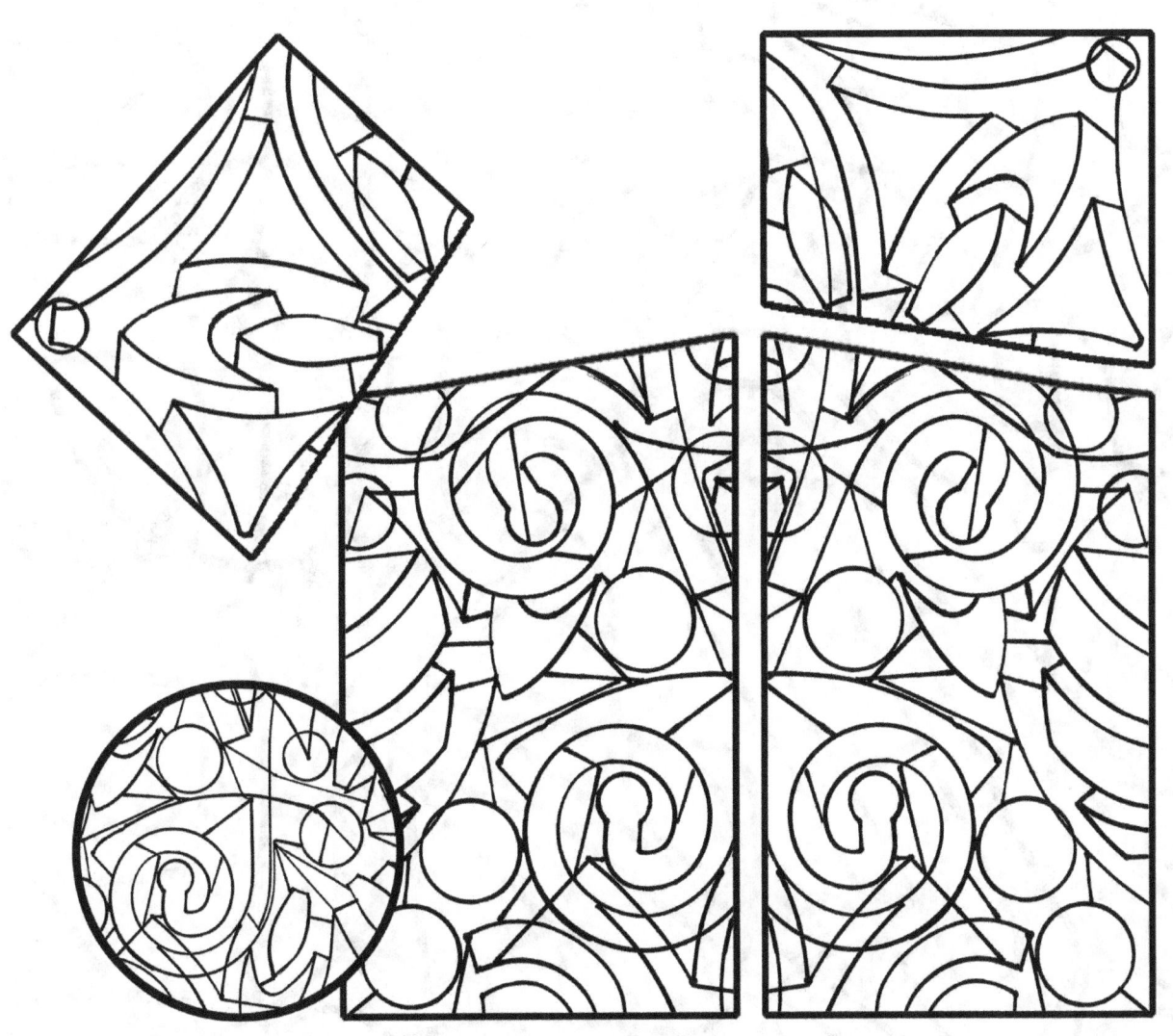

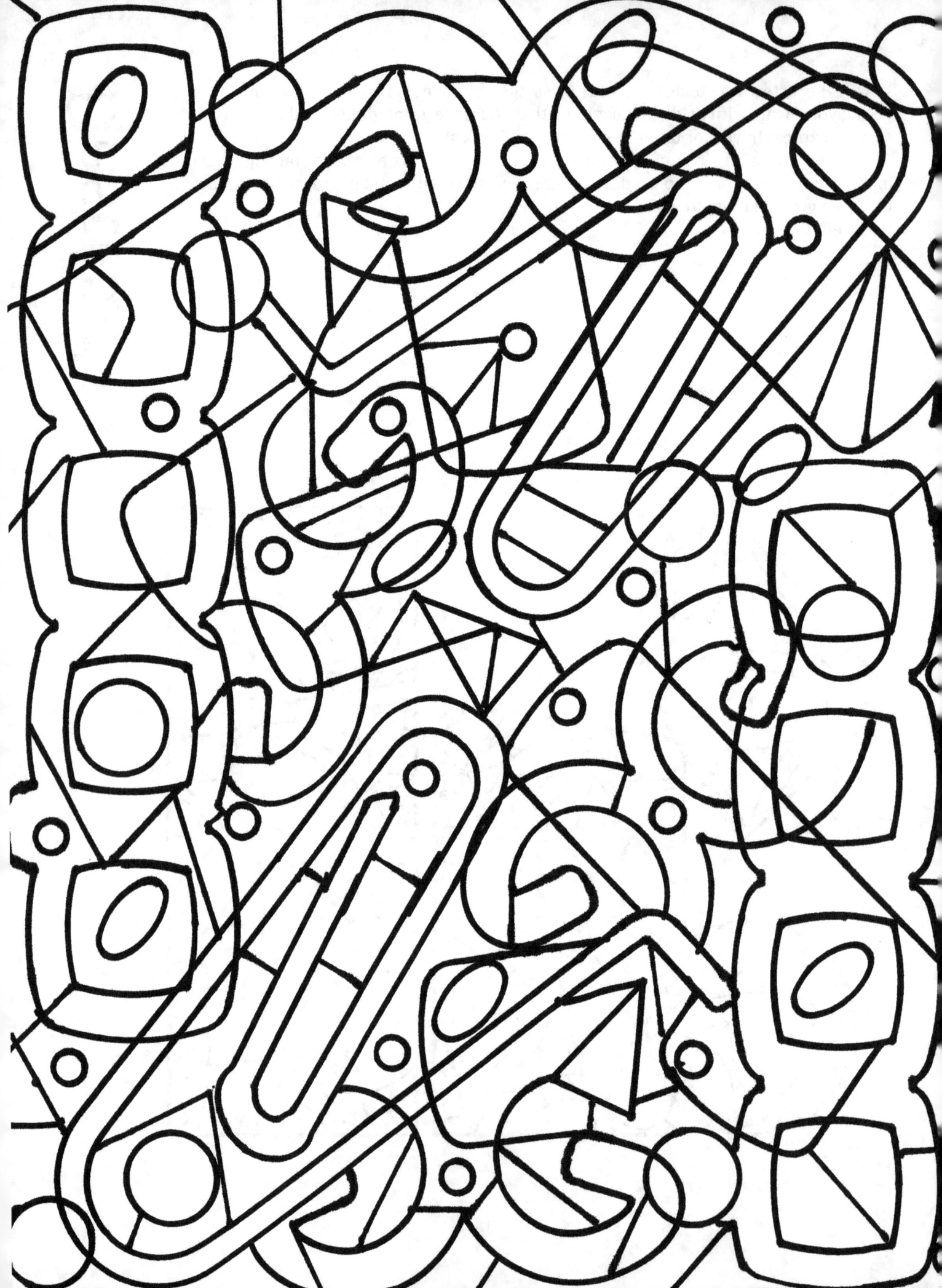

One of the most emotionally and spiritually damaging things we can do to someone is to deny or block their right to their own mind and soul.

We do this by presenting our own opinions and convictions as inflexible religious obligations, particularly during the beginning of a person's learning process when they trust us most.

Whenever I see inflexible, black-and-white responses to permissible disagreement, my heart breaks. I don't understand why so many of us guilt believers into following us instead of encouraging them to sincerely research and consult their Lord.

What makes us trust ourselves more than we do our Creator?

And what makes us so convinced that we are right that we can now completely disregard another point of view, or deem it as unworthy of even mention?

And more tragically, what inspires us to mock and scoff at those who disagree with us?

Unfortunately, the latter creates cult-like behavior that, quite literally, destroys a person's emotional and spiritual health—and encourages emotional and spiritual abuse in the worst form.

One thing I've learned from my own spiritual struggles, as well as supporting others through theirs, is that much of our pain stems from being in environments that assaulted our sense of self, and blocked access to healthy individuality. These environments punished us for the slightest disagreement with a prevailing opinion or for not showing enough "respect" to the group's favored personality.

And the more vulnerable we were during this time—whether in childhood or when first learning about our faith—the more traumatic our suffering and the more difficult and tumultuous our healing.

Each day I'm surprised and saddened to find that there are so many of us—and so many who have given up on faith and spirituality altogether.

Because it's rare to find a religious community that respects the right of each person to his or her own mind and soul. Most communities are so fixated on the worldly outcomes of behavior control and group or leader validation that the spiritual goals of sincere guidance and salvation in the Hereafter are completely lost.

These groups forget that ultimately God is in charge of hearts and souls, and that it is actually a mercy that He has not placed this burden on us…

And that it is a form of oppression—of self and others—to place this burden on ourselves.

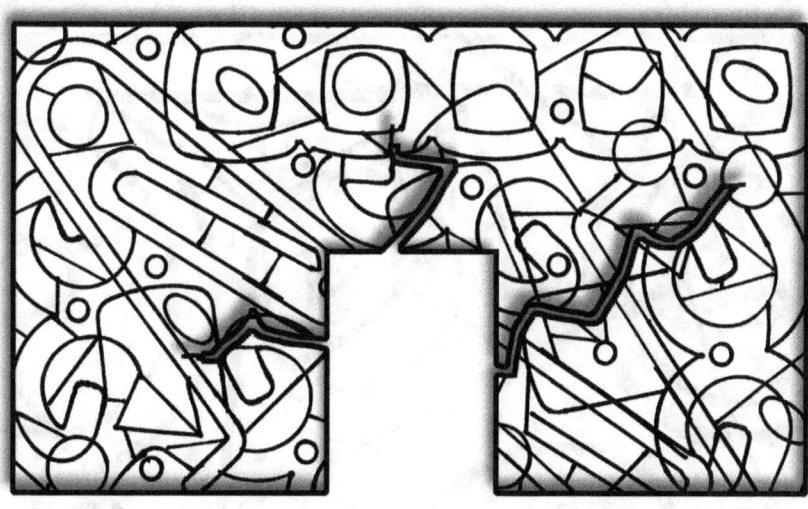

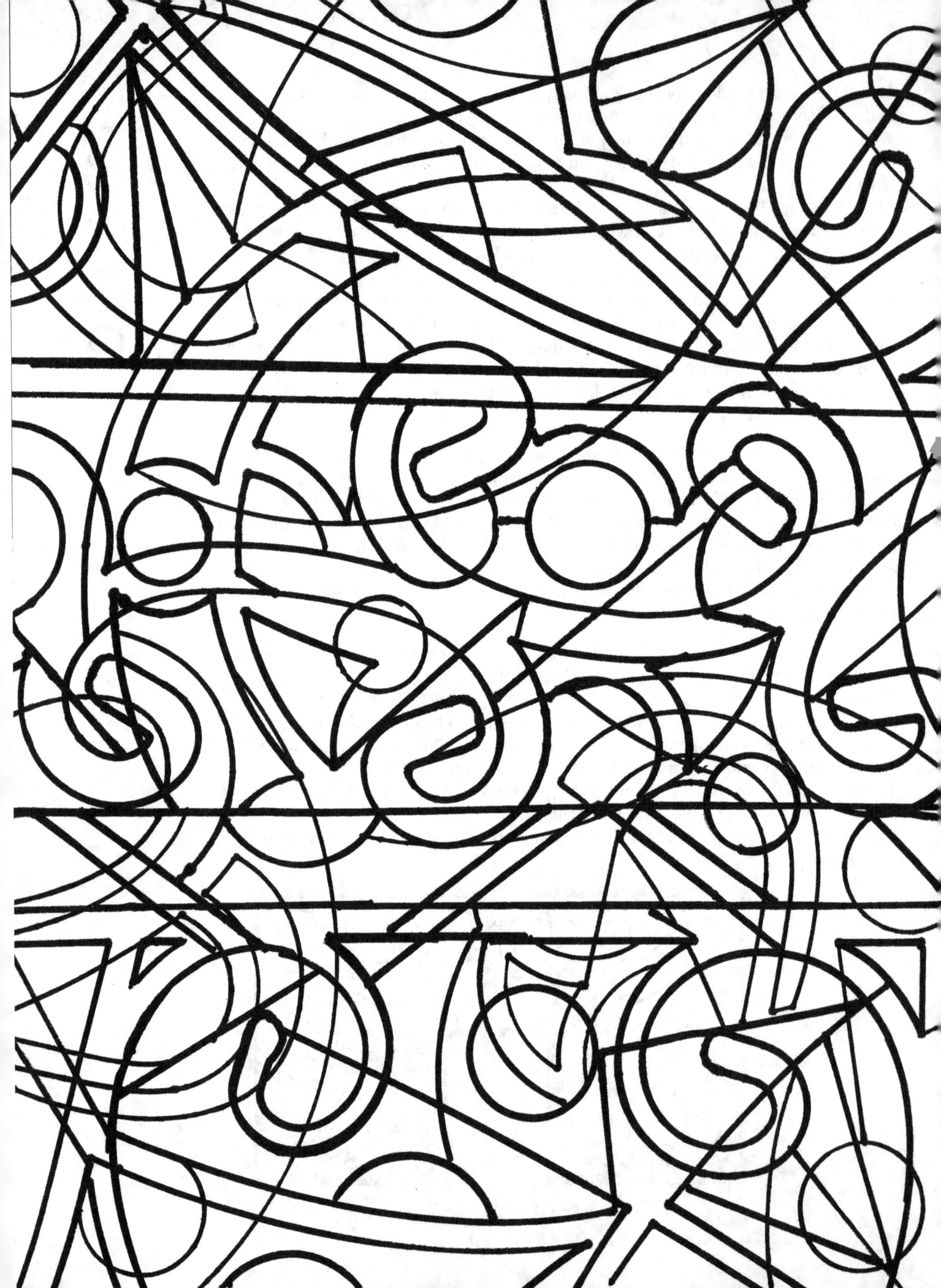

There's a reason we're told to make excuses for each other.
And it's not only because the truth is often in one of those seventy excuses.
It's also because making excuses for others makes *us* better people.

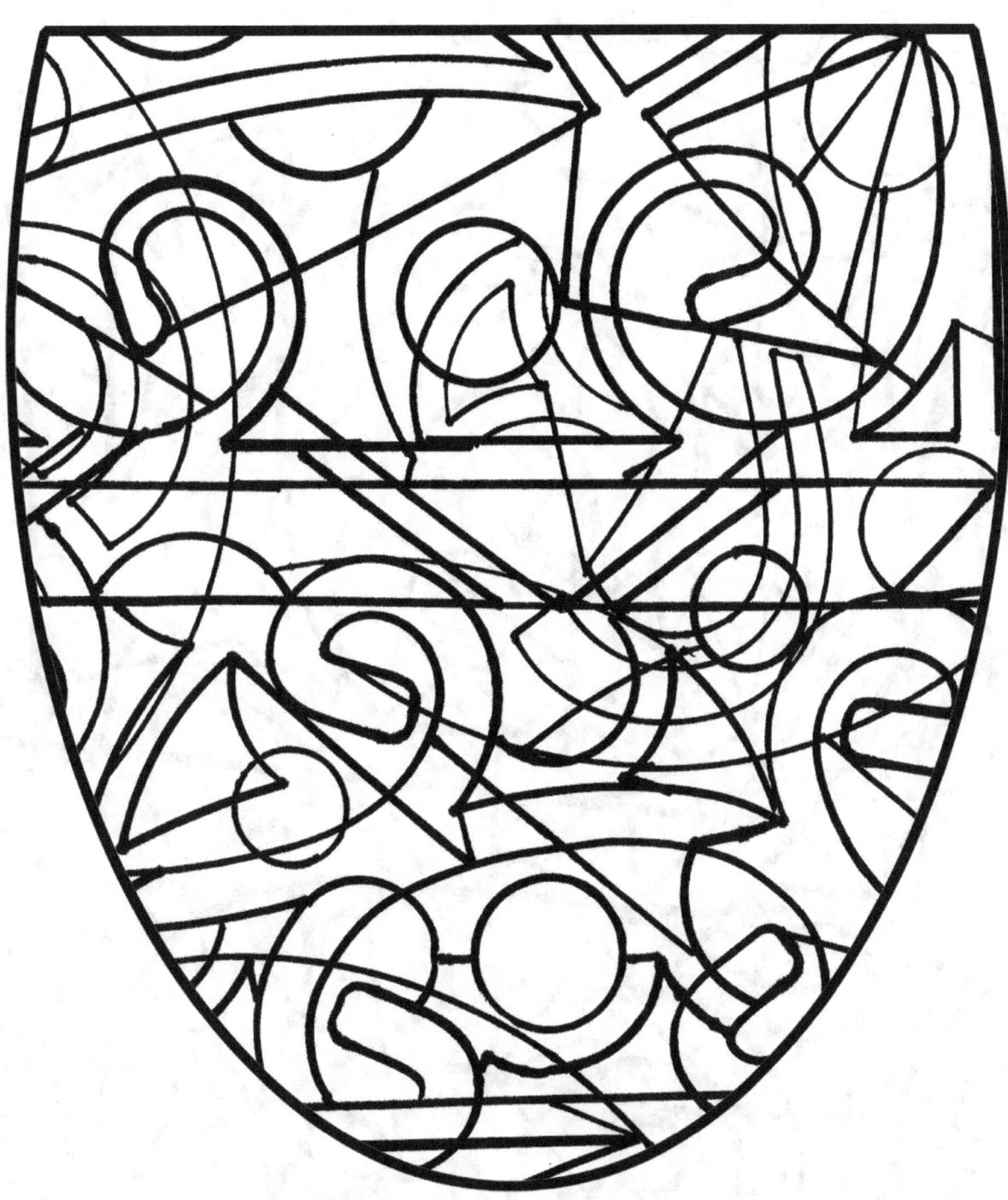

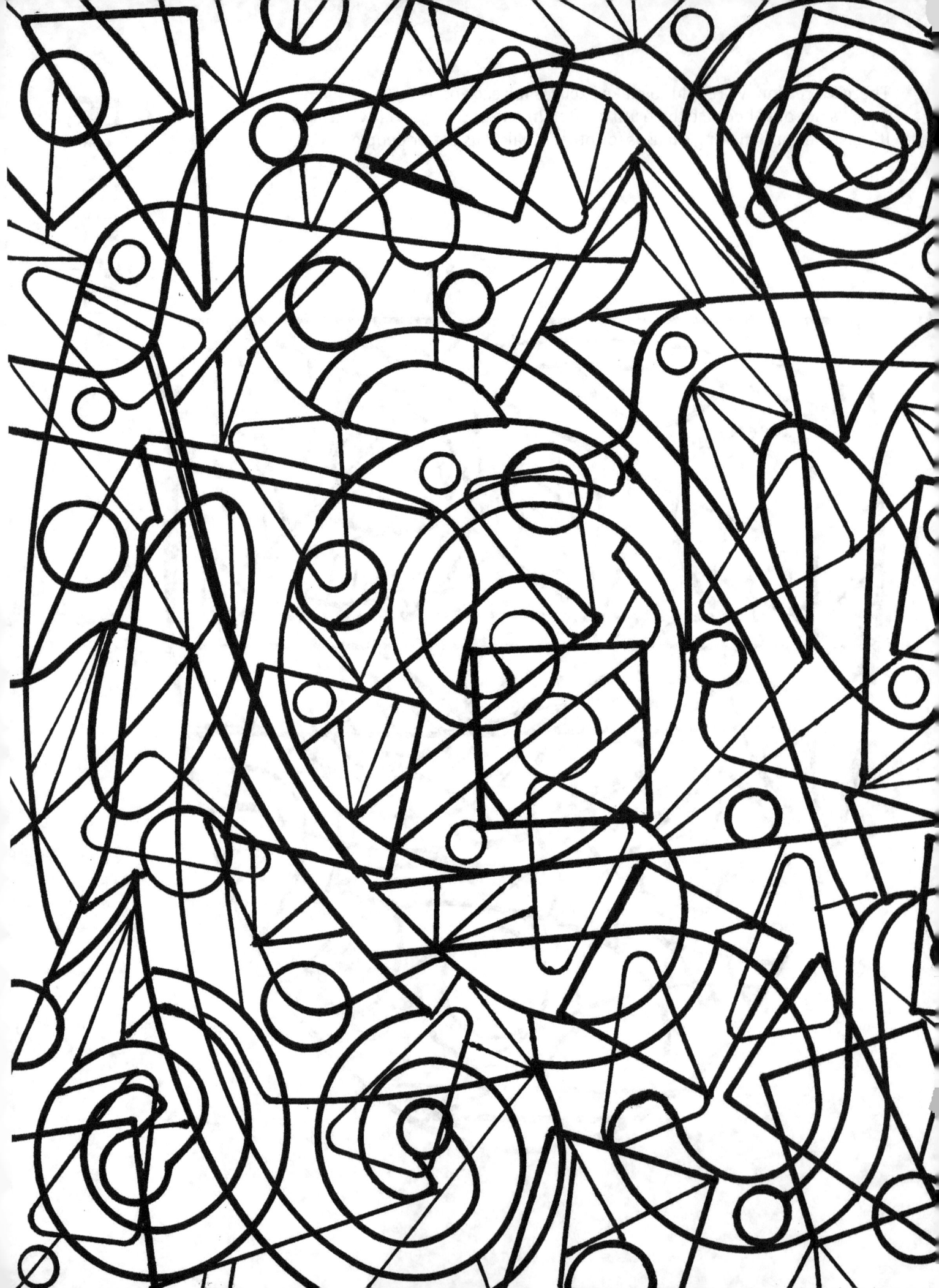

Connection with the right person for marriage is like a communication from God to your heart, then from your heart to your mind, such that your whole being knows this is right for you.

Any time you have to force ideas into your mind in hopes of convincing your heart—while nursing deep feelings of reluctance and anxiety—then you know something is very, very wrong.

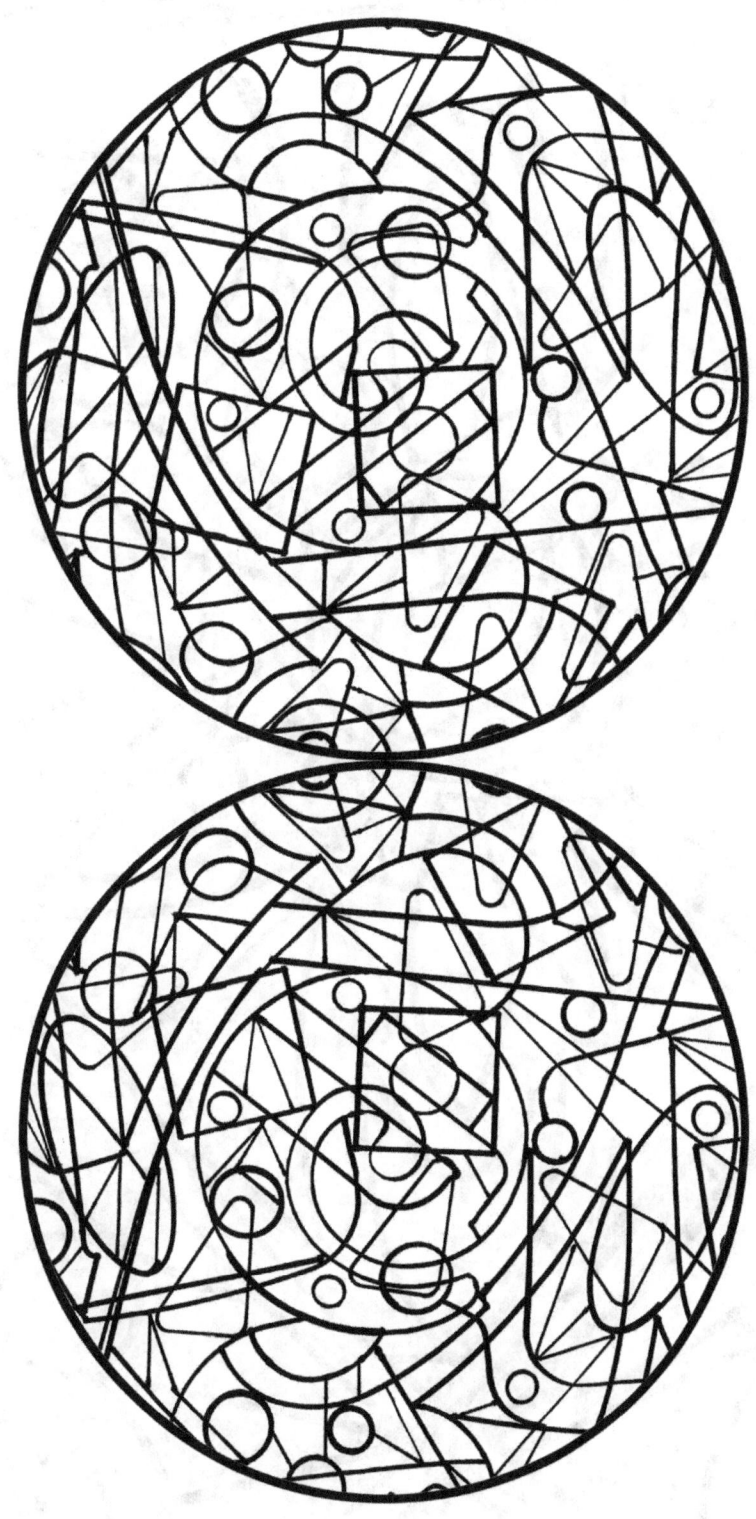

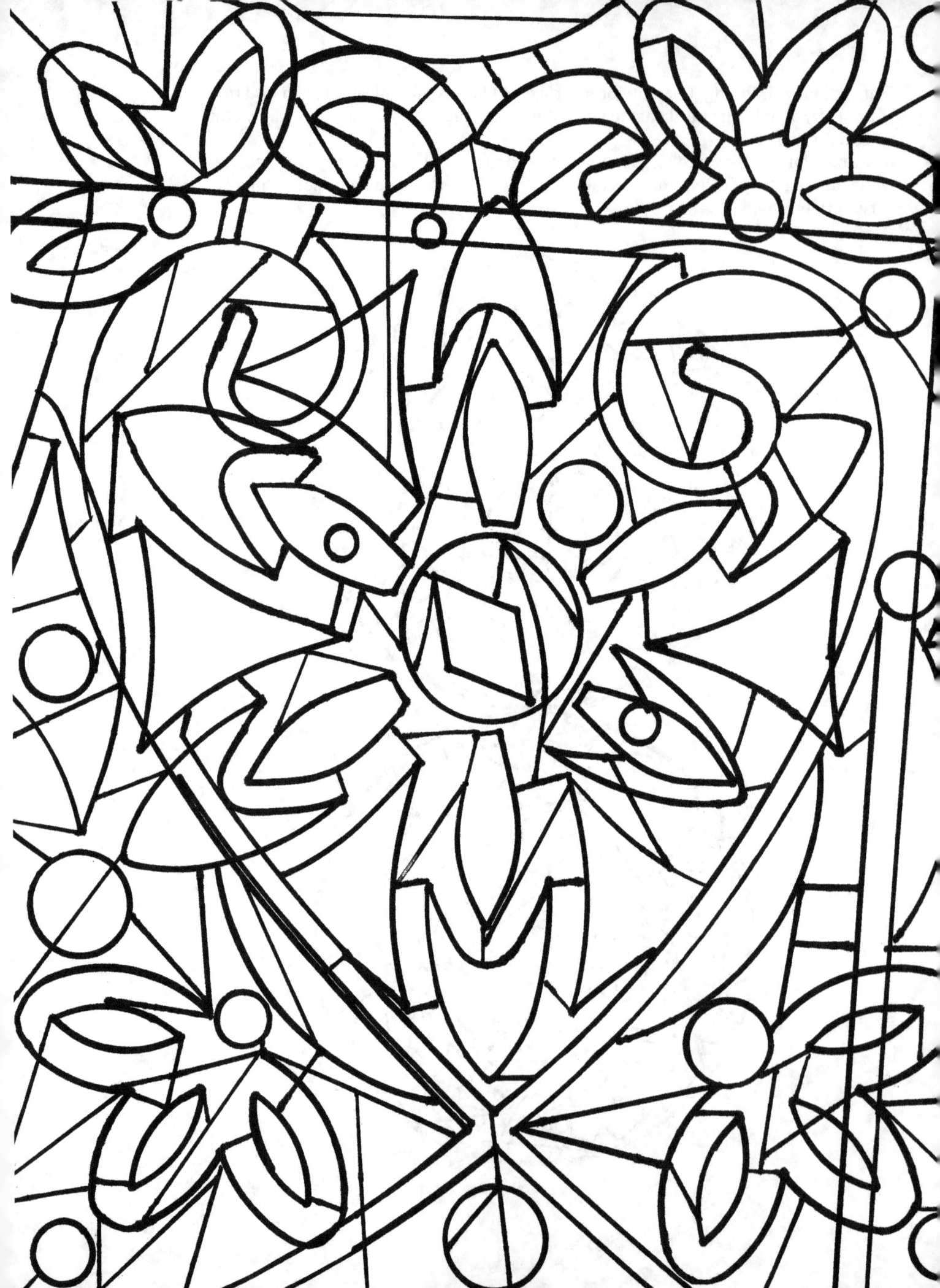

Some lessons simply cannot be passed on in words,
no matter how heartfelt, earnest and clear.
Some of us must be touched by the fire of experience
before we understand the destructiveness of the flame.

Fire.

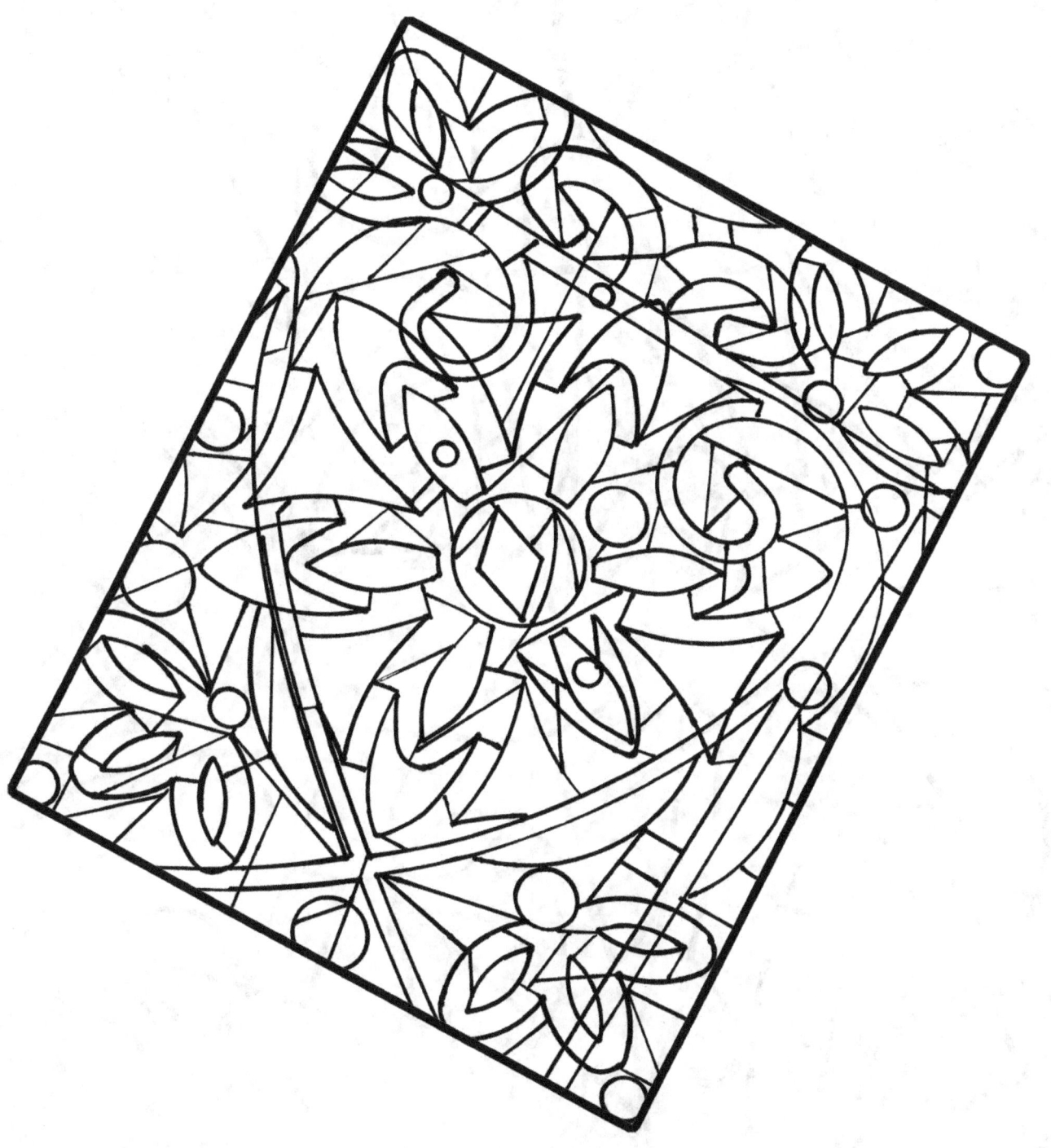

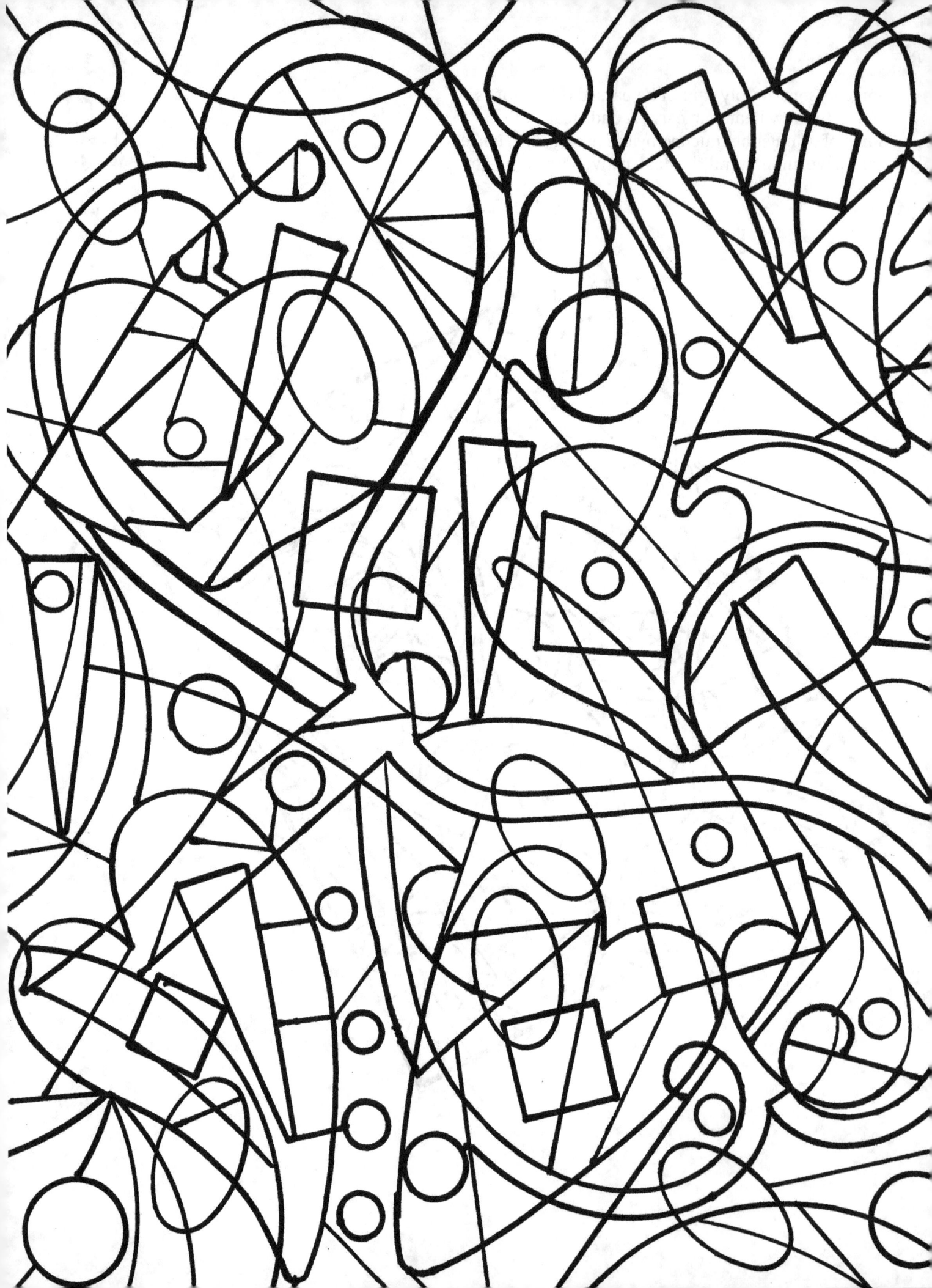

"Why did God make this happen to me!" is a senseless question—unless you're unaware of your purpose on earth, or are completely ignorant of what a test is. The purpose of life is to worship and obey your Creator, and the meaning of a test is that a problem or challenge has been handed to you— with the expectation that you're fully capable of passing the test.

And both faith and life are filled with tests.

In fact, both faith and life *are* tests.

So don't become frustrated with the exam paper.

For certainly, the One who gave you the exam has also given you the answer key.

Don't fail just because you're angry that it actually requires energy to fill in the answers—or because you imagined that *your* test should have only parts you want or enjoy.

Tests.

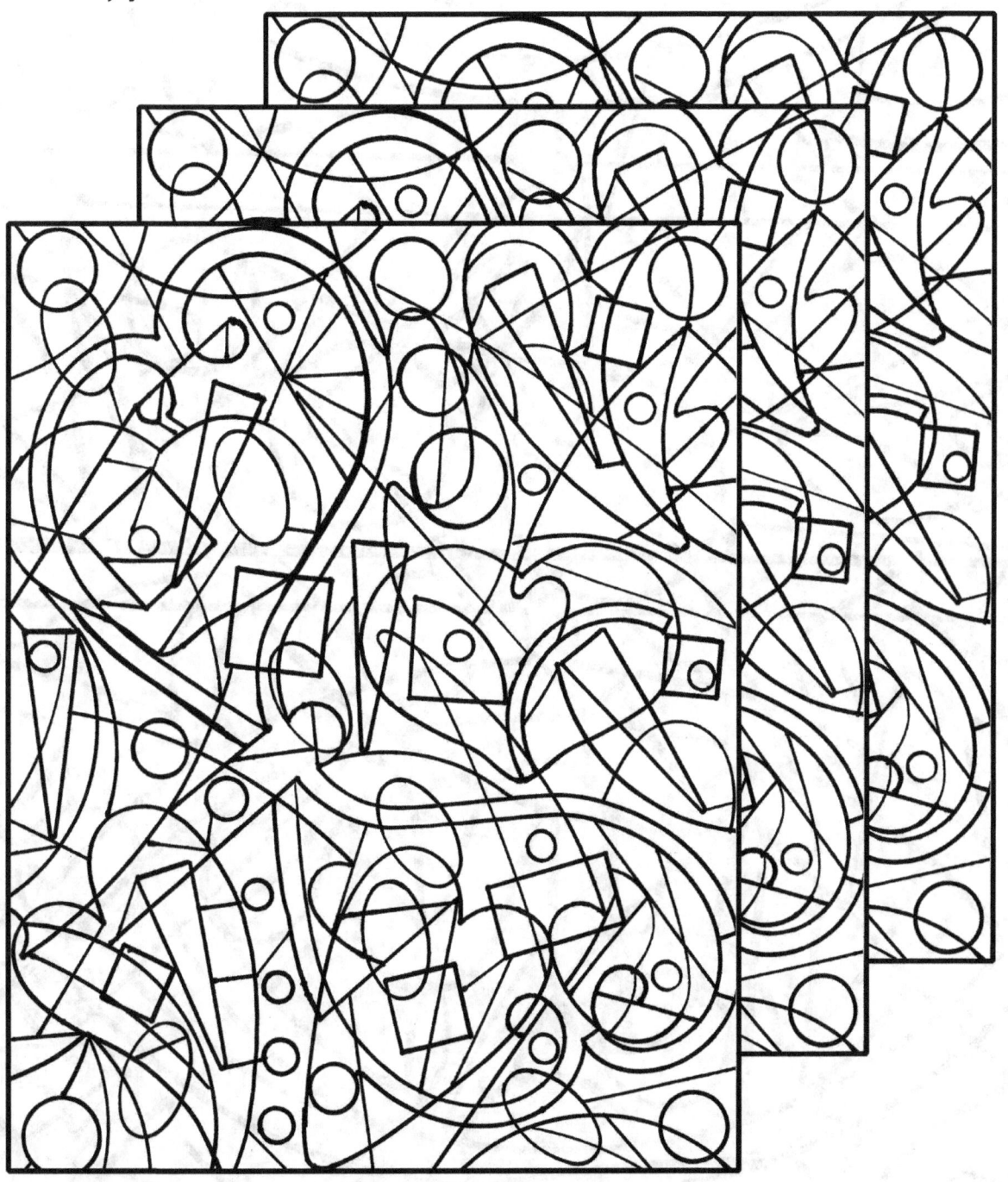

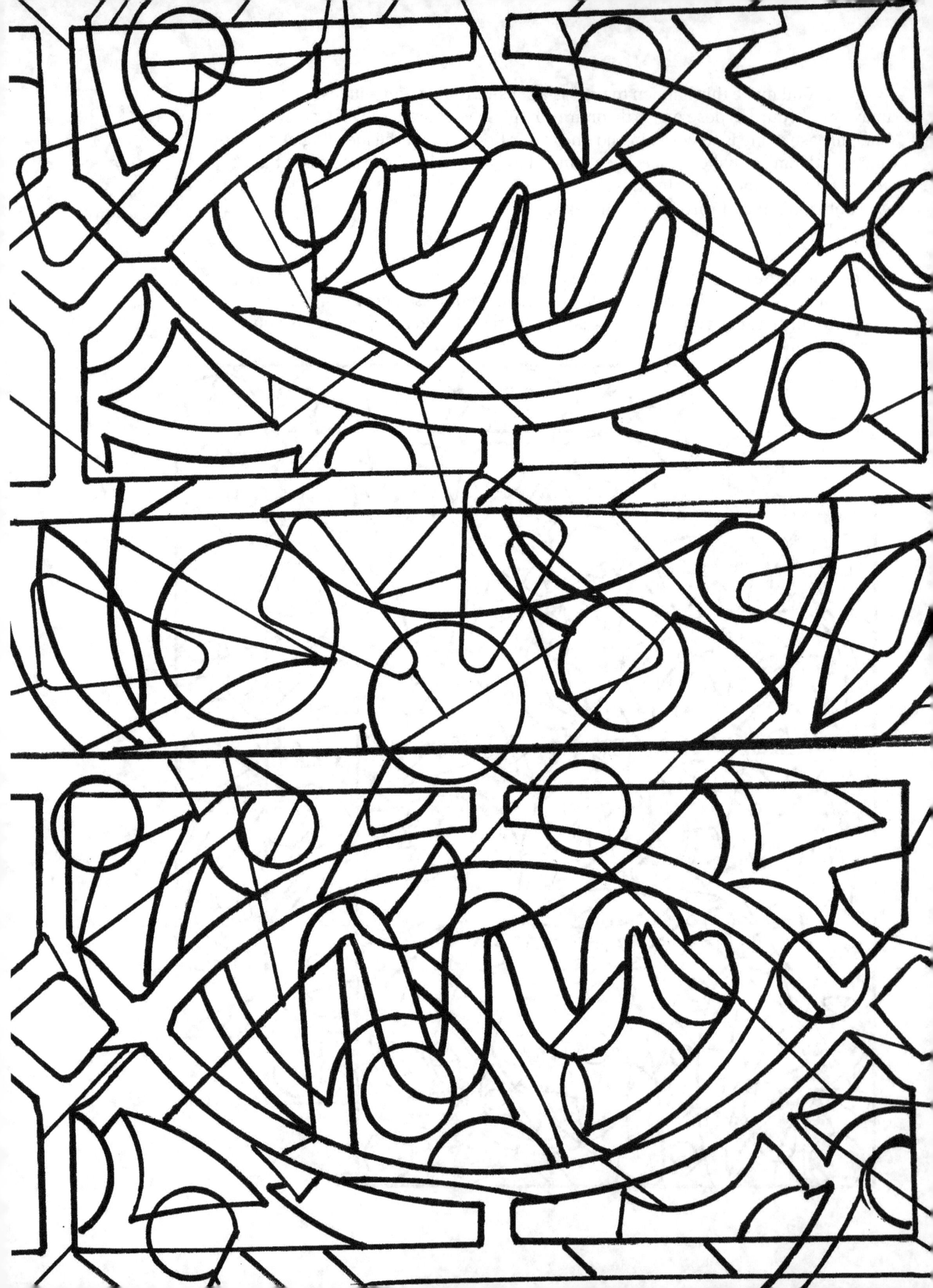

Who is your Lord?
Stop. Before you rush to answer, take a moment and let your soul bear witness.
When we're asked this question in the grave, it is not about the right answer.
It's about the true answer.
And as with all personal truths, the answer lies more closely to the word "your"
than it does to the word "Lord."

We all know that God is our Lord.
But who is *your* Lord?
Who or what is the ultimate authority in your life?
Who or what inspires your beliefs about right and wrong—about what to stand up for,
about what to oppose?
Who or what inspires your conversations whispered late into the night?
Your frustrations and victories throughout the day?
Your posts online?

If your soul cannot firmly bear witness that the answer to each and every one of these
questions is the Master of the Day of Judgment,
then the right answer and your *true* answer are not one.
So there's much work to do...
Before you are lowered beneath the ground.

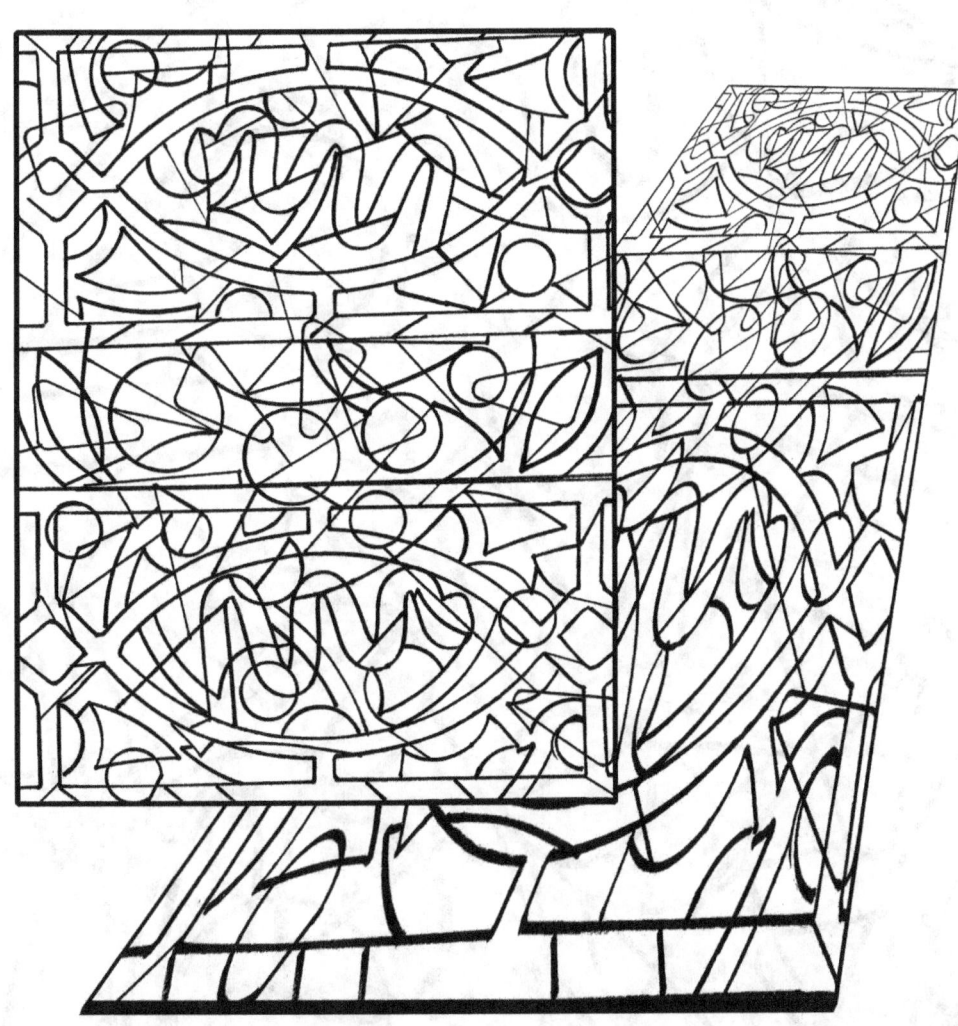

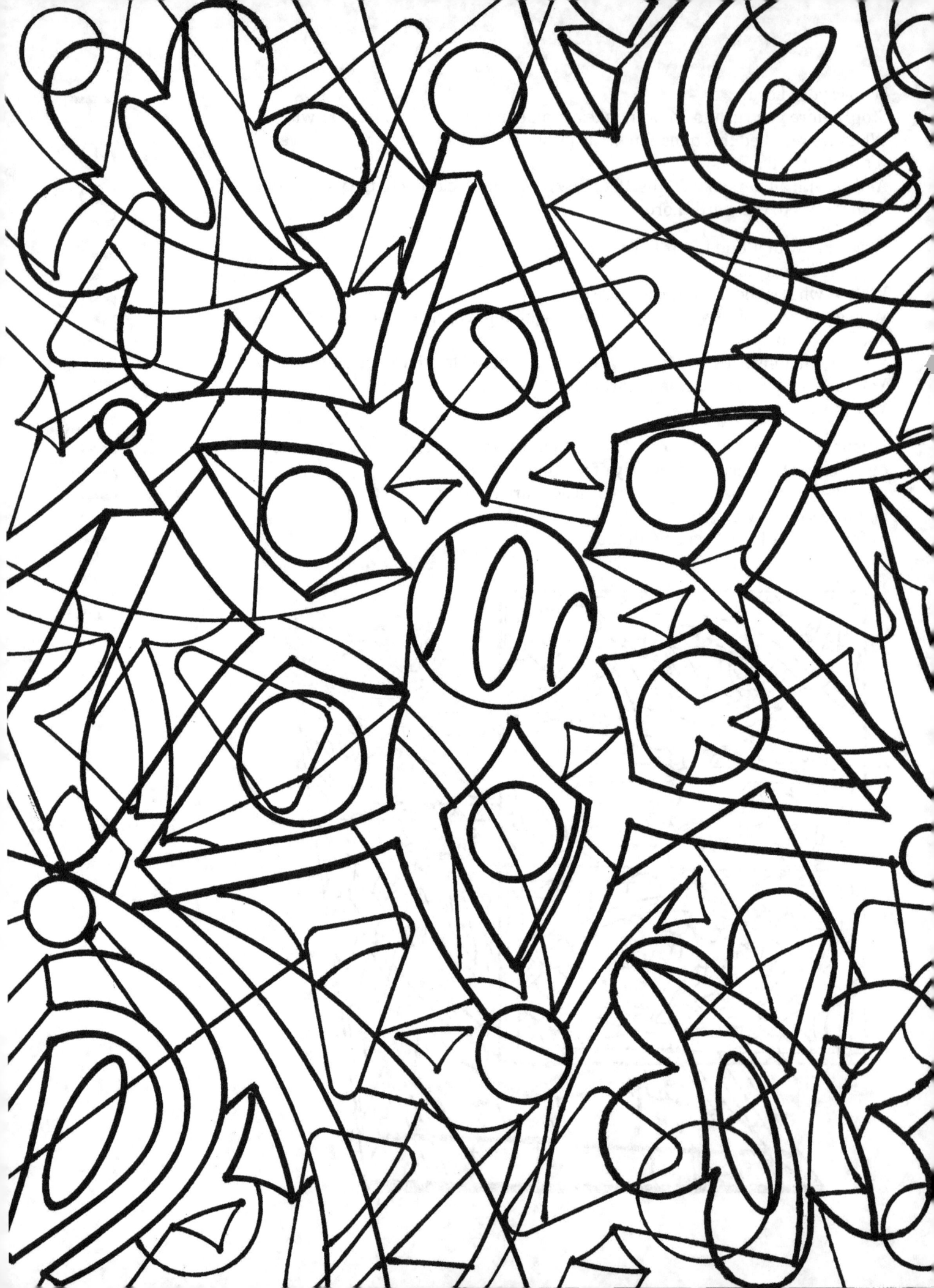

True faith isn't about walking through life completely happy and undisturbed in every circumstance. It's about staying sincerely connected to your Lord despite the inevitable ups and downs in life.

But giving your problems to God and having complete trust in Him is not always a smooth, tranquil process. When you're really stressed out, hurt, or confused, you don't always feel good or a sense of peace right away, even if you're constantly praying and asking for guidance.

Many times, the process continues to be an internal battle for a very long time.

But this isn't a sign of weak faith. It's a sign of the natural fragility of the human heart—and a sign of the believing soul seeking purity.

For having true faith and trust in God isn't about perfection.

It's about remaining in sincere remembrance of your Lord and in humble obedience to Him, whether you're enjoying times of ease and happiness or enduring times of tremendous pain and difficulty.

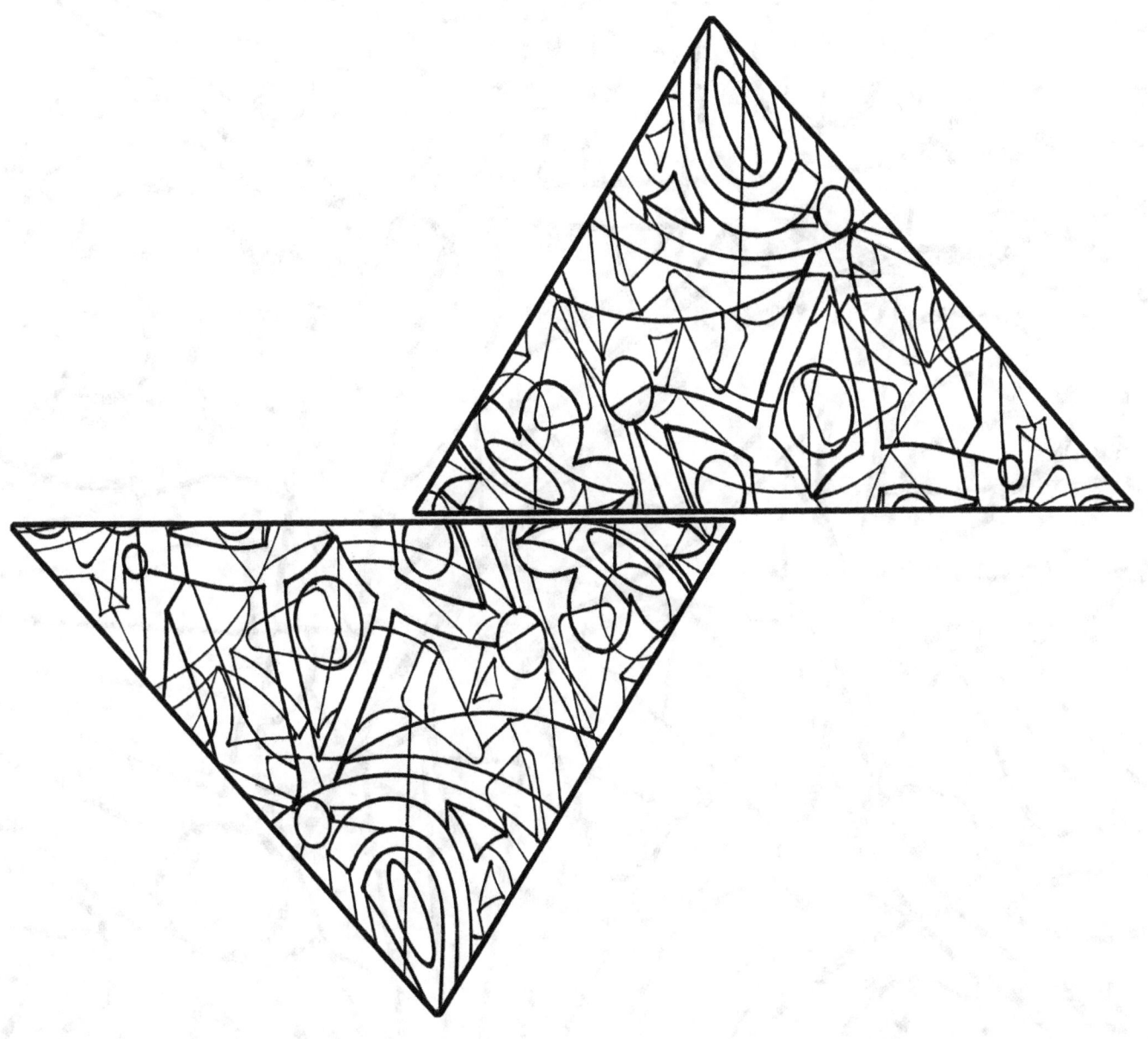

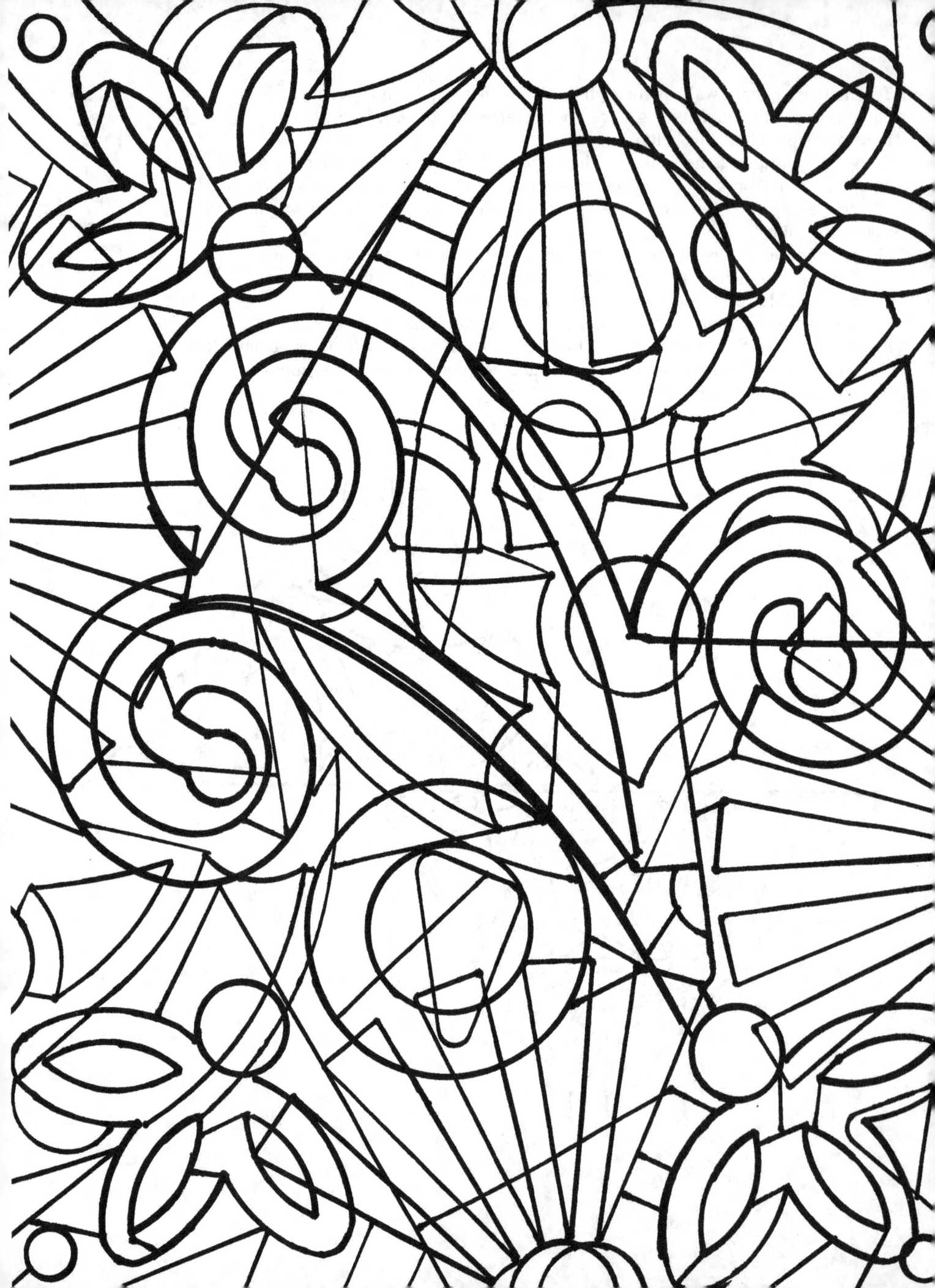

Why do you hesitate to turn to your Lord?
Why do you not bend your knees in prayer or rest your head on the ground, prostrating in humility?
Why do you not raise your hands, begging with tears in your eyes?
"I don't deserve mercy and forgiveness!" you say.
And you're right.
None of us do.
But that's the goal of life in the end—to be granted the mercy and forgiveness that none of us deserve.

Humility.

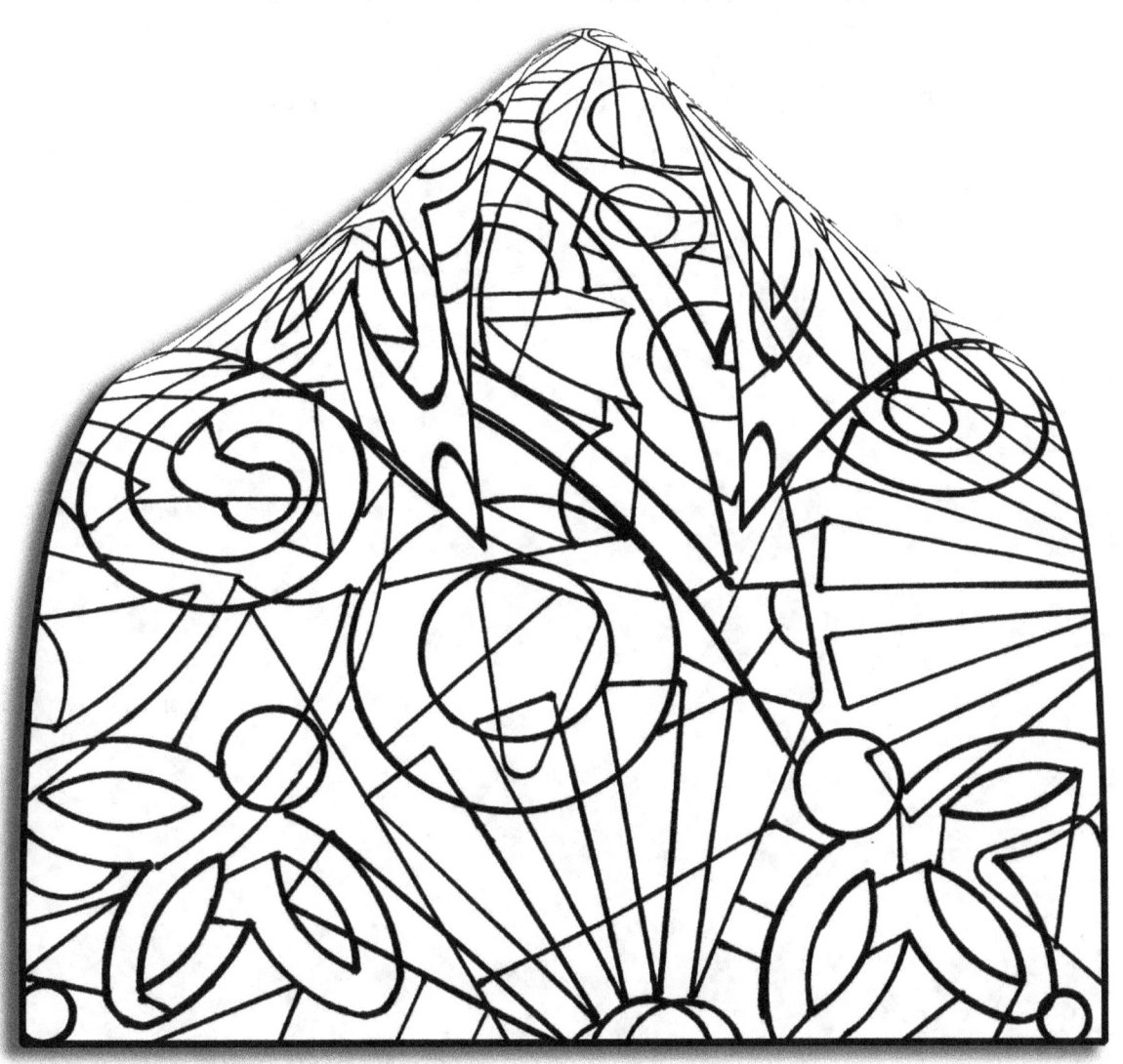

Also By Umm Zakiyyah

Pain. From the Journal of Umm Zakiyyah
Let's Talk About Sex and Muslim Love
UZ Short Story Collection
If I Should Speak
A Voice
Footsteps
Realities of Submission
Hearts We Lost
The Friendship Promise
Muslim Girl
His Other Wife

Order information available at ummzakiyyah.com/store

Read more from Umm Zakiyyah at uzauthor.com

About the Author

Daughter of American converts to Islam, Umm Zakiyyah (also known by her birth name Ruby Moore), writes about the interfaith struggles of Muslims and Christians, and the intercultural, spiritual, and moral struggles of Muslims in America. Her work has earned praise from writers, professors, and filmmakers and has been translated into multiple languages.

To find out more about the author, visit ummzakiyyah.com or uzauthor.com, subscribe to her YouTube channel: uzreflections, follow her on Twitter and Instagram: uzauthor, or join her Facebook page at facebook.com/ummzakiyyahpage.